PRAISE FOR JENNIFER BROWN
& *INCLUSION*

"Inclusion, in the true sense of the word, is no longer a soft issue. It is unequivocally a business imperative. In order for organizations to thrive and be profitable, we must cast the widest net to bring in the best talent from every source around the globe. This means diversity of thought, style, approach, and experience, which if done right and the company culture supports it, allows for better engagement, productivity, innovation, and a direct and proven impact on the bottom line.

Given the changing times and the uncertainty we face in the world today around safety, trust in the system, and globalization of the economy, we need to create safe places for everyone to be themselves and bring their authentic selves to work and home. No one should feel unsafe or unprotected or fearful of not being accepted due to any difference they may have. They should feel unique, special, and valued. It is our job as change agents to make this a reality.

Jennifer Brown's book is a real testament to driving change in this new era. It's a call to action, with a useful and practical set of tools that can be implemented by those who truly care and want to make things happen. Having known Jennifer and her work for some time, I'm a real believer in her passion, talent, and the innovation she brings to the discipline of diversity and inclusion. She truly gets it and is a real role model for many in this field and beyond."

—**Patsy Doerr**, global head of corporate responsibility and inclusion, Thomson Reuters

"Given the current state of events tearing at the diverse fabric of what has made America great, Jennifer Brown and her new book, Inclusion:

Diversity, the New Workplace & the Will to Change, is a must for those who want to absorb Jennifer's thoughts, ideas, concepts, and personal courage. She is a must-follow on social media and a global thought leader on diversity and inclusion.

Keep a highlighter handy and readily accessible on your diversity journey with Jennifer. Everyone needs a mentor, advisor, and guide like her that has walked the walk."

–**Fields Jackson, Jr.**, founder and CEO, Racing Toward Diversity

"It is my pleasure to begin by saying that Jennifer Brown is a friend. Over the course of almost ten years, we've worked together on what matters most to Jennifer: enlightening everyone to the endless possibilities for opportunity and growth in workplaces and as a society. Her passion for seeing the way forward toward equality is energizing. I have drawn from her energy and insight and always look forward to sharing stories with her because in that exchange I always learn and renew my own commitment."

–**Dr. Rich Goldberg**, Rich Goldberg Consulting LLC; inaugural fellow, Stanford University Distinguished Careers Institute

"Most all organizations say they strive to be a meritocracy…one where people get ahead based on talent and effort and where unconscious bias plays little or no part in hiring, promotions, compensation, assignments, and other key career steps. For the leaders that realize that those ideals are so very hard to achieve in reality and understand that much help is needed along the way, Jennifer stands out as a powerful guiding light. She is passionate yet reasoned in her commitment to working with organizations to understand their specific challenges and get them 'to a better place.'"

–**Adam Quinton**, CEO, Lucas Point Ventures

"Jennifer uses cutting-edge data, digital prowess, and a thorough experiential understanding of diversity as it currently stands to present a clearly defined path to compel true change. As the founder of Lesbians Who Tech, I know how crucial it is to have a road map for anyone seeking to understand the objective reality of what diversity in the workplace means and why it matters, with optimism moving forward to elevate us all."

−**Leanne Pittsford**, founder, Lesbians Who Tech

"Diversity is more than who's in the room, inclusion is more than a box on an organizational chart, and success isn't holding an annual seminar. Managing change is hard, but failing to change means losing the skills, talents, and insights of today's workforce. Diversity and inclusion must be part of an organization's DNA and implicit in each employee's mission. Jennifer Brown brings fresh insights, girded with real-world examples, to a field in need of reinvigoration."

−**Annise Parker**, former mayor of Houston; current fellow, Doerr Institute for New Leaders at Rice University

"When I am searching for a new perspective, a fresh idea, or a strong voice in diversity, Jennifer is the person I rely upon. She has not only inspired me with my own personal diversity story but to successfully drive culture change as a diversity and inclusion leader in my global organization. As Jennifer says in the book, 'it's complex,' but she has the ability to shine a bright light on the most critical issues."

−**Jim Rottman**, global head of diversity and inclusion, Roche Pharmaceuticals

"Jennifer Brown's position working with leaders from across multiple industry sectors allows her to see trends and observe needed change from a unique vantage point. And with that advantage, she hits the nail on the

head about what is needed in our organizations: change on a vast scale—and not limited to just the internal workplace environment, but most critically, the external, social environment of our world. As evidenced by recent turbulent events, we are at a crossroads in America. Our future as a unified, prosperous country depends on the directions we take now. Jennifer's guidance comes at that tipping point, and I hope her readers will take her advice and tip us in the right direction."

–**Steve Humerickhouse**, executive director, The Forum on Workplace Inclusion, University of St. Thomas

"Long overdue—practical and in-your-face truths for a more inclusive work environment."

–**Patricia A. David**, managing director and the global head of diversity, JP Morgan Chase

"The ever-growing research on the business value of an inclusive workplace is overwhelming. The hard job is no longer making that argument. The hard job is grounding these aspirations in actual decisions and behaviors in the workplace. Jennifer Brown is a leader of this focus on data- and outcomes-driven change. This book is an exceptional opportunity to learn how to build a better company."

–**Dr. Vivienne Ming**, neuroscientist and entrepreneur, researching the future of human capital

"Change is hard. And if you are serious about truly creating a diverse and inclusive workplace, there is no better source of tough love coupled with pragmatic solutions than Jennifer Brown. I have had the privilege of working closely with Jennifer on multiple projects that create lasting change even in the most rigid of companies. The tremendous respect I have seen her command in a room is earned by demonstrating a passion for

helping others presented through practical, tangible shifts in both practice and thinking. You owe it to yourself and to your business to take Jennifer's nuanced and experienced advice to heart. Diversity is good for business, and few are better for expanding diversity than Jennifer Brown."

–Jonathan D. Lovitz, vice president of external affairs, National Gay & Lesbian Chamber of Commerce® (NGLCC); director, NGLCCNY

"Jennifer understands the importance of relationship building in challenging microinequities and creating change. She has a genuine appreciation for the need to step out of one's comfort zone when expanding one's circle in order to truly live as an agent of change."

–Carmelyn P. Malalis, commissioner and chair, New York City Commission on Human Rights

"Any organization, big or small, could consider making diversity and inclusiveness a part of its culture. The business value is proven—organizations generate more revenue, innovate more, and attract and retain high performers as a result of it. To reap the benefits, D&I needs to be factored into all key business processes and day-to-day decision making. Jennifer Brown's book offers organizations practical advice for building a workplace that represents the needs and best interests of everyone. It provides readers with fresh insights and a straightforward framework for companies that are seeking to enact true progress and ensure that both diversity and inclusion are top of mind for their leadership."

–Karyn Twaronite, diversity and inclusiveness officer, EY Global

"Jennifer Brown brings a unique voice and a powerful perspective to shine a spotlight on the importance of what really matters when it comes to diversity in the twenty-first century. Her insights shatter barriers that

reveal opportunities to guide companies to secure a bigger return to the bottom line. Period."

–Leo Preziosi, Jr., executive director and founder, Live Out Loud

"Inclusion: Diversity, the New Workplace & the Will to Change is a conversation with Jennifer Brown. Her voice is clear, and her perspective blends experience, research, and current events, which tell a story that cannot be denied. It is compelling. Jennifer's thought leadership in the field of diversity and inclusion will undoubtedly help shape a larger vision for what is possible and inform the questions we should all be asking ourselves and one another. This book will inspire all of those who have felt disengaged and disconnected, who struggle to find their unique voice—their truth—and bring their fuller selves to any part of life."

–Dr. Shelton Goode, director of diversity and inclusion, Oshkosh Corporation; author, *Diversity Managers: Angels of Mercy or Barbarians at the Gate*

"Jennifer Brown is a leading global authority on diversity and inclusion, helping senior leaders from companies large and small achieve higher profitability through equality for all employees. Inclusion: Diversity, the New Workplace & the Will to Change *captures Ms. Brown's wisdom and insights for companies to immediately implement and create an environment where all employees can help with the bottom line."*

–Valerie M. Grubb, operations consultant and trainer, Val Grubb & Associates, Ltd.; author, *Clash of the Generations: Managing the New Workplace Reality*

"I have had the opportunity to see Jennifer Brown speak on a number of occasions over the past several years, and as both an out lesbian and a

media professional, I have benefited personally and professionally from her insight on workplace diversity."

—**Brooke Sopelsa**, managing editor, NBC OUT

"Jennifer Brown is a quintessential change maker and thought provoker. She forces us to think about change in a strategic and intentional manner that embodies new cultural norms in both our professional and personal lives. This is a must-read for anyone looking to make an impact on their ecosystem in a different, out-of-the-box kind of way. Kudos!"

—**Candace Waterman**, MCA, chief of staff, certification and program operations, The Women's Business Enterprise National Council (WBENC)

"Jennifer Brown's Inclusion: Diversity, the New Workplace & the Will to Change *is a compelling read, focusing on the pivotal changes in society that are influencing workplace equality with innovative, practical solutions. Jennifer Brown has been a great partner and is a powerful force in driving change within corporations. This book is a must-read for managing in the twenty-first century."*

—**Ana Duarte McCarthy**, global diversity practitioner; former chief diversity officer, Citi

"In an evolving national and regional landscape that brings real challenges for workplaces, Jennifer Brown's guidance can help organizations build a strong foundation for growth and serve as an example for others. Don't miss the opportunity to tap into her experience shared in Inclusion: Diversity, the New Workplace & the Will to Change.*"*

—**Alphonso David**, chief counsel to the governor, New York State

"Jennifer Brown is a lifelong student of diversity and inclusion. If you want to truly create a diverse and inclusive organization, her book Inclusion: Diversity, the New Workplace & the Will to Change *is a must-read."*

–**Paul Grossinger**, entrepreneur, angel investor, and syndicator; founder of Gaingels

*"*Inclusion: Diversity, the New Workplace & the Will to Change *pulls back the curtain on real challenges facing leaders who are ready for change but don't have the resources. Jennifer's success in leading organizations through these challenges demonstrates that it is possible."*
–**Terry Young**, founder and CEO, Sparks & Honey

"Jennifer Brown is one of the smartest and most innovative voices in the world of workplace diversity. If you want to make your company a more successful, profitable, and inclusive environment, read this book."

–**Dorie Clark**, author, *Reinventing You* and *Stand Out*; adjunct professor, Duke University Fuqua School of Business

INCLUSION

INCLUSION

DIVERSITY, THE NEW WORKPLACE
& THE WILL TO CHANGE

JENNIFER BROWN

PUBLISH
YOUR
PURPOSE
PRESS™

Publish Your Purpose Press
141 Weston Street, #155
Hartford, CT, 06141

PUBLISH
YOUR
PURPOSE
PRESS

The opinions expressed by
the Author are not necessarily those held by Publish Your Purpose Press.

Ordering Information: Quantity sales and special discounts are available on quantity purchases by corporations, associations, and others. For details, contact the publisher at the address above.

Cover design by Katie Biondo
Printed in the United States of America.

ISBN-10: 1-946384-10-0
ISBN-13: 978-1-946384-10-2
Library of Congress Control Number: 2017942716

The information contained within this book is strictly for informational purposes. The material may include information, products, or services by third parties. As such, the Author and Publisher do not assume responsibility or liability for any third party material or opinions. Readers are advised to do their own due diligence when it comes to making decisions.

Publish Your Purpose Press works with authors, and aspiring authors, who have a story to tell and a brand to build. Do you have a book idea you would like us to consider publishing? Please visit www.PublishYourPurposePress.com for more information.

DEDICATION

This book is a love letter to all those who have felt disengaged and disconnected, who struggle to find their unique voice, their truth, and bring their fuller selves to any part of their lives—but especially to their professional lives.

Whatever stage of the journey you're on—from just picking up this book because you're wondering what all the fuss is about when it comes to diversity, to someone who thinks about inclusiveness daily and wonders, *What else can I do?*—my hope is that these stories and examples provide a rich road map for you. The book describes multiple facets of creating a better, safer, more welcoming and inclusive workplace, where all kinds of talented people can feel truly Welcomed, Valued, Respected, and Heard[SM]. It also clearly delineates what's in it for us, what's in it for companies, and what's in it for society, *if* we do this well. So many voices are not feeling included in the narrative right now, and this is hurting us all . . . and generations to come.

As you gain clarity and strength around sharing your own diversity story and it becomes woven into your leadership, know that you are also healing and realigning parts of you, a process which can make you a more resonant, more powerful leader whose strength others will see and want to willingly follow. The amount of time talented people spend wandering, navigating the line between safety and authenticity, covering aspects of who they are in their professional environment—without examples of success they can relate to around them—is heartbreaking to me, and inefficient for the business world.

I've endeavored to lay out the tools for evolving ourselves and our organizations into a new, healthier future.

Let's redirect the precious energy so many are spending on that dilemma—the seemingly impossible choice between assimilation and taking the risk of telling our truths—toward becoming the amazing, successful human beings we can be. For those of us in relatively more privileged positions, for whom the path has been easier, we must build our awareness of the struggles others with relatively less privilege face; acknowledge and absorb how exhausting the suppression of self is; and utilize our position to advocate, to protect, and to further the conversation. It is so much less risky for those with greater privilege to do so. This is the only way large-scale change in organizations will occur.

We might have played smaller, and minimized our power, for survival, but those days are over. Let's set a new tone for business, and for the world, that honors each and every one of us, our contributions, and our very presence.

TABLE OF CONTENTS

FOREWORD xxi

PREFACE xxv

ACKNOWLEDGMENTS xxvii

ABOUT THE AUTHOR xxix

CHAPTER ONE 1
Change Is Hard

CHAPTER TWO 27
Origins of Change

CHAPTER THREE 51
Change Agents: The Roles We Play in a Diverse Workplace

CHAPTER FOUR. 79
The Change Has Already Begun

CHAPTER FIVE 111
Gender at Work: It's Not a Woman's Problem

CHAPTER SIX 135
What's Your Purpose?

CHAPTER SEVEN 155

The Workplace of the Future: Breaking the Mold, Letting Everyone In

CHAPTER EIGHT 189

The Changing Marketplace and Our Diverse Customers

CHAPTER NINE 205

ERGs: Change Can Be Tribal

CHAPTER TEN 241

Talking Diversity: Leading Your Diversity and Inclusion Revolution

IN CLOSING 267

GLOSSARY 269

RESOURCES 275

REFERENCES 281

FOREWORD

When Jennifer approached me with a request to contribute to the foreword of her book, I felt extremely honored. I consider Jennifer to be a trusted thought leader and a dear friend. We easily move from holding deep, strategic conversations about social justice and diversity to giggling over silly events involving family and friends.

But I felt pressure to write comments on point with what is happening today in our country around diversity and inclusion. Honestly, my will to change has leveled up like the obsessed Pokémon Go gamers wandering the streets across America. Our systems are broken, our country is wounded, and we must have the will to create change to heal. My role within society as a diversity and inclusion manager does just that: create change. And unfortunately, in this country filled with growing struggles and tensions across groups, this role is critical.

By the time I received more details on Jennifer's book, our country had heard more reports of police officers shooting African Americans, woken up to news of the Orlando nightclub attack, and just experienced the sniper's attack on police officers in Dallas. Putting this in context with the concept of *Inclusion: Diversity, the New Workplace & the Will to Change* made it easy for me to craft my thoughts to this foreword. I am delighted and humbled to be afforded this opportunity to put into writing my respect and admiration for Jennifer and her work.

When I joined my company eighteen years ago to work in corporate diversity, I had no idea what I was getting myself into. My definition of "diversity" was limited to race and gender. Like most people, my thoughts focused on protected classes; I saw this position as an opportunity to give voice to the underdog. I joined corporate America in the late nineties and found very few role models for me to emulate. Where could I possibly find individuals like me—a Gen X, Asian-Pacific American, LGBTQ ally, and single mother of a biracial child with disabilities—who were running companies and calling the shots? Diversity became a concept I connected with immediately; it revealed itself as one of the only ways I felt that I could make an impact in my company and leave a legacy.

The concept of "inclusion" hit me as very fresh and exciting, an opportunity to bring straight white men over forty into the conversation and really make the culture change effort for everyone. After all, I quickly learned that culture change is not about taking anything away from one group to give to another; it isn't a "fight the power" theory. Rather, it is about creating space for all individuals to fully contribute and thrive. And corporate culture change must be focused on the bottom line: working toward keeping a competitive advantage in these uncertain economic times, driven by a will to change.

Creating change is often a lonely place. Finding the will to change, and to create *real* change, requires passion and patience. One needs passion to create change, passion for what is possible, and passion about seeing results. If a person becomes involved with diversity and inclusion for monetary rewards or recognition, it is doubtful that he or she will be successful. This work is about service to the company and to others. The ultimate goal is higher performance, which only comes about when people are feeling valued, supported, and respected for their individuality.

My mom once asked me to describe what I do for a living. I answered, "Well, it feels like I bang my head against the wall of resistance to create change. At times, the wall of resistance actually cracks, which gives me a moment to rest and inspires me to continue." The will to change requires a lot of patience and a strong persistence. Patience is about realizing that change happens when one convinces his or her constituents to slow down and adjust behaviors so they can speed up the way they do business. As we travel this challenging but gratifying road, my advice is to allow yourself to see the signs of change, acknowledge the necessary work you put in, and celebrate the victories, no matter how small. You are making a difference, whether it's easy to perceive or not.

> At times, the wall of resistance actually cracks, which gives me a moment to rest and inspires me to continue.

The will to change must come from deep inside the change agent. No one can artificially manifest that sort of will. Jennifer Brown has laid out real-time examples of how we must find our own voices to create change. Don't be your toughest critic and minimize your accomplishments; this work takes time, this work takes dedication, and this work takes patience. Keep that in perspective when someone tells you that you haven't been successful. It all begins with understanding your own value and connecting to your motivation to thrive through being true to yourself and contributing your gifts in today's turbulent and uncertain world.

—Jennifer "Jae" Pi'ilani Requiro, national manager of diversity and inclusion, Toyota Financial Services

PREFACE

Change is hard. Newsflash, right?

Most of us have an aversion to change once we've grown comfortable, or even familiar, with our current conditions. The longer those conditions persist, the more we take root in them and the harder they become to change, even if the reasons to do so are valid and beneficial. Getting out of bed early on a Monday morning requires a change most of us rarely want to make. And the longer we resist it, the more difficult it becomes until we're rushing out the door, late for work and behind schedule.

Whether it's our attitude, our social environment, or even our diet, changing something deeply ingrained in our lifestyle is challenging for us all. Even the simplest of tasks can be complicated by the notion of change. The reasons surrounding this phenomenon have a lot to do with the psychology behind how we view change in the first place, and perhaps, even more so with *how a particular case for change* is presented to us.

If someone tells you to change an article of clothing, for instance, you would probably first want to know why your clothes are inadequate before making the effort to redress yourself. If the answer is convincing and there are, in fact, a few stains you missed, then changing into a clean shirt or a fresh pair of pants is a painless endeavor.

But imagine if the change were cultural and system-wide. Undressing indoctrinated social norms and beliefs certainly asks a lot more of us than a change of clothes, but it follows much of the same rationale. It demands that we have the courage to embrace uncertainty and suspend disbelief and look at the facts—however painful. It demands that we accept that there is a gap between what is and what should be, or needs to be. When we evolve to or adopt new truths, these may conflict with our previous beliefs. And all of this demands a clear vision for what needs to change and how; it demands great leadership initiative. But most of all, it demands the self-discipline to actually change and *stay* changed. With all those variables, no wonder we resist.

So I'll be blunt with you: If you have picked up this book and believe we have nothing to improve in today's workplace, that the current state is acceptable (or you don't even care to know the current state because it doesn't affect you), I want to say this isn't the book for you. However, respectfully, it is the perfect book for you. Awareness is the first step—just the openness and curiosity to learning more about the topic of inclusion could shift entire workplace cultures. After working across the Fortune 500, I will share exactly what's broken, how it became broken, and what you can do about it. If you feel awakened and impatient after the first chapter, you're in the right place.

Let's get to it!

ACKNOWLEDGMENTS

Many hands, and hearts, helped me shape this book. I have viewed it as a true collaboration from the beginning and could never have had the courage, or logistical know-how, to bring it into the world without the perseverance of my team, the encouragement of my supporters, and *lots* of solid project management!

To my book team—Niki Gallagher-Garcia, Jenn T. Grace, Veronica Pirillo, and Kate Powers—your steadfast march alongside me has made the process as enjoyable as it could have possibly been, and your encouragement to push my own boundaries has been formative to my growth into a bolder evangelist. To my reviewers, I am humbled by the time you made to review our arguments, facts, and figures with a lovingly critical eye.

Words cannot begin to thank my fearless JBC team for their tremendous passion, vision, and dedication in carrying forward our mission to build more inclusive workplaces for all: Robert Beaven, James Childs, Dave Ciliberto, Niki Gallagher-Garcia, Jenn T. Grace, Holly Kalyn, Nancy Mace, Emily Nugent, Alison Oxman, Veronica Pirillo, Kate Powers, Sharon Smith-Mauney, Jeffery Smith, Michael Spinella, Claire Tse, Ash Varma, and Andrea Ward.

And to the many clients, subject matter experts, and colleagues who generously provided their case studies, research, and testimonials—we consider it such a privilege to bring your organizational triumphs into the light. It is our deepest hope that this book gives you another important tool in your change arsenal.

For my family, who has loved and supported me and consistently celebrated my journey toward greater authenticity and honoring my truth, becoming allies yourselves in the process, I am tremendously blessed.

And finally, for my partner in life and advocacy, Michelle Alvarez, may we march together for another twenty years, because as we both know deeply in our bones:

"We choose only once. We choose either to be warriors or to be ordinary. A second choice does not exist. Not on this earth."

—CARLOS CASTANEDA

ABOUT THE AUTHOR

Jennifer Brown is an award-winning entrepreneur and owner of the strategic leadership and organizational management firm, Jennifer Brown Consulting (JBC). As a leading diversity and inclusion expert, speaker, and social equality advocate, Jennifer's workplace strategies have been employed by some of the world's top Fortune 500 companies and nonprofits to help employees bring their *full selves* to work. Jennifer's groundbreaking work in talent management, human capital, and intersectional theory have redefined the boundaries of talent potential and company culture.

Jennifer founded JBC in 2006 to bring her successful strategies in consultative training and thought leadership to the C-suite. She and her team have since facilitated and coached thousands of leaders all over the world on critical issues of strategy, leadership, and integrity. Her focus today is on identifying emerging workplace trends and building more enlightened and inclusive organizations with client work and outreach where all kinds of talent can feel Welcomed, Valued, Respected, and Heard^{SM}. Her areas of expertise include catalyzing diversity to drive innovation and business results; business resource group evolution; growing leaders in the new global, generationally diverse and technologically connected workplace ecosystems; and aligning corporate strategy with individual, team, and societal values.

Jennifer Brown Consulting is proud to hold diverse supplier certifications by both the Women's Business Enterprise National Council (WBENC) and the National Gay & Lesbian Chamber of Commerce (NGLCC).

CHAPTER ONE

CHANGE IS HARD

"When we speak, we are afraid our words will not be heard or welcomed. But when we are silent, we are still afraid. So it is better to speak."

–AUDRE LORDE

Whenever I talk to a group about change, most people stiffen with worry, concerned about the *kind* of change I might mean. I understand the feeling. Change is vague, seemingly limitless, and it's uncomfortable, even scary, to think that something you're familiar with may be at risk of going away, especially for reasons you do not fully understand. This is especially acute if that change could take something—you're not sure what—away from you.

So let me begin by easing the tension. When we talk about "change" relative to diversity and inclusion, we're talking about something as simple and obvious as how our workplaces adapt to the opportunities and challenges current and incoming employees encounter every day in their work and lives. This is the basic equation of what makes workplaces, well, "work." While it might be simple and obvious as a focus, unfortunately we don't do it very well. This book will lay out the reasons for that and the many available paths forward toward change.

Regardless, to avoid becoming obsolete, our workplaces and business practices must evolve alongside society and its prevailing culture. We have no choice. So *change*, in not only the conceptual sense but from a practical point of view, is not only beneficial to a company's success; it's vital. As we say, change is the only constant— or another favorite: change or die.

Where we initiate change matters, and I'll share constructive and creative ways to begin your organization's diversity and inclusion journey later in the book. But for change at work to begin, we first have to understand what the conversation about diversity and inclusion is, right now, in the current day. Because of our work, and the sheer number of corporate leaders and employees we speak with every day, we sit at the eye of the storm—and these days, it's nearing a Category 5.

Those of us who've spent any time in corporate America are likely familiar with the dreaded "diversity training" as epitomized in a now-famous episode of the show, *The Office*. We know the drill: a brief lecture given by obligation or compliance, followed by uninspired and limited policy changes, executed by a beleaguered and bewildered management team, and then inflicted on a begrudging workforce. Let the collective eye rolling begin.

If I had believed that organizational change began and ended with such trainings, I would never have felt inspired to join the ranks of people who specialize in the reinvention of the workplace. What *The Office* episode *does* show well is discomfort—to hilarious effect— and discomfort plays a big role in change. As we said earlier, we spend our lives avoiding discomfort—it's only human. But organizations and people need a nudge—and more often a strong push—to change behaviors, to think differently about the cultural norms to which they've grown accustomed. In today's fast-changing world, organizational leaders will need to do some fresh soul searching, reevaluating much of what they've built their leadership identities upon—as well as see other people differently, more deeply, and more accurately—and most importantly, how they *want* to be seen. We will need to acknowledge our own relative privileges or access to opportunities not available to others and be a part of leveling that inequality in the workplace. A change will not occur on its own, and if it does, but it wasn't planned or is forced, there is the potential for lasting collateral damage—not just in terms of morale from a tone-deaf leadership team, but in real business bottom-line terms, too.

> We will need to acknowledge our own relative privileges or access to opportunities not available to others and be a part of leveling that inequality in the workplace.

The conversation about the haves and the have nots at work can be off-putting to some, especially without proper context. It is uncomfortable to acknowledge that we all have some responsibility for the systems we labor in when their flaws are pointed out—sometimes, very publicly. But understand that we're in it together. All of us. Each and every one of us struggles to resolve the riddle of what the workplace and our careers seem to demand and what we deeply desire for ourselves. Exploring this apparent dichotomy is central to the work of diversity and inclusion. That's why we first need to understand what the current changes impacting the workplace are, and why we can't afford to ignore them, before we can address them head-on.

Thankfully, we have a new tool at our disposal to spot some of these changing opportunities and challenges in real time. Social media has created a profound shift in how we engage with one another, as well as how many people see the world around them, often for the first time. Instead of digesting the image presented to us, we can peek into the actual reality. And once we see that reality, it is hard to "unsee" or "unknow" it. People may not be any quicker to address an injustice or an inequity than they were years ago, but with tools such as Facebook, Twitter, Tumblr, Instagram, Snapchat, mobile-phone cameras, and blogs, a broader community can be reached, and inequity becomes harder to hide or ignore. Our actions—and importantly, inactions, especially as leaders—are there for all to see. On the plus side, connecting with our *affinity* and exploring common challenges together has become easier than ever, and we've seen just how quickly change can result from these connections and mobilizations in the global news arena—for good and for bad.

> Our actions—and importantly, inactions, especially as leaders—are there for all to see.

A larger but connected trend is the democratization of decision making as a society. We see this in the way people crowdsource purchasing decisions, evaluate an employer before interviewing or taking a job, and in the way most of us leverage social media. The individual is growing in knowledge, empowerment, and authority, while at the same time our organizational hierarchies are stuck in the 1950s. Younger generations are challenging traditional hierarchies by questioning whether the "senior" person is automatically deserving of respect or assumed to be knowledgeable, just because of where that person's name appears on the organizational chart. They want to know the "why" behind everything, and they want to know the leader as a "full" person—who doesn't just get a pass because of an impressive title. Many leaders I work with seem to not be aware of this expectation, or they are hoping that it dissipates as incoming talent matures and becomes "just like everyone else, with mortgages, kids, and responsibility." Not so fast.

If I can take a little generational credit, this democratic shift has its roots in the disenchantment of generation X (the generation born between approximately 1965 and 1976)—coming of age in the 1980s—and how disaffected we were, losing faith in institutions, starting to view authority with a critical eye, and experiencing the lack of employer loyalty firsthand as we watched its effect on our parents' safety nets and lifetime employment and job security. We were the first to see our mothers in the workforce in substantive numbers and to see divorce rates skyrocket, too. For the millennials, often referred to as generation Y (the generation born between approximately 1977 and 1995),[1] the trend toward autonomy, meaning, purpose, and being embraced for who they are feels like a strong reaction to the generation before them. Their self-awareness and validation began with their doting parents and continues into their present workplace. Although their wants and needs might be criticized as entitlement, it behooves every employer to heed this message: if you value me, then invest in me, and see all of me, so I can do my best work for you. Whatever our stereotypes about this newest generation in the workforce, this is a powerful equation to consider.

GENERATIONS BY BIRTH YEAR

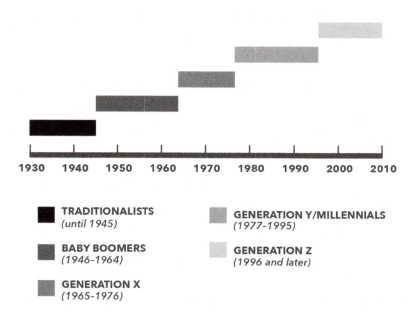

TRADITIONALISTS
(until 1945)

BABY BOOMERS
(1946-1964)

GENERATION X
(1965-1976)

GENERATION Y/MILLENNIALS
(1977-1995)

GENERATION Z
(1996 and later)

Note: There is some disagreement about birth year ranges for the Millennial and Generation Y cohort(s); we have consulted the following: http://genhq.com/faq-info-about-generations/. For more information on the various generations, please see: http://www.theatlantic.com/national/archive/2014/03/here-is-when-each-generation-begins-and-ends-according-to-facts/359589/.

The solidarity and collective energy of workplace cohorts finding each other in the darkness, discovering their collective voice, and influencing their organizations toward greater health, vitality, and yes, innovation, is something we witness on a daily basis in our work. The courage we see in our clients, and in so many employees, is exhilarating and props up our faith. But the individual change maker—that brave soul who stands up—still plays the most pivotal role in triggering change. If that person speaks from the heart and backs it up with action, one move can cause a landslide.

A SPARK IN THE FIRE: HOW ONE MAN BROUGHT CHANGE TO TWITTER

In the fall of 2015, Leslie Miley, a former engineering manager at Twitter, wrote a blog post explaining his decision to leave one of the world's most revered tech companies. While some organizational restructuring hastened the tough call, Miley claimed his departure ultimately hinged on the social media giant's poor response to diversity issues, specifically those revolving around its hiring practices and the low representation of black[2] and Hispanic workers in its workforce.[3]

The only black engineer in a leadership position quitting Twitter over diversity issues seemed ready-made for headlines. And it was. The revelation rang loud and wide, creating ripples of raised eyebrows and difficult questions across the tech world and beyond. How bad would an experience need to be to justify quitting a job that most in your field would do anything to have? How important must the issue be to pass on a healthy severance package *just so you could talk about it*? And even more puzzling, how could a company so publicly supportive of diversity and social causes struggle with the same issue, in its own hallways?

At the time, Twitter was a company with "#BlackLivesMatter" literally painted on the walls of its San Francisco headquarters. It hosted large events advocating for race and gender equality. It took pride in creating a platform where voiceless communities could gather and share ideas that facilitated social and political change all around the world. If there was a group speaking loudly about diversity and equality, Twitter was likely to be holding its microphone.

With Miley's post came a deluge of stats and revelations that painted an unexpected image of the hip, young company worth billions: 30 percent of Twitter's users were black or Hispanic, yet black and Hispanic workers accounted for only 6 percent of their workforce, (technical and nontechnical roles combined).[4] Following his exit, Miley stated that Twitter "no longer has any managers, directors, or VPs of color in engineering or product management."[5] While it wasn't a declaration of outright racism, Miley's departure was evidence of a large racial gap that Twitter seemed either unaware of or unsure how to address.

THE VIRAL EFFECT

A company best known for innovation and disruption, Twitter was thrown off balance by Miley's accusations. A company that worked to cultivate corporate transparency as well as social empowerment found itself fumbling both of these mission-critical balls in front of all its constituencies and stakeholders, and the irony was too much to ignore. Within days, Miley's post went viral on social media and news outlets, even on the scrolling feeds of Twitter itself. The more the story reverberated throughout the media industry, the more we learned about what had gone wrong and how common Twitter's challenges were across the entirety of Silicon Valley.

Prior to his exit, Miley had questioned his bosses on why black and Hispanic engineers were so underrepresented, and they had agreed to look into the disparity. An investigation into hiring data traced the problem to a low percentage of black and Hispanic talent in Twitter's hiring pipeline.

When all roads lead back to blaming the pipeline—as they often do in my experience—most managers consider the case closed, saying with a shrug that it's outside of their span of influence. The refrain is that diverse talent is hard—nay, impossible—to find, especially for technical roles. In our data-driven world, and especially for technology companies, we expect numbers and the data to hold all the answers, so when certain affinities are missing from the pipeline, it's not the company's fault that there is a systemic issue, right?

The answer, perhaps, lies buried beneath our silence, as we all instinctively avoid uncomfortable, potentially difficult conversations about problems that are nuanced and complex and have many sources. In an interview with NPR in November 2015, Miley gives voice to a palpable concern about how corporations begin, or don't begin, those conversations: "[T]he moment you say 'diversity,' I think a lot of people think you're calling them racist or a bigot. They automatically go on the defensive, or they just don't want to have the conversation."[6] We never even get started on the path.

> [T]he moment you say 'diversity,' I think a lot of people think you're calling them racist or a bigot. They automatically go on the defensive, or they just don't want to have the conversation.

I have experienced this reaction myself and believe we need to enter these conversations in a radically different way, including *radically different stakeholders* in those conversations. If we spend all of our time saying, "show me the data" and then decide it's not our fault, we are missing a key accountability of leadership, which is of course—you guessed it—to lead. To ask the tough questions. To put ourselves in the role of the learner, over and over again, and acknowledge there is much we don't know. To lead through service to others.

THE RISING AWARENESS OF UNCONSCIOUS BIAS AND MICROINEQUITIES AT WORK (AGAIN)

I say "again" because many of us have been studying and discussing bias in the workplace of course for years, but the topic is experiencing a resurgence at the moment, and with a twist. Miley's experience at Twitter may seem less dramatic when compared to past stories of seemingly more overt discrimination, but what makes his experience so important to contemporary society lies much farther below the surface. Twitter playing a starring role couldn't have been cast more perfectly, a fact that helped make Miley's story that much more compelling for viral consumption. A tech giant of the digital age revealing its own struggles was simply too momentous for the public to ignore. The story elucidates not only many of the ways in which a company's relationship to the public is changing through transparency and accountability but also the challenges of beginning to implement a powerful and transformational diversity and inclusion strategy that connects the workforce to the workplace, to the marketplace, and back again, in one inclusive ecosystem.

While Miley was implying Twitter had some particular challenges with race, he was doing it in a way most had never seen before. The disparity in Twitter's diversity numbers had a lot more to do with systemic issues and practices—such as the relative weight given to schools attended, credentials, individual merit, and the lack of focus on creating an environment of inclusion in its work culture—than it did a conscious effort to exclude black and Hispanic employees. Miley raised the point that discrimination today is often an *unconscious act*, the result of how we tend to believe that the norms and experiences of our own social group—whether defined by race, class, gender, sexual orientation, disability, religion, or some other qualifier—are, or should be, the same for every other social group. And the realization that they are radically different.

These misperceptions are more formally known as ***unconscious bias***, and it is hard-wired in all of us. In fact, it's one of the main reasons why fostering change in the workplace is so challenging, because many of us aren't aware there's a problem, especially if things have been relatively easier for us. This is how we are unconscious. If we're white, male, and maybe, heterosexual—and we consider ourselves progressive people too—it might not have crossed our minds that our old friend bias is still around and playing a detrimental role in a work environment we assume to be a meritocracy.

When we are missing a piece of information, when we are acting quickly, talking fast or maybe too much, or hiring quickly to match our company's growth, we make an assumption that is more informed by our own background and experience and our own comfort level than it is by the facts. Not noticing there is a disparity in our workforce or team demographics, we'll naturally gravitate to certain resumes over others, we'll think to promote certain folks over others, and we'll build teams that look like us. And then when we look around and see that our workforce doesn't represent our world, we'll blame schools, the educational system, or some other external factor. We don't like to have our biases pointed out, and it is very tempting to blame "the system."

The occurrence of overtly sexist, racist, and homophobic comments and jokes has decreased in some workplaces, which may be the good news, but today we are experiencing a related but different twist on exclusion: the pernicious ***microinequities*** or ***microaggressions***. The term, minted by Columbia Professor Derald Sue, refers to "brief and commonplace daily verbal, behavioral, or environmental indignities, whether intentional or unintentional, that communicate hostile, derogatory, or negative racial slights and insults toward people of color."[7] These can apply beyond race and ethnicity and are experienced by many with historically stigmatized identities.

I call this "death by a thousand cuts" in the workplace. For Twitter, even without overt discrimination, the impact on Miley, of subtle oversights, of not being included, of not feeling valued, was the same. After Miley's public declaration, the company had to address a problem that, in the dominant, Euro-centric workplace culture that seems to reign in certain quarters of the business world, we have simplified and dismissed for decades.

Twitter's head of engineering quickly issued an apology and a statement outlining the company's plans to improve its diversity and inclusion mission. Inclusion training courses for employees would now be mandatory. Recruiters would step up their presence at historically black colleges and universities and at Hispanic-serving institutions. Management teams at all levels would begin collecting, and more thoroughly analyzing, data on retention variations between ethnic groups. Twitter made a public commitment to increasing the number of blacks, Hispanics, and women within its workforce.

Fast forward to early 2016, when I found myself presenting on the topic of building more inclusive workplaces to a packed room of lesbian technologists at Twitter's San Francisco headquarters. Jeff Siminoff, the company's new diversity lead and a personal friend, welcomed us with enthusiasm, making a point to tell us that the company was proud to host this growing community and the evolving conversation on *LGBTQ* issues and empowering allies at all levels. So much has improved in the aftermath of Miley's blog and the media scrutiny, including the appointment of Siminoff to the role of overseeing diversity at the company.

His appointment and onboarding though were anything but smooth and touched off another firestorm. Siminoff is a white, albeit gay, *cisgender* man. Those angered by the news of his appointment argued that the decision displayed Twitter's continued resistance to appointing people of color and women to executive positions. In my opinion—and as an organizational change practitioner who happens to be white—this dialogue diminishes an entire community of change makers by implying that leaders of certain identities cannot be effective. At the same time however, I strongly believe passionate discussion is needed on this topic about how critical it is to diversify so many companies' leadership ranks with less-represented talent and how powerful some choices are in sending messages that so many crave—messages that say "you're important" and "we heard you." This appointment might have felt tone-deaf and defeating to some, while at the same time empowering and strategic to others. I'll speak more about the power of allies in later chapters.

We don't need to reduce these dialogues to right or wrong; the goal should be to become fluent in seeing both sides of issues and training ourselves with enough first-person data and research to be aware of our lens and then to look through the lens of others at the exact same information and imagine how it might impact us and others. I find that having a strong opinion on either side is not as useful (although it has created some big names in the diversity space).

Regardless, the Twitter saga is an effective cautionary tale for why companies need to prioritize getting their diversity house in order.

THE AGE OF DATA TRANSPARENCY

Twitter isn't the only company to experience the whiplash of a hyperconnected global society. It has rattled entire industries of all kinds, and a surge of action has occurred as companies try to field the myriad of issues arising from total mismatches between their internal employee demographics and the demographics of the clients or customers they depend on. Transparency is making this disparity more and more difficult to hide.

If you've tuned in to the news in the last year or two, you've likely witnessed technology companies issuing a deluge of workforce data. Thanks in large part to social media pressure and callouts by so many to fix the problem, and the rising preeminence of younger workers who are the most vocal generation in decades, we now live in an age where companies are revealing closely held company information as a sort of "throwing up of hands" at the problem and a public plea for help in addressing seemingly insurmountable diversity challenges ("It's the pipeline!"). The spark that started it all is widely considered to be Tracy Chou, a twenty-seven-year-old coder at Pinterest who, in 2013, took the simple but provocative step of uploading a spreadsheet—to the code-sharing platform Github—that companies could use as a template to make public the number of female engineers in their ranks. Chou didn't intend to be an activist, but it was a shot heard throughout the Valley.

Female employees at Facebook had increased one percent globally in a year, while there was no change in the numbers of black and Hispanic employees.

And what has been the reaction, and more importantly, the progress since all of this supposed transparency? Some good news is that companies are now in the routine of sharing their demographics; the bad news is that the numbers haven't changed since the sharing, despite efforts and a public focus on the issues. Facebook reported that female employees at Facebook had increased

14

one percent globally in a year, while there was no change in the numbers of black and Hispanic employees.[8] So much for the power of transparency.

The company attributed their recruitment challenges to the early education system and to how children are prepared for jobs in Silicon Valley; the company is directing its energy now toward launching a five-year $15 million partnership with Code.org to provide students opportunities to learn computer science and programming skills, much of it going toward training K-12 teachers so that they in turn can instruct kids.

A positive step, to be sure. Let's explore the pluses and minuses of other actions, and inactions, a bit further.

BACK TO THE FUTURE: UNCONSCIOUS BIAS TRAINING

Many organizations responded to the data release by attempting to increase understanding of how we naturally gravitate to people like ourselves (seeking comfort, of course) and how organizations have shaped themselves around this unchecked tendency, to the detriment of our team effectiveness and innovation. The fact that demographic disparities haven't been top of mind for most organizations has led to the incredible homogeneity we see in the top layers of organizational leadership and, in some companies, throughout all layers of the organizational hierarchy.

Because specifically technology companies love data and science, but almost all *C-suite* and executive leaders love it just as much, the reaction to these systemic problems has been largely focused on training on unconscious bias. There exists a lot of research on the topic; therefore, if the argument is scientifically based, people should be convinced, and maybe we can all move on. Training is just one of many change tools, and clearly more is needed to shift the numbers.

Facebook isn't alone. An industry focus is helpful when looking at this topic, and certain fields are indeed especially challenged on the diversity front. US Census data show that blacks, Hispanics, and women are underrepresented in the fields of science, technology, engineering, and mathematics (STEM). For example, blacks and Hispanics combined made up 26 percent of the total US workforce in 2011, but their share of STEM occupations was only 13 percent.[9] Self-reported demographic data from many of the Silicon Valley tech firms reflects similar numbers. In October 2015, Airbnb shared that its workforce is 54 percent male, 63 percent white, 7 percent Hispanic/Latino, and 3 percent black. *USA Today* reported in March 2016, "In major Silicon Valley tech companies, men greatly outnumber women, accounting for as much as 70 percent of the workforce."[10]

When Google released its diversity data in 2014, Stanford University's Vivek Wadhwa said, "Frankly, Silicon Valley is a boys' club. It's like a frat club run wild . . . They don't understand why they have to be inclusive . . . And this is why it's important for companies like Google to be at the forefront of change, and encouraging women to join them . . . That could cause dramatic change within five years if they started focusing on it today . . . this is a really, really significant announcement that they have made." And Laszlo Bock, Google's SVP, People Operations, shared these thoughts following the release of their data: "One big thing is unconscious bias and diversity. In the privileged strata we occupy as Fortune 500 and global Fortune 1000 companies, we don't see a lot of overt sexism, racism, or homophobia, but you do see discrimination, and it's an outcome of people unconsciously being biased against one another."[11]

But inequity is not limited to tech. In January 2016, Bono was tweeting from the World Economic Forum in Davos, expressing the need for greater gender parity there. Only about 18 percent of the participants at Davos are women. Barri Rafferty, CEO of Ketchum North Americas, a PR firm, told *Fortune* in January 2015 that she was repeatedly mistaken for an attendee's wife.[12]

In January 2016, across industries, the Center for American Progress reported that fewer than 20 percent of all C-suite executives and 4.6 percent of CEOs are women at Standard & Poor 500 companies. "The lowest number of women in leadership roles are in the consumer products, transportation services, computer software, technology, chemicals, energy and utilities, construction, industrial manufacturing, and automotive and transport industries," writes Adrienne Selko in *Industry Week*.[13] That's a lot of industries in need of understanding why minorities are so underrepresented in leadership roles.

PROFILING CHANGE: A LOOK AT THE NUMBERS

While 13.2 percent of the US population is black, according to the Census Bureau, as of this writing, there are only *five* black CEOs at the country's five hundred largest companies: Kenneth Chenault of American Express, Delphi's Rodney O'Neal, Merck's Kenneth Frazier, Carnival's Arnold W. Donald, and Ursula Burns of Xerox.[14] This number is about to change and not in the right direction. Burns, the first black woman to run a Fortune 500 company, will step down following a split planned later in 2016. With her departure, there will be no black women heading a Fortune 500 company. There are only twenty-one female CEOs on the list, down from twenty-four last year.

In 2015, Hispanics/Latinos comprised 17 percent of the US population; there were nine Hispanic CEOs at Fortune 500 companies. As of this writing, there are ten Asian American CEOs in the Fortune 500, while Asians comprised 5.6 percent of the population. Tim Cook at Apple is the first, and currently only, openly gay Fortune 500 CEO.[15]

In January 2016, Richard Felloni, writing for *Business Insider*, observed the off-balance diversity at major companies, comparing the lagging numbers with the benefits that more level rates of diversity add to the company's competitive advantage. "Studies show that diverse organizations actually perform better than homogeneous ones, and so by changing the way we approach diversity, we are making ourselves a more competitive company."[16] Indeed, according to a 2015 McKinsey report, *Why Diversity Matters*:

> In the United States, there is a linear relationship between racial and ethnic diversity and better financial performance: for every 10 percent increase in racial and ethnic diversity on the senior-executive team, earnings before interest and taxes (EBIT) rise 0.8 percent.

McKinsey found that companies in the top quartile for racial and ethnic diversity are 35 percent more likely to have financial returns above their respective national industry medians, and those in the top quartile for gender diversity are 15 percent more likely.[17]

Cristian Deszö of the University of Maryland and David Ross of Columbia University studied the effect of gender diversity on the top firms in S&P's Composite 1500 list, a group designed to reflect the overall US equity market. First, they examined the size and gender composition of firms' top management teams from 1992 through 2006. Then they looked at the financial performance of the firms. In their words, they found that, on average, "female representation in top management leads to an increase of $42 million in firm value."[18]

In order to reach our innovative potential as employers, producers of new goods and technologies, and corporate citizens, we have to effect some profound change in addressing our gaps. That responsibility doesn't fall on any one group; change is going to challenge all of us.

LESSONS LEARNED: CHANGE IN SILICON VALLEY

Many of the major tech companies, having shared their diversity data from late 2014 to early 2016 and now making it a regular reporting activity, are stepping up their diversity and inclusion efforts following the flood of media scrutiny.[19] They've created jobs, departments, and initiatives dedicated to increasing their diverse talent and cultivating inclusion in their workplaces.

- In 2015, Intel unveiled a five-year, $300 million diversity program to build a workforce that mirrors the level of diversity among tech graduates.[20] CEO Brian Krzanich said the company is "missing opportunities" because its workforce doesn't represent the population.

- Apple has awarded scholarships to young developers from forty-one different countries in the past year. The company's website says, "We believe the more perspectives we have, the more innovative and powerful apps can be." In 2015, in the United States, nearly 50 percent of Apple's new hires were women, black, Hispanic, or Native American.[21]

- Facebook overhauled its unconscious bias training in February 2015, posting a one-hour version online in

July 2015. "It's best to start by having individuals reach a personal understanding of their possible biases and then have them work together through real world examples," shares Maxine Williams, global head of diversity at Facebook. "We look at our internal surveys: Is the hiring rate increasing? Are employees indicating that they feel connected and that they feel a sense of belonging?"[22] TechPrep is an online resource hub that Facebook launched in partnership with McKinsey in October 2015, designed to welcome underrepresented minorities to computer science.[23] Facebook University creates internships to cultivate underrepresented populations.

- In January 2016, Pinterest recruited Candice Morgan, who worked for nearly a decade at nonprofit Catalyst Inc., where she advised companies across industries on how to create more inclusive cultures.[24]

- Judith Williams, Google's global diversity and inclusion programs manager, started at Dropbox in October 2015.

These may all be small steps, but they are significant. Creating diversity officer positions in early-stage, fast-growth companies whose sole focus is driving more diverse and inclusive workplaces—and leveraging talented leaders who've achieved success elsewhere in the filling of these positions—is a wise move. As we've discussed, change doesn't just happen, especially on the uncomfortable (for many) topic of diversity; proactive, consistent, and relentless focus is needed in the form of a team who's accountable for progress and in the form of executive leadership who take a stand and make real investments.

The search for solutions to workplace inequities may get harder—and more costly—before it gets easier. With so many deeply ingrained conventions that need to be addressed before inclusion can be successful, we have to trace the origins of existing problems to discover their solutions. That search will lead deep into history, back to our fundamental management orthodoxies and, ultimately, to our deep challenges with equality as a country.

ENGAGING THE WHOLE WORKER

The need for change surfaces just about everywhere in an organization, if you know where to look. We poll employees endlessly about their levels of engagement and are becoming increasingly convinced that workplace cultures influence everything from recruitment to retention to the very value of brands worldwide. It is much harder to please shareholders or investors with your results when the vast *majority* of your workforce would describe themselves as disengaged.

A disengaged workforce is not an innovative one, as innovative behaviors and actions spring from minds that are open, from people who feel their voice is heard and respected and who trust their colleagues. According to a 2013 Gallup poll measuring employee engagement in the workplace, a meager 13 percent of employees across 142 countries worldwide report feeling engaged in their jobs—that is, they are emotionally invested in and focused on creating value for their organizations every day.[25] That

> It is much harder to please shareholders or investors with your results when the vast majority of your workforce would describe themselves as disengaged.

means a whopping 87 percent are focused on something else. What do you imagine that is costing an organization's bottom line?

I know from my own experiences, as both an employee in corporate America and as a consultant, that so many employees are withholding that valuable "discretionary effort" they *could* bring to work but don't, or won't, *if* they don't feel Welcomed, Valued, Respected, and Heard[SM]. Those of us who don't feel commitment take that energy elsewhere, and while our performance is diminished and we may be harming our careers, the company loses the most. Put very simply, consider the following:

- Engaged employees are the ones who are most likely to drive innovation, growth, and revenue that their companies desperately need.

- Actively disengaged employees continue to outnumber engaged employees by nearly two to one.

We'll let you do the math.

Companies lose great employees like Leslie Miley, who walk off the job rather than contend with a hostile or indifferent corporate culture. Many like Miley grow weary of expecting or hoping for change. "Companies turn over great employees because they're not organizationally strong enough to support rapid development within their ranks. In many cases, that is a recipe for discontinuity in service and product offerings as well as disloyalty in the ranks," shares Brendan Burke, director at Headwaters.[26]

Striving to be more transparent about diversity and inclusion is a good first step, but the road to lasting and deep culture change requires time and commitment. If transparency is followed by inaction, or a lack of visible attention (which amounts to the same thing), a slow but toxic fire can be kindled. This window of time between measurement, announcements, and real action is very important. The brownie points companies get for sharing their flaws openly last for a brief time, and then accountability for action kicks in. If there isn't visible, sustained, and meaningful action by leadership, it can almost make it worse to have discussed challenges—and made in the end false promises—in the first place.

We consult to a regional bank that contacted us because they had learned they were close to losing a huge bid—an existing client relationship—partially because they had without noticing sent an all-white and all-male team to the sales meetings. In giving the feedback to the bank, the potential buyer also shared that it was disturbing to walk through the halls of the bank and notice the lack of visible diversity. As we scrambled to put the bank's first ever diversity strategy together so they could at the very least discuss their awareness of their challenges and their road map for change, they ultimately lost the deal. Their prospective client represented a diverse group of constituents who needed to feel confident that their banking partner would understand their world. This experience was a huge wake-up call for the bank. I often say to my clients, "If you think you haven't lost a bid or a relationship at least in part because of diversity metrics, you're probably wrong—it's just that nobody has had the courage to give you the honest feedback."

As we know, profound and lasting organizational change toward more diverse and inclusive cultures can be very hard to get right. Training has, historically, been a go-to solution for culture change, but it's only one tool in what needs to be a much larger and multifaceted arsenal, as we point out above. And when not handled in the right way, it can be counterproductive, which demonstrates the delicacy of this topic and the issues that it raises for people. A January 2016 article in the *Harvard Business Review* stated, "The most commonly used diversity programs do little to increase representation of minorities and women. A longitudinal study of over seven hundred US companies found that implementing diversity training programs has little positive effect and may even *decrease* representation of black women."[27]

The rhetoric of diversity that sometimes shows up in traditional diversity training can result in inaccurate and counterproductive beliefs. In a recent experiment, it was determined that some training not only makes white men believe that women and minorities are being treated fairly—whether that's true or not—but it also makes them more likely to believe that they themselves are being treated unfairly.[28]

Sadly, this type of data is commonly used to refute the usefulness of training. I would argue that training design and approach matter enormously; our firm has had great success leading programs that are properly customized and buttressed by the right change-management practices that focus on organizational change and the role of the leader in taking concrete steps to lead the conversation about inclusion. We are emphatic about the fact that no training exists in a vacuum. Without understanding the pros and cons of a company's prevailing culture, workforce engagement, workplace dynamics, and the potential impact a younger, increasingly diverse talent pool will have on all of it, many traditional diversity training seminars *will* feel outdated, out of touch, and worst of all, insincere.

As a Gen-Xer specialist in the space, I've been able to witness firsthand how today's company leadership who largely hail from the baby boomer generation is failing to connect with today's workforce, despite good intentions. It's very difficult for us to step outside our worldviews, and yet step outside them we must. Organizations are failing to tap into the wide variety of values, beliefs, and needs of the multiple generations in the workplace as they update their approaches. For example, the failure to develop internal culture and workforce strategies alongside societal changes has severely diminished traditional companies' success in recruiting talent and engaging new and existing workers rattled by the transition to corporate life and the bureaucracy. If a company is unable to engage today's workforce, it's most likely the result of not developing new strategies capable of accommodating the needs and wants of a new age. Considering the overwhelming number of technological, economic, social, and generational changes worldwide just within the last two decades, it's understandable that large companies are struggling to pivot with the impact, but it's not excusable.

Part of the work of inclusion is helping those already in the workforce to feel safe bringing more of themselves to work, versus what they have done historically, such as downplaying parts of themselves for purposes of assimilation. Companies need every single person's knowledge, skills, and overall input, but employees won't bring all of this unless there is a trusting relationship between employer and employee. Where and how and why a company begins to take steps toward this looks different for every company, which we'll discuss in the next chapter. What's most important is to start—somewhere.

CHAPTER TWO

ORIGINS OF CHANGE

"Owning our story can be hard but not nearly as difficult as spending our lives running from it."

–BRENE BROWN

You never know how, or when, change is going to come, but we do know one thing: it's inevitable. When change comes to companies that sign up for it, the *why*—and its origins—are critical. Somewhere, somehow, someone has raised the flag, signaling for help because the workplace seems riddled with invisible problems that can neither be solved internally nor ignored.

Miley's experience at Twitter resonated with me as a parable of all the missed opportunities in our workplaces today. We see similar patterns in nearly every company we consult to. The conversations are initiated by a senior leader, or perhaps the diversity team, because they are witnessing high-profile departures of diverse talent, like Miley's from Twitter, and they fear the implications, both internally and externally. One of the last things companies want in their workforce is that revolving door, as diverse talent specifically seems to be leaving a particular business unit or leader in large numbers. Given how difficult it is to source this talent in the first place, as we discussed in chapter 1, it's especially expensive to lose it and, of course, demoralizing to see it lost.

Take women in engineering, where a long career is far from guaranteed. "Women engineers are twice as likely to leave a company," says Diana Bilimoria, a professor and chairwoman of organizational behavior at the Weatherhead School of Management at Case Western Reserve University. "Those who leave often exit in their thirties, feeling as though they're in an environment where they can't succeed," she says.[1]

Other times, I hear the *cri de coeur*, "We want to do better," which can mean several things, all of which I welcome because they are all openings to change. Anything that gets us through the door so that we can roll our sleeves up, we will take!

But let's explore more closely where the appetite for change begins to better understand the diversity and inclusion problems that today's companies experience most frequently. We call them change originators, and they're prevalent in companies small and large across virtually every industry. We will share our top five, which range from personal motivation to reputational pressure to bottom-line sales. Sometimes all are present in one company, which just means even more energy for change; but sometimes, all you need is one to begin the process.

CHANGE ORIGINATOR: THE CEO

"I want us to do better, and I know it starts with me."

Although C-suite leaders are paid precisely to set a bold vision and lead others through the difficult landscape of business, when it comes to diversity and inclusion, those who need to change might be— you guessed it—C-suite leaders themselves. Power and authority are changing so fundamentally that the very premises around which many leaders have built their careers, and perhaps, organized their lives—and even their sense of self—are being challenged. Today's workplaces are full of outdated management practices from a bygone era, and the most unaware population are often those at the top of the house, who grew up when times were different and have succeeded by mastering a well-worn but increasingly irrelevant playbook.

On the flip side, some leaders might feel like *they're* the ones stepping back in time. A CEO might switch from one company, where diversity and inclusion are a big priority and embedded everywhere, to another where no thought has been given to the topic. As they evaluate the demographics of their new organization and hear the stories about fractures within the workplace culture, a problematic picture emerges. If they're paying attention, they'll ascertain through internal feedback and data, as well as information in the public domain or from customer circles (or from their social circles), that they are lagging behind their industry competitors. No one likes to hear that, especially anyone who's competitive enough to reach the C-suite. And many senior leaders become concerned about their reputation sooner or later if they have a short time to leave their mark on the organization. Thoughts of legacy can certainly light a fire for change. Finally, some just have an unshakable and proven commitment to creating more opportunity for others and being a positive civic actor. These are

Thoughts of legacy by an executive can certainly light a fire for change.

the leaders who would say inequality and unhealthy cultures won't occur "on their watch." We feel blessed to meet people like them, with their intrinsic motivation and steadfast commitment to change.

They are the absolute best clients to work with because they are eager to use their platform to instigate.

Lately, we are starting to see CEOs and companies engaging in activism around diversity issues in the news, which represents an encouraging change. Howard Schultz, CEO of Starbucks, for example, intended to spark a national dialogue about race in response to the killings of Michael Brown and Eric Garner in 2015 and the subsequent civil unrest by launching the company's #race-together campaign, in which baristas would write the phrase "Race Together" on Starbucks cups.[2] The goal was to unleash conversations on the topic through baristas and the enormous Starbucks customer community, and while, ultimately, the initiative didn't resonate and receded from view, it was a bold step for a leader—a white one at that—to take.

Two additional examples of strong advocacy by senior leadership on behalf of employees come to mind. First, ninety executives had spoken out against a North Carolina law that eliminated antidiscrimination protections for lesbian, gay, bisexual, and ***transgender*** (LGBT) people as of March 2016.[3] And in 2015, I found myself in good company amidst another important show of leadership solidarity. As a CEO, I represented one of hundreds of businesses large and small that signed the Amicus Brief for the right for LGBTQ couples to marry that went to the Supreme Court.[4] Our company's name shared the signature page with many of our large Fortune 500 clients.

Behind closed doors, certain senior leaders worked tirelessly to create consensus that signing the brief would be the right thing to do; I am certain individuals took uncomfortable stands vis-à-vis each other, their boards, and their legal counsel to push their companies into the dialogue. Some were successful, and some were not. It's interesting to note that one particular client of ours decided not to sign, fearing a backlash. For the companies that signed, no backlash occurred. Times are changing.

It should be said that all this external and visible commitment, while tremendously empowering to employees of those companies, doesn't necessarily mean that the organization is free from work to do when it comes to their internal workplace culture. I will address this dichotomy throughout the book, as it continues to be a strong and noticeable contrast and should be a point of focus for *change agents*. Great intentions at the top of the house—and even great actions, great scores on all the indices and lists, and a whole host of awards—do not guarantee a healthy culture for all.

For the companies that signed, no backlash occurred. Times are changing.

Regardless, we do need to assess where leadership stands on the issues. When JBC begins work to create and launch diversity and inclusion efforts, I always ask about the CEO. Invariably these days, the CEO is usually driving the conversation on the topic, and that's an immeasurable benefit (almost a necessity) to the initiative's success. I had the privilege of working with the CEO of a European bank who was not satisfied with the bank's inattention to the issue and was a constant and relentless supporter who held his direct team accountable for change. Through our conversations, I knew that he related deeply to the issue of equality, based in part on the fact that he had daughters and couldn't imagine them working on a trading floor where they would be subjected to sexist or homophobic jokes and banter. He became gravely concerned when he considered how this impacts not just women but all kinds of talent who may be underrepresented and not have the wherewithal, courage, or air cover to speak up, risking their job in the process. He knew the onus was on leadership to set a different tone and monitor itself, as speaking up is very risky for so many. Cultures change from the top, and leaders need to speak often, and consistently, about the environment they expect. There is direct accountability between a leader and the next level or two down, and each CEO can and should set clear expectations around culture, behavior, and the workplace environment. Every movement made at the top of the house—everything that is said, as well as what is unsaid or not talked about—will cause ripple effects throughout the organization.

> He knew the onus was on leadership to set a different tone and monitor itself, as speaking up is very risky for so many.

Because this particular CEO was on board, we spent less time focused on the *why* of the initiative and more on the *how*, working on talking points for his executive team meetings and the kickoff to our training sessions for three hundred senior leaders. He was the one leader we didn't need to strongly pull through the business case, kicking and screaming. He didn't need to be convinced. He just wanted to know how we could most quickly and accurately tackle culture change. A year later, the conversation about diversity and how it's critical to the bank is still continuing, and ***employee resource groups*** (more on these in a later chapter) have been formed and launched, with more appearing every several months as employees are seeing that the conversation and the commitment is going to stick. It's starting to feel safe; they're on their way.

CHANGE ORIGINATOR: THE ECOSYSTEM

"We're feeling the pressure from the
people we do business with."

One of the most exciting emerging business cases for having inclusive workplace cultures where diversity is a priority is that the ecosystem surrounding the company is starting to exert pressure. When seeking a vendor partner, customers and clients issue requests for proposals (RFPs), which are, essentially, large-scale bids for work. RFPs are dreaded by many in the consulting world because they are exhaustive and run the supplier through the gauntlet; however, they are starting to ask questions about the bidder's diversity metrics, programs, and progress and are becoming a compelling change tool. In the bid itself for a whole host of unrelated goods and services the buyer wants to procure, the buyer also wants to see evidence of organizational commitment and some traction on diversity. All bidders are judged on their ability to answer these questions, and they are sometimes even given a relative percentage score for each section of the RFP.

When suppliers—and when we say suppliers, we mean small companies to huge professional services companies—have no program to describe, and certainly when they bring an all-white, all-male sales team to the RFP presentation meeting, like our regional bank client did, it can concretely hurt their prospects for winning the business. Sam's Club CEO Rosalind Brewer appeared on CNN in 2015, and in discussing Sam's Club's commitment to diversity, she explained that she talks directly to current and would-be Sam's Club suppliers about diversity and gives them feedback when they send an all-white, all-male team to a meeting: "Every now and then you have to nudge your partners. You have to speak up and speak out. And I try to use my platform for that. I try to set an example." As a discouraging side note, the story spurred backlash, with people calling Brewer a "racist" and "anti-white," encouraging a boycott of Sam's Club stores using the hashtag #boycottracistsamsclub.[5] However, the boycott never gained steam, and Walmart stood by Brewer. "For years, we've asked our suppliers to prioritize the talent and diversity of their sales teams calling on our company," Walmart CEO Doug McMillon said. "Roz was simply trying to reiterate that we believe diverse and inclusive teams make for a stronger business. That's all there is to it, and I support that important ideal."[6] Brewer was lauded by many for her stand.

Threatened backlashes aside, many of our clients are starting to connect the dots between their diversity and the bottom line. It's a wake-up call. I have been waiting for this to play out, and I knew that it eventually would. Given that it so tangibly hurts the bottom line, it can be motivational for companies—especially the C-suite—to feel the financial penalty of inaction.

It can be motivational for companies— especially the C-suite— to feel the financial penalty of inaction.

The good news is that companies just getting started, while their demographics may not yet reflect their nascent efforts, can get bonus points for effort and for having something underway. Much of my education for executives revolves around understanding comparatively abstract workforce strategies. Unlike so much in their world where they can create change in markets, business structures, and products overnight if they wish, workforce composition will only change when you do two things: proactively hire more diverse talent on the front end *and* maintain a longer-term, consistent commitment to creating an inclusive workplace where all kinds of talent are attracted to your company and want to build their career there. You might be able to hire your way into a better picture, but those hires won't stay long if you don't apply focus to the culture they are entering. And culture takes work—it can move backward as well as forward. A merger or acquisition between an inclusion-focused and diversity-valuing company and a company with no understanding or commitment to those things can go either way, culturally—it depends on which company's culture takes the lead. Small hint—it is not always the more progressive culture of the two, in the lead position. Did I mention that change is hard?

> ## Change is not a machine; it's us, in all our multifaceted complexity.

Change is not a machine; it's us, in all our multifaceted complexity.

The big companies that have been investing in diversity best practices for decades, and those that haven't but want to create a cycle of accountability and positive change and have some big contracts to hand out, can and should throw their weight around in the sales process and in their selection of suppliers, like the Sam's Club example. They have an ecosystem to influence, and they carry a big stick.

CHANGE ORIGINATOR: THE MARKETPLACE

> *"Our demographic make-up doesn't always reflect the markets we serve."*

Reflecting your market's demographics can be a powerful impetus for a diversity and inclusion initiative. Companies have, sometimes, unwittingly created insensitive products or approaches to new markets that misread or fumble the ethnicity, gender, culture, or geographic issues at stake. This is particularly easy to do if the leadership team, and the layers of direct reports beneath them, are principally white; principally men; principally very similar in education, background, and experience to one another; and likely not reflective of a particular target customer community. Nike, for instance, infamously had to recall thousands of products when a decoration intended to resemble fire on the back of its shoes resembled the Arabic word for *Allah*.[7] Mexican billboards allegedly printed a translation of Frank Perdue's tag line, "It takes a tough man to make a tender chicken," to read, "It takes a sexually stimulated man to make a chicken affectionate."[8]

©Randy Glasbergen
glasbergen.com

"They say we're not placing enough emphasis on diversity."

At JBC, we recently received an inquiry from a regional construction company that works with one of our large retail clients. The retailer, a forward-thinking company on issues of diversity and inclusion, had expressed concern about the complexion of the construction company's leadership. A quick glance at the latter's website showed an overwhelmingly white and male team. The CFO-turned-budding-diversity-champion at the construction company had given us a call as he had been charged, of course, to protect the contract and investigate what could be done. It was dawning on them that they would need to change the composition of their leadership team to reflect the communities they served and the customers with whom they did business. Their clientele was now demanding it. It is better to not wait for this kind of pressure.

CHANGE ORIGINATOR: THE EMPLOYEES

*"Our senior leadership and/or our board
don't reflect the rest of our workforce."*

Not seeing yourself and people who share your identity—however you define your identity—reflected in any leadership roles at the company you work in can cause pain, frustration, and ultimately, disengagement on the part of employees who long to see themselves and their identities in positions of leadership. I can't overstate the impact leadership-to-workforce representation has.

Representation matters. Actress and activist Geena Davis, in speaking about the staggering underrepresentation of women in feature films, has said about young women, "If she can't see it, she can't be it." Promising employees who look at the org chart and don't see themselves wonder whether there is a path to leadership for them. When a high-profile or executive- level leader leaves—and if that person

If she can't see it, she can't be it.

is diverse in ethnicity, a woman, an "out" LGBTQ executive—I have seen fast and broad ripple events through the employee population. They imagine the worst and internalize a message that "people like me can't be successful here." This is often the net effect of the departure, even if the executive's separation from the company might not have had anything to do with identity or the fact that he or she is "the only" of a particular background at that level, in that company. There was a high-profile departure of an out executive at one of our technology-company clients; I was working with the company's LGBTQ employee resource group at the time and had a bird's-eye view of the unintended impacts that can happen.

For a little background, as is true for many LGBTQ networks in the corporate arena, this group maintained an official "public" mailing list and also a "bcc" list, meaning there were still many who wanted to stay informed but not go public about their membership in the group due to fears about being "out" at the company. When this executive left suddenly, many on both lists interpreted it to reflect poorly on the company's "true" support of LGBTQ talent versus its stated support, which, in the case of this company, was very strong. This was one of those companies with many, many awards by all the big names, and walked the talk, too. As news spread of the executive leaving, I heard anecdotally that many on the bcc list became afraid of even that list (are corporate lists ever *really* secure?) and asked to be removed, and some on the public list did the same in the days after the departure, effectively going underground.

I share this story often to communicate, especially to executives, how delicate employee engagement truly is, especially for diverse talent who are constantly scanning the horizon, trying to discern if they are genuinely supported, or if it's just lip service. At my company, we know how difficult it can be to create awareness and understanding among those who are part of the traditional majority in workplace leadership, who haven't personally experienced this "got to see it to be it" factor, and therefore dismiss it as griping or blame it on the low numbers in the pipeline instead of hearing the plea that it is: to be seen, heard, and represented in the pipeline to leadership. Employees who crave seeing others of their heritage or background in leadership positions seem to be looking for reasons to stay, and the organization should bend over backward to provide them.

CHANGE ORIGINATOR: HELP WITH THE "HOW"

"We know why we need to be better; we just don't know how to get started."

A company that says its leadership is clear on the *why* for change might seem like the optimal starting point.

> Employees who crave seeing others of their heritage or background in leadership positions seem to be looking for reasons to stay, and the organization should bend over backward to provide them.

When we, as consulting partners, can spend less time and effort making the business case (the *why*) and move directly to designing strategy and execution (the *how*), we breathe a sigh of relief. We think to ourselves, *Now we can really get to work.*

An understanding of why diversity is important, however, can vary from person to person: How deep is that commitment, for each leader, and in concrete terms, for the company? Lack of clarity and varying levels of buy-in and a sense of urgency can fragment senior teams, who need to unify and speak with one consistent voice on the topic to create the momentum needed to shift an entire company in a new direction. We need leaders to investigate the problem, confront the pain points with honesty and openness, invest time and thought into their own *how*, and execute on it, individually and as a group. We need them to *own* the how; the figuring-it-out part of the journey is where they develop ownership and put their so-called skin in the game. I am happy to provide the road map, but their involvement in its development is critical.

In a post on Medium.com, cofounder and CTO of Pandawhale and blogger Joyce Park writes about how strange it is that so many view diversity as a chore:

> Diversity isn't like choking down spoonfuls of oat bran because it's supposedly good for you! It's literally like eating out at a wonderful new restaurant every day. Diversity is the foundation of the products with the biggest or deepest markets, and therefore of the economic regions with the most growth. Diversity is the driver of competition, which makes things better for end-users by forcing more innovation and lower prices. Diversity is the reward for pushing past your fears and embracing the inevitability of change. Diversity is about going for the awesome in life instead of settling for what you're comfortable with. Diversity is about each individual maximizing their impact on the world, instead of everyone trimming their personal stories—the traumas, the talents, the struggles—down to fit some imagined mold.[9]

As a consultant, I relish being handed the wheel to a company's diversity vehicle, but culture change around diversity demands a strong, authentic, consistent hand and voice from each internal senior leader and from the team, articulating their own narrative and their commitment to the work of inclusion. We work hard to get them as excited as Joyce Park is, in describing the promise of diversity. We have often worked with senior leadership teams to help them articulate their personal value propositions for this work and have armed them with strategies, behaviors, and language to lead the efforts. Only senior leadership teams can make it real and make it resonate, but they need to find a connection point that excites them—an angle they can internalize and believe in.

There is no one answer for every company. Leading culture change requires a balance of skill and will: skills to address what's uncomfortable or perceived to be unfair, and the will or desire to change it. Talking about diversity and inclusion can be painful, awkward, and fraught. It can be a delicate conversation that may seem to lead in exhausted, pointless circles or into an abyss where everyone is dissatisfied, offended, and angry. But we have to risk that conversation if we want to move forward.

> Only senior leadership teams can make it real and make it resonate, but they need to find a connection point that excites them—an angle they can internalize and believe in.

In delivering focus-group feedback to leadership teams, my team and I have seen so much discomfort. As in Elizabeth Kubler-Ross's five stages of grief, we've observed raised voices, flushed faces, tears, anger, indignation, denial, disavowal, and everything in between. The feedback we present on behalf of the workforce—in their own words—doesn't just paint a grim picture of the employees' working-day experience; it may also sound like criticism to well-intentioned senior leaders. The resilience and emotional intelligence to listen, to avoid defensiveness around intent, and to be curious about the information and passionate about the solution—*that's* where we can begin to make progress.

WHY YOUR CHANGE INITIATIVE CAN FAIL

Diversity and inclusion strategies generally fail for one of two main reasons: (1) we believe simple will be simpler than it really is, or (2) we make simple more difficult than it needs to be. Either way, the work must be done (and diversity can be complex), and regardless of all that is unique about companies ("but we're different!"), there is a recipe, a proven and well-worn path, to follow. Many things don't need to be reinvented, and this is one of them. Don't make simple overly difficult, in other words. Getting started is half the battle.

Many companies in older industries look to Silicon Valley to have their strategies either be validated or to check themselves on "what Google is doing." Respectfully, some more mature companies that have been applying themselves for decades and have robust diversity efforts that span hundreds of thousands of people impress me most and have been great teachers for me over the years as I've assembled my consulting tool kit. There is a reason that some longtime household names make some of the most respected lists, such as Fortune's "Best Workplaces for Diversity." When I walk into those companies, there is a baseline understanding amongst anyone who leads people that valuing diversity and being evaluated on inclusive behaviors is something they will be accountable for. They have been all the way down the path, beyond the asking of "Why do we need to do this?" to the "How are we doing this?" They have built the HR systems to support and measure inclusion. I encourage younger companies to learn about the journeys, challenges, and triumphs of their elder peers and leverage their lessons, while innovating around and perhaps beyond them, too. In a perfect world, the learning flows both ways.

Speaking of tried, true, and simple, a must for any change initiative is an in-depth assessment of the current state of an organization's culture. Before speeding ahead and introducing your KPIs (key performance indicators, which some companies live by), it is vital that you are informed about the real pain points, the structural inequities, and the unintended or invisible barriers to inclusion.[10] The formation of the current state "snapshot" is critical. Next, as we've just discussed, a successful strategy begins with a firm commitment at the top to the critical importance of building a culture of greater inclusion. Once that commitment is established, all involved set out on a path to understanding, well, just how much they don't understand! I promise, this is a good thing—and progress.

If you're confused already, that's okay. Before we go any further, let's take a look at a few of the key points you'll need to know if you're working on diversity and inclusion in your organization.

FIVE SIMPLE TRUTHS ABOUT DIVERSITY AND INCLUSION[SM]

There are a few realities to keep top of mind as you or anyone in your organization moves from status quo toward embracing diversity and building an inclusive culture.

1. Change is hard.

2. Most of a company's untapped diversity and inclusion knowledge lives in the middle and entry levels.

3. Equality is good for people and for business.

4. Workplace diversity and inclusion means respecting all people's inherent differences equally.

5. Unconscious biases and unexamined cultural values and standards affect everything.

Change is hard.

Fear of the unknown—often about backlash and resistance—makes implementing and maintaining any new strategy demanding for managers and employees alike. When the topic is diversity, fear plays a big role for two critical populations: those who haven't spoken up but who are being asked to offer more insights about their experiences of inclusion and exclusion, and those who feel they know little about the topic but sense they will be on the receiving end of criticism. This can lead to paralysis and no progress.

There are powerful tools to make these conversations more productive and certainly more enjoyable. Previous generations of diversity training were described as "shame and blame" sessions for a reason. As a relatively young practitioner, I have heard many stories from before my time as a facilitator about multiday, tearful, deep and painful explorations of stereotypes that cast some in the room in an extremely hurtful—and not always accurate—light. While those programs were powerfully transformative in helping many confront their privilege for the first time, we have, thankfully, moved toward a conversation that includes all voices and honors all experiences and points in the journey, without devolving into an "us and them" paradigm. We acknowledge that those with greater privilege have a unique opportunity to lead from a place of *allyship*, to stand for and drive outcomes that many lack the positional power or social capital to lead.[11] Leadership today comes with this added responsibility.

The ability to lead inclusively is a top competency for leaders in the new age. From the factory floor to the executive suite, all have a role to play and are asked to stand up and get involved in the best inclusion efforts. No one in the workplace should feel that his or her voice isn't included, but we can't always rely on those whose voices are absent to do "all the changing."

The ability to lead inclusively is a top competency for leaders in the new age.

Most of a company's untapped diversity and inclusion knowledge lives in middle and entry levels.

Corporate America suffers from a leaky workforce pipeline. If women and people of color do not see themselves represented in the senior leadership team, if they see themselves repeatedly passed over for opportunities, if they perceive that they have to work twice as hard to get on the radar screens, they will eventually either disengage from their work or begin to look elsewhere. It is critical to construct a system that guides and cultivates talent from the entry level, creating channels of communication through which every group has a voice and everyone benefits by listening; this is the beginning of forging the path to workplace equality.

Those in the middle and below in organizations also carry an outsized amount of wisdom about the external world—about customers, partners, and incoming talent—because they are closer to the ground and further away from the so-called ivory tower. They have close relationships with external partners. These are your cultural informants, inside and outside the organization.

Equality is good for people and for business.

We now have access to a myriad of statistics, demonstrated return on investment (ROI), and anecdotal feedback about the bottom-line impact of diversity, as well as the role that the *perception* of equal opportunity plays in building successful enterprises, of all shapes and sizes.[12] Reality and perception are equally important for success, and I'll share more insight on this as we go.

Workplace diversity and inclusion mean respecting all people's inherent differences equally.

The golden rule, treating others as you would like to be treated, is out. The platinum rule is in: treat others as *they* would like to be treated. You will have to learn to ask what that entails, and the answer will be different for different members of your organization. People need to understand that others' experiences are different, but just as valid as their own, before they can really learn how to treat their colleagues in the way that they prefer to be treated. We will need to become expert at understanding our lenses, and then seeing the world, and the workplace, through the lenses of others, to create real change.

The platinum rule is in: treat others as *they* would like to be treated.

Unconscious biases and unexamined cultural values and standards affect everything.

In this case, everything can mean from hiring requirements to work environments to how some continue to believe that the workplace is a meritocracy (quick tip: it's not). Providing the same starting line for employees doesn't mean that everyone actually starts from the same place. It is essential to understand how employees get to the starting line in the first place—the hurdles they face in the career race that may be invisible to you—in order to create truly

> Providing the same starting line for employees doesn't mean that everyone actually starts from the same place.

equal opportunities in the workplace. We use an exercise called the "privilege walk" in some of our programs, which we'll go into detail about later in the book and which demonstrates in concrete terms the relative privileges of each of us, to each other. It's a powerful, eye-opening moment for many.

A favorite teaching tool of ours is the Johari Window.[13]

Based on a four-square grid, the Johari Window prompts questions about what is known and unknown about the self and what is known and not known by others. There are a myriad of opportunities for cross-cultural and diversity sharing to occur when we consider especially what is known about ourselves that others do not know. What do we keep from our work teams and colleagues, and why? What are our mutual, undiscovered biases that are keeping us from connecting and keeping our workplace cultures from truly changing? We will explore the particular and transformative power of finding the answers to this question in later chapters.

JOHARI WINDOW

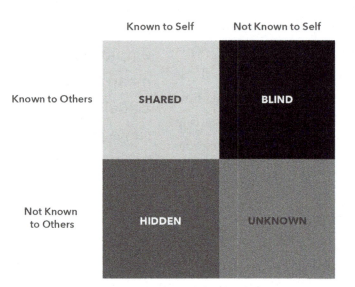

The key to managing and leading through change is to understand the need for it—where the pain point is, the *why* for change—and then to rally your change drivers and tools to tackle the *how*. As people who feel inspired to be catalysts for any kind of change, we must continue to look through multiple lenses at the challenge—from the individual

What are our mutual, undiscovered biases that are keeping us from connecting and keeping our workplace cultures from truly changing?

all the way to executive leadership—and understand what might enlist them as partners in the effort. We can speed change by educating ourselves and others about the negative effects of bias.

CHAPTER THREE

CHANGE AGENTS

The Roles We Play in a Diverse Workplace

"The most common way people give up their power is by thinking they don't have any."

–ALICE WALKER

A colleague who works at a major hotel chain recently shared my TEDx talk on "Finding Your Voice in the Workplace[SM][1] as part of a sales training he was leading. About halfway through, he hit the pause button and asked, "Who do you think this woman is?" He collected all kinds of answers, and then he hit play again. Once he got to the section where I detail my experiences with coming out as LGBTQ (more on that in a moment), and how my identity impacts my experience as a business owner, people were astonished. In just a few minutes, they had formed so many assumptions about me— about my family, my work, what's important to me—and most of them were wrong.

All of us make assumptions based on what's visible about someone, and then we fill in the blanks about the rest, often based on our own lens or filter. That old friend, unconscious bias, creeps in. Many of us, in our everyday lives, think in terms of stereotypes and have no experience of things that are beyond our conception of the norm. We just haven't been exposed to difference. The Johari Window mentioned in the previous chapter demonstrates that we have areas where we may be overconfident in what we know, rather than acknowledging that there is so much we don't know—our many blind spots, in other words.

Sharing my personal story in these training sessions involves my personalizing the issue of stereotypes and unconscious bias. I use myself as a teaching instrument. If the audience is largely white, given I'm a white woman, they might be slightly more comfortable with what they perceive as our "sameness," and I'm aware that I might have access to conversations and influencing opportunities because of the comfort my audiences feel or a certain unearned status they bestow on me.

When they learn even more about my identity, further along in my story—when I come out, for example, as LGBTQ—my audiences are forced to confront the fact that there are some aspects of me they may not be so comfortable with or even familiar with. Foreign or surprising aspects about someone can trigger a negative judgment.

Intersectionality is the ability to hold in our minds all of who someone is, simultaneously, a skill that we can learn through practice and discipline.

If you'll pardon the saying, it's often not so black and white, or even clear to us—let alone those meeting us for the first time. The concept of an individual having multiple aspects and truths—the idea that someone can be privileged in some ways but not in others, or have multiple identities that intersect and impact each other, including gender, race, and sexual orientation—is called *intersectionality*, a term coined by Kimberle Crenshaw in 2014. It is the ability to hold in our minds all of who someone is, simultaneously, a skill that we can learn through practice and discipline.[2]

When the opportunity presents itself, I may hesitate to reveal more of my own diversity story, depending on the assumptions—potentially inaccurate—that I'm making about the risks involved in revealing further personal details and in being true to myself. This dynamic prevents so many in today's workplace from feeling their worth is recognized, and it takes a toll on their sense of self. We'll talk about this dynamic, identified as *covering*, later in the book.

But when we do share our stories, it provides a powerful opportunity to open up the dialogue and leverage our identities to create greater understanding of the ways in which people view, and often misperceive, the world through the tinted lens of their own experiences. We are each a powerful instrument and demonstration of the beauty of the intersections. If we all can better understand how unconscious bias works and cultivate awareness of our individual biases, then we can avoid limiting or damaging our ability to lead, to make decisions, and to be better colleagues. Whether those decisions involve recruiting, hiring, staffing a project, choosing a mentor or a supplier, or even how we engage with another human being on the street or in the subway, unconscious bias is always present in us. But how much better would it be if we knew we were making the decision based on the best information possible, rather than based on a snap judgment? As Google's blog states it: "Combating our unconscious biases is hard, because they don't feel wrong; they feel right. But it's necessary to fight against bias in order to create a work environment that supports and encourages diverse perspectives and people."[3]

Google cites, as a relatively simple demonstration of unconscious bias, the fact that when YouTube launched its video-upload app for Apple, approximately 10 percent of the uploaded videos were upside down: "Were people shooting videos incorrectly? No. Our early design was the problem. It was designed for right-handed users, but phones are usually rotated 180 degrees when held in left hands. Without realizing it, we'd created an app that worked best for our almost exclusively right-handed developer team."[4]

Learning to manage your unconscious bias isn't just a soft skill. A lack of awareness of it and a lack of vigilance about it can limit your ability to deliver a functioning product. This is another case of—as the Johari Window showed us—"You don't know what you don't know."

I myself am still prone to bias when confronted with disparate dots that my brain automatically—and often incorrectly—connects. Even those of us who do this work for a living still struggle with our all-too-human wiring. When I walk into a room of all-white male executives, for example, it's easiest for me to make assumptions about who they are, only to discover as I ask them to share what diversity means to them that most of them also have a story associated with identity or background, and the experience of exclusion, which may be related to ethnicity, socioeconomic class, political affiliation, and family, to name a few. Almost as often as I make these assumptions, I discover that I've made an error that says more about me than it does about the other individual. This is an important reminder to me—and

Everyone knows something about diversity.

should be for all of us—that everyone knows something about diversity. It's also critical for me to discuss this connection in my conversation with those who enjoy privilege—namely, the men in the room who have the power to influence changes that would affect many in their organization. It is critical that they too see themselves as having a story to share.

Rather than view unconscious bias as an unwelcome intrusion in my thoughts, I see it as a reminder to be watchful and to keep learning, to share my process and progress with others, and to put myself into situations where I am confronted with a broader array of examples of "different from me." Others certainly may not enjoy this journey as much as I, getting stuck in resistance, stubbornly defending their own lens as the only way to look at a situation. They protect themselves and their beliefs and shore up their power and position for what they think is survival and maybe self-protection, but their behavior actually has the opposite effect and can send damaging ripple effects outward, especially in organizations where so many still look upward for cues about norms, behaviors, and what's acceptable. Leaders are watched very closely.

I have taught myself to try to see all people, regardless of how they appear, as people I don't truly know, whom I can't know from a stereotype or a quick assumption about their education, culture, or upbringing. This awareness has been reinforced time and again in the classrooms where I facilitate; I am often amazed by what senior leaders choose to share, sometimes for the first time, as we work and get comfortable with each other. They reveal how they are very much caught up in the same unconscious bias dynamic, on both sides of the equation:

- An executive who identifies as Jewish revealed his faith to his colleagues in my executive session, presumably for the first time, by relaying a story from the year before. When he first began in his role, he said, a critical annual company meeting was scheduled during a Jewish holiday. But because he feared he might be judged or excluded, he stayed silent about it and ended up attending the meeting—across the world. His sharing the story that day was the first time he'd mentioned it. He hadn't thought it mattered until that point.

- An executive who identifies as a Democrat shared that when marriage equality was affirmed by the Supreme Court, he felt he couldn't express his excitement on his Facebook page or in the workplace. When asked why he'd suppressed his feelings, he revealed that he feared repercussions because of the conservative beliefs of his peers on the executive team and the conservative nature of the company as a whole. In my session, he bravely shared this for the first time with his peer team.

We know that prejudice is irrational, but it's nearly unavoidable, a kind of vestigial instinct meant to protect us from whatever may cause us harm. Since, however, we are no longer hunting and gathering in the wild, and we know that the fight-or-flight response likely doesn't serve us as effectively in the modern world, we need to make the effort to slow down and not be a victim of our instincts. Our interpretation of especially what we know little about, or have no experience with, can be even more distorted. We often accept our own skewed interpretations of what we can't fully comprehend in an attempt to bring apparent order to the world. It feels good in the moment. Or, because we fear what we can't comprehend, we seek to avoid it.

At Google, more than twenty-six thousand employees have participated in unconscious bias training as of this writing.[5] We discussed in an earlier chapter that this was one of the company's solutions to their demographic challenges and the fact that women and people of color are so poorly represented at the company. Google has also articulated guidelines for inclusive behaviors that we at JBC enthusiastically endorse, such as making a habit of asking who has been included and who has been excluded. It's so simple and obvious, and yet examples of *not* doing this well are everywhere, when you begin to examine it—such as names on conference rooms:

> "…Googlers pointed out that of the dozens of conference rooms named after famous scientists, only a few were female. Was this our vision for the future? No. So we changed Ferdinand von Zeppelin to Florence Nightingale—along with many others—to create more balanced representation. Seemingly small changes can have big effects."[6]

No one set out to send a message that women weren't welcome at Google when they originally named the rooms. They probably just wanted to name the conference rooms in an aspirational way after—you guessed it—very well-known names in the scientific field, and the most documented names that history has recorded are mostly male. Unconscious biases, though, informed the naming process and created an unintended message about who is welcome—and who is worthy of celebration and recognition—and who is not.

I've worked with a small handful of smart senior leaders who refuse to

Unconscious biases, though, informed the naming process and created an unintended message about who is welcome—and who is worthy of celebration and recognition—and who is not.

begin interviewing for an open position until they have a diverse *slate* of candidates. I've also worked with leaders who shrug and say, "We didn't get any applicants who were women or people of color. They must not be interested," rather than asking if their job description might have contained exclusionary or prejudicial language, or if they posted it only in locations that might not invite or welcome those constituencies.

In June 2015, Nobel Prize winner Tim Hunt spoke at a conference about the "trouble with girls" in the laboratory: "Three things happen when they are in the lab; you fall in love with them, they fall in love with you, and when you criticize them, they cry."[7] Women scientists took to social media, with both humor and righteous indignation, under the hashtag #distractinglysexy, to challenge Hunt's assertion.

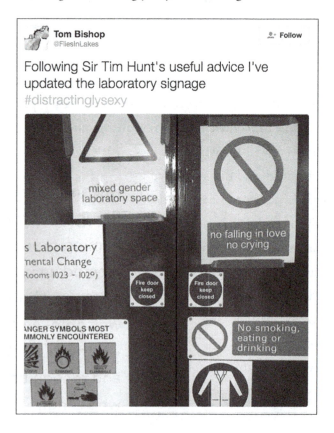

Shortly thereafter, Isis Anchalee Wenger, a female platform engineer at OneLogin, appeared in the company's recruiting campaign and received comments about her appearance, which also questioned her qualifications.

Mortified by her sudden celebrity but determined to use the opportunity to address inequity and unconscious bias in engineering, Ms. Wenger wrote, "I've had men throw dollar bills at me in a professional office (by an employee who works at that company, during work hours). I've had an engineer on salary at a boot camp message me to explicitly 'be friends with benefits' while I was in the interview process at the school he worked for."[8] While taking pains to clarify that neither of these were *bad* guys, Wenger went on to talk about a larger cultural bias that permeates her work environment:

> There is a significant lack of empathy and insight toward recognizing that their "playful/harmless" behavior is responsible for making others inappropriately uncomfortable. This industry's culture fosters an unconscious lack of sensitivity toward those who do not fit a certain mold…mild to extreme personal offenses that they've *just had to tolerate.*[9]

Wenger also mentioned that people expressed skepticism about whether an engineer could look like her, and she took issue with the idea that she was meant to represent *all* engineers. "News flash: this isn't by any means an attempt to label 'what female engineers look like.' This is literally just *me*, an example of *one* engineer at OneLogin."[10] And thus began a second social media campaign, under the #ILookLikeAnEngineer hashtag, as well as a larger initiative to "facilitate concise plans of action" in order to create a real shift toward greater inclusion and acceptance for women engineers and developers.

We may inevitably perceive the world through our own lenses, but we can also challenge our perception that everyone else is working with the same understanding and perspective. If we work to cultivate a better understanding of how others experience the same environments and situations, we'll raise our own intuition about our interactions. That intuition is essential to building workplaces and market spaces that are more welcoming, more comfortable, and more inclusive.

Let's keep exploring this notion of *one's lens*. Many white people bristle at the suggestion that they have an inherent—and sometimes unearned—privilege relating to their ethnicity; they judge that they have worked hard, struggled, and, through sheer effort, earned everything that they've achieved. Acknowledging privilege recognizes that the playing field is far from level and that some start on higher ground than others do.

> Acknowledging privilege recognizes that the playing field is far from level and that some start on higher ground than others do.

It's only once we can recognize and acknowledge the ways in which our race, gender, class, ethnicity, nationality, sexual orientation, disability, and other identity markers have offered us certain advantages and disadvantages that we can begin to understand ourselves and our experience more evenly. With that self-awareness, we see much more clearly how we interact with and experience the world around us, and hopefully, we find it that much easier to discover our role within it and then of course advocate for those who are relatively more challenged.

ACKNOWLEDGING PRIVILEGE: MY STORY

I was born into an upper-middle-class, conservative, Christian family with a stay-at-home mom and a physician father. I grew up in Orange County, California. I went to private school and then to an exclusive liberal arts college. As I moved out into the world, I had all the privileges that those early experiences afforded me. They didn't protect me from heartache, disappointment, or shame, but they opened certain doors for me and created access to conversations, people, and opportunities.

When I came out as a lesbian during my undergraduate years, I discovered that my community of origin described previously didn't quite fit me. But I also discovered that, inside my newfound LGBTQ community, some people also made assumptions about me. I tried to dress to fit into that community because I wanted so badly to belong. I thought I had to wear the uniform at the time—involving combat boots and big flannel shirts and short hair—that would allow me to be seen as a community member. For marginalized communities such as the LGBTQ community, which was incredibly more marginalized twenty-three years ago than it is now, finding that community was critical.

The only problem was dressing like that wasn't comfortable for me. I didn't have this word at the time, but that uniform didn't align with my truest gender expression. In the years since, as so many in the LGBTQ community have become more comfortable, safer, and feel less compelled to conform in *any* direction, I have had more freedom to find a comfortable expression of my gender, which happens to involve a more feminine one.

The very fact that I didn't fit into either community—my community of origin, or my community of choice—was an important lesson, as it enabled me to experience another insider/outsider dynamic and raised my awareness that we all have multiple communities of identity, and of choice, and that there can be pressure to conform to all of them. At the same time, it's critical to differentiate ourselves; the striving for authenticity shapes and forms who we are and combats stereotypes of all kinds.

It's critical to differentiate ourselves; the striving for authenticity shapes and forms who we are and combats stereotypes of all kinds.

It's powerful to feel you've transcended the limitations, and sometimes the confinement, of a certain community. I embrace the outside. We'll talk about the power of experiencing hardship and challenges related to exclusion in a later chapter.

I have experienced setbacks, disappointments, and heartbreaks in my career, but I also know that my current gender expression (a more predictably feminine one) is its own form of privilege. Let me explain. It helps people in my community of origin (straight, white, and conservative) to hear what I have to say. I am able to return to that community to bring a message about valuing diversity in all its forms, as I come in a familiar, safe package. This isn't bad or good, fair or unfair—it is just a fact.

As change agents, we all have our best roles to play—our strongest cards. Each of us contains change tools, which include not just what we know, but who we are and how we appear. Our awareness of how we might be stereotyped plays a role and is called ***stereotype threat***, but we can't concede to the fear.[11] Rather than judging ourselves for those aspects, the more useful question is: Am I effectively using everything I have been given to create positive change?

When I reflect on what others assume about me based on my appearance and dress, I am reminded of my friend and current diversity leader at Twitter, whom we mentioned earlier. He is a white, cisgender gay man, whom the media assumed could never successfully effect change on behalf of workplace communities that reflected a different ethnicity from his.[12]

Although we did discuss earlier the need of many to "see it, to be it" and the pain of a lack of role models for so many people who aren't white and male, the assumption that a white cisgender man can't be effective as a change agent is also limiting. He and other white men who dedicate their careers to diversity and inclusion are trailblazers, whom I honor, and who are necessary for progress. They shock, surprise, and give a new face to the word *diversity*. This is powerful.

We all play a role in how others feel about themselves. Often, it's the smallest things that help those outside the norm feel included, respected, and valued, not just at work but also in everyday life. I want my role to be one that helps people who have fewer advantages than I have to succeed with equal effort and be valued by their employer. Equally, I want to grapple with my more stigmatized identities—being a woman and LGBTQ, for example—and utilize them in the most productive way possible to increase understanding and to ensure my voice is strong and steady.

As I ask you to think about what your role will be, I think it's necessary to spend some time on privilege.

> It's the smallest things that help those outside the norm feel included, respected, and valued, not just at work but also in everyday life.

FEELING OUR IMPACT: GETTING HONEST ABOUT WHITE PRIVILEGE IN AMERICA

In her 1988 essay "White Privilege: Unpacking the Invisible Knapsack," Wellesley College Professor Peggy McIntosh wanted to understand the implications of her whiteness. She set out to explore the ways in which being part of a racial majority served as a benefit, as a creator of opportunity and access for her, and to illuminate the hidden advantages many whites don't consciously perceive themselves to have, even as people of color may be painfully, shamefully aware of these cultural subsidies. Here are a few of McIntosh's fifty observations about white privilege:

- "I can if I wish arrange to be in the company of people of my race most of the time."

- "I can turn on the television or open to the front page of the paper and see people of my race widely represented."

- "I can talk with my mouth full and not have people put this down to my color."[13]

JBC PRACTICAL EXERCISE

With our clients, we often explore both unconscious bias and the ramifications of privilege through an exercise called the "privilege walk" (https://www.buzzfeed.com/dayshavedewi/what-is-privilege). Participants stand in a straight line in the middle of an empty room. JBC's facilitator reads a series of statements, every one of which addresses some small privilege that is based on gender, race, ethnicity, class, sexual orientation, or disability. They include:

- If your ancestors came to the United States by force, take one step back.

- If there were more than fifty books in your house growing up, take one step forward.

- If you ever felt unsafe because of your sexual orientation, take one step back.

- If you studied the culture of your ancestors in elementary school, take one step forward.

Each of these statements confirms or refutes a set of assumptions we might make about our colleagues, friends, neighbors. Over the course of the exercise, individuals move forward or back as they answer the questions, eventually finding themselves spread widely across the room. Many are afraid to look around the room or feel shame about being in the very front, or very back. There are often tears and apologies. The discussions that follow the exercise are heartfelt and vulnerable. They enable participants in the exercise to see the disparities in any group of individuals—those unique combinations of advantages and disadvantages all individuals are given—and, ultimately, allow them to connect with the responsibility of privilege as well as the less-advantaged parts of us.

Archbishop Desmond Tutu is credited with the following description of the African understanding of mutually beneficial coexistence:

Africans have a thing called *ubuntu*. It is about the essence of being human. It is part of the gift that Africa will give the world. It embraces hospitality, caring about others, being willing to go the extra mile for the sake of another. We believe that a person is a person through other persons, that my humanity is caught up, bound up, inextricably, with yours. When I dehumanize you, I inexorably dehumanize myself. The solitary human being is a contradiction in terms. Therefore you seek to work for the common good because your humanity comes into its own in community, in belonging.[14]

Ubuntu is a Zulu or Xhosa word meaning "I am because we are." In organizational management, we might call this kind of mutually beneficial coexistence—you guessed it—*inclusion.*

REVERSING THE PRIVILEGE EQUATION

I see this type of **mutualism** most clearly in our work designing cross-identity mentoring programs in the workplace.[15] In the diversity and inclusion space, these programs are known as **co-mentoring**, or sometimes **reverse mentoring**, and when applied to the development of underrepresented talent, they work to identify up-and-coming leaders and pair them with more senior leaders explicitly of different backgrounds where possible. The "reverse" part acknowledges that with so much knowledge that's needed for organizations to flourish existing in the lower segment of the organizational pyramid, we must invest in harnessing this knowledge and driving it *upward*, not just pulling it from the top down. Both ends of the spectrum need each other.

The cofounder of Fast Company, Alan Webber, describes reverse mentoring this way: "It's a situation where the old fogies in an organization realize that by the time you're in your forties and fifties, you're not in touch with the future the same way the young twenty-something's [are]. They come with fresh eyes, open minds, and instant links to the technology of our future."[16]

Companies such as Cisco and GE have turned to reverse-mentoring programs in recent years, and their success has shed light on the benefits within their respective STEM field especially. There is symbiosis between executives who make time to build cross-identity relationships (across lines of race/ethnicity, gender, sexual orientation, disability, generation) to solve a company problem (retention of a certain segment of talent) by helping those outside the power structure navigate up the pipeline, while ideally retooling their own skill set in the process through the mentorship of a younger professional. Many make time for it because it's the right thing to do, and they are personally committed to, and enjoy investing in, emerging leaders. Others view it as solving a costly corporate problem. As we've talked about in earlier chapters, getting to each person's *why* and positioning around it with any initiative, but especially diversity-related efforts, is critical.

Creating pairs for mentoring programs might still look hierarchical—one senior person paired with one more junior person—but in today's programs, leaders have an opportunity to see the workplace, and the world, through a different lens than their own. When mentees share their challenges and struggles in a system that wasn't built for or by them—a system that has been more hospitable to the people that don't look like them—the differences can be stark, instructive, and compelling. There are multiple opportunities for those "a-ha" moments.

CEOs experience their "a-ha" moments, too, and turn them into real-time learning for others. In August 2012, I interviewed Jim Turley, former CEO of Ernst & Young (EY), at the National Gay and Lesbian Chamber of Commerce (NGLCC) conference. He shared two especially compelling stories about his own moments of discovery and deeper understanding of all that privilege can enable, and who exercises their privilege without awareness of doing so. In reference to the day that EY launched a mentoring program specifically targeting female talent, Turley recalled,

> At about 6:30 p.m. that night, a young man sticks his head in my office door and asks if we can talk. He said, "I was at the launch today. It sounds like an interesting program, but I'm feeling disadvantaged." I sat there for a second and then I looked at him and said, "You're a third-year person with us, a senior accountant. I'm the managing partner of the office. Did you have an appointment to see me?" He didn't. So, I said, "Let's get this straight: You came to talk to me, sight unseen, about something that really worries you. A young woman in your shoes might not have the comfort and confidence to come talk to me. She would walk out of the firm." The guy said, "You're right. If something bothers me, I'll come talk to you about it. This is a great program." And he walked out the door.

EY is of course a leader and inspiration to so many when it comes to representation of women and gender in the workplace. While there are many powerful and well-known female leaders at the firm who also wouldn't have hesitated to approach the CEO with concerns, Turley's point is well-taken generally, about who may or may not believe that their concerns matter or will be addressed. In discussing stereotype threat previously, we pointed out that those not traditionally represented in executive leadership and with a relatively more stigmatized identity—women, people of color, people with a disability, LGBTQ individuals—are often more hesitant to raise concerns, for fear of being labeled unfavorably. Women might keep their head down, for example, rather than speak up, not to appear too strident. What the previous example shows me is the great lengths we still need to go to educate male colleagues about the gendered difference in these behaviors, *why* the differences exist, and that they need to do more in support of shifting empowerment and opportunity to those who struggle with perceiving they have less of a voice. Turley utilized this interaction with another man as a teachable moment.

Turley also talked about his collegial collaboration with Beth Brooke, an openly gay senior partner:

> She is my right hand, not just on diversity and inclusion but also on public policy and regulatory issues, which are central to our profession. Beth and I have been working very closely for years. There have been no secrets between us, and we have had some very open discussions.
>
> I am just so proud of her for being honest with herself and who she is. And I'm proud of our organization because, frankly, people don't care. They just care about her talent. They care about her being part of Ernst & Young.[17]

Turley summarizes, in a very real way, what diversity and inclusion's ultimate purpose really is. People are, well, just people. They want the same opportunities, the same benefit of the doubt, and they want to be viewed and treated the same as anyone else, regardless of their differences. Nothing more, nothing less. Good diversity training isn't about glorifying one group over another, nor is it about vilifying or humiliating the white men who have seemingly won the privilege lottery. Diversity conversations are a time for people to talk about what makes them whole, to explore both their shared and divergent experiences in order to more accurately understand who they are as a team and ensure that each person feels comfortable and energetic about contributing.

THE FOUR STAGES OF INCLUSION^{SM}

Diversity conversations are a time for people to talk about what makes them whole, to explore both their shared and divergent experiences in order to more accurately understand who they are as a team and ensure that each person feels comfortable and energetic about contributing.

Our company's mission statement describes our goal of building more inclusive workplaces, where all kinds of talent can feel welcomed, valued, respected, and heard. This is a simple way to understand what we mean by a culture of inclusion: everyone wants to feel welcomed; everyone wants to know that she has been heard. Most of us feel included when our coworkers affirm that (1) we belong, (2) we matter, (3) what we do matters, and (4) "they" hear what we say.

We developed an inclusion model in our consulting work called the Four Stages of Inclusion^{SM} that speaks to those deepest human needs and is easy to understand because the concepts are universal. Even the first step of defining each of those words *through our lens* (welcomed, valued, respected, and heard) is instructive; we are each likely to define them through the prism of our culture, style, and experience. This is where bias can creep in, as we make immediate assumptions even about definitions of so-called common concepts like feeling "welcomed."

We prefer our own definitions, as that's the world we know, but we can't stop there.

Others will see these concepts through their own lenses, and perhaps they will define them differently. The very presumption that welcoming behavior, for example, looks and sounds the same to you as it does to another can be an immediate bias that provides a teachable moment. I invite you to be curious about how others define and experience these concepts, instead of assuming that they will agree with your definition. How do we do this? We ask, we seek to learn more, and we listen, *really* listen, to others. This process of seeking to see through others widens our vocabulary as leaders and provides an important check-and-balance on how we might tend to blindly prioritize our lens over that of others. This is just one building block of inclusive behavior.

The Four Stages of Inclusion can be thought of as a step-by-step progression, but they don't necessarily need to be applied in this order. Being mindful of our own various lenses at JBC, we've provided just a handful of possible definitions here, while acknowledging that there are so many more to learn about (and we're always learning!):

This process of seeking to see through others widens our vocabulary as leaders and provides an important check-and-balance on how we might tend to blindly prioritize our lens over that of others.

- An inclusive culture is one where all employees feel **welcomed;** when every employee is invited to join the conversation, or a project team, or a social gathering, morale and intergroup collaboration soar. Welcoming isn't a single act, performed once. It's an ongoing set of behaviors that welcome all voices, particularly those different from your own in identity, style, or background, to build an environment where inclusion is a priority for all and a habit in every business interaction.

- Once employees know that they are welcomed, we can take another step: making them feel **valued**. As employees grow more comfortable with their workplace, they become more confident in their work, more assertive in discussions, and assume a greater sense of responsibility for a project's success. Leaders need to make sure employees are challenged by assigning proportionally important work and giving more visible assignments to increase and reinforce employees' sense of their value.

- As employees meet these expanding expectations, they need to be rewarded for their accomplishments. Leaders who regularly express gratitude to high-performing workers ensure that employees feel personally and professionally **respected**. This can include publicly highlighting the accomplishments of all team members, for example, or examining the distribution of responsibilities to ensure that there is truly equal opportunity.

- If an inclusion effort addresses the behaviors above, the employee's voice is much more likely to be **heard**. Being heard in the workplace isn't just a suggestion box in the lunchroom or quiet tolerance in a staff meeting; it's creating opportunities for employees to make, or at least contribute to, important decisions. Hearing implies potential action, if appropriate, on the part of the leadership team, or at least an intentional honoring of input, ideas, and effort. It also implies openness to constructive feedback, which may be difficult, but important, to receive.

An effective inclusion strategy creates practical benefits for everyone involved. When a company commits to diversity, it also has to commit to inclusion. Diversity is the mosaic of people who bring a variety of backgrounds, styles, perspectives, values, and beliefs as assets to the groups and organizations with which they interact. Inclusion enables us to strive to have all people represented and included within our organization (and in our society), ensuring that all employees feel welcomed and valued, not only for their abilities but also for their unique qualities and perspectives. Simply put, diversity is the *what* or the *who*, and inclusion is the *how* of transformative performance.

EXCLUSION IS COSTLY

Companies can hire voraciously to fix their lack of representation, but an inclusive culture that embraces all differences is the way organizations can actually *keep* that talent. Diverse talent, as we saw in chapter 1, will not stick around to be excluded. And as the following chart from Bersin by Deloitte implies, that revolving door is very expensive to maintain.

> Companies can hire voraciously to fix their lack of representation, but an inclusive culture that embraces all differences is the way organizations can actually *keep* that talent.

What I find fascinating about Bersin's model is to think about all the points along an employee's life cycle at a company where they can get derailed, even before they have provided value back to that company. If the goal is to retain our talent long enough so they begin to return the investment we've made in them, not managing inclusion effectively is an obvious and frequent derailer, costing us money when we don't do it right, in the form of talent walking out the door before they've even reached the threshold of returning value.

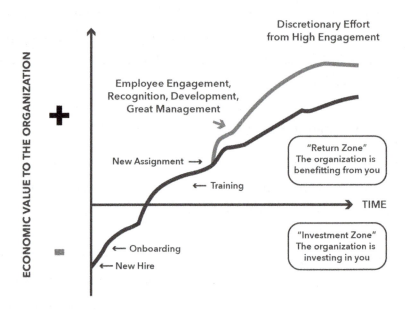

COST TO VALUE OF AN EMPLOYEE

Source: Bersin by Deloitte, 2014.

There is a similar dynamic with teams. Sometimes, we hear resistance to the challenges inherent in diverse teams. Isn't it more work? Won't it take longer to get up and running? It may appear so, at the beginning. Colleagues with similar educations and cultural backgrounds will, initially, work together better. They pretty much hit the ground running because of a natural alignment, but ultimately, they don't perform as strongly.

Katherine Phillips, Paul Calello Professor of Leadership and Ethics at Columbia Business School, writes in *Scientific American* about her research:

Decades of research by organizational scientists, psychologists, sociologists, economists and demographers show that socially diverse groups (that is, those with a diversity of race, ethnicity, gender and sexual orientation) are more innovative than homogeneous groups.

It seems obvious that a group of people with diverse individual expertise would be better than a homogeneous group at solving complex, nonroutine problems. It is less obvious that social diversity should work in the same way—yet the science shows that it does.

This is not only because people with different backgrounds bring new information. Simply interacting with individuals who are different forces group members to prepare better, to anticipate alternative viewpoints and to expect that reaching consensus will take effort.[18]

> Simply interacting with individuals who are different forces group members to prepare better, to anticipate alternative viewpoints and to expect that reaching consensus will take effort.

While it might take a diverse team's members longer to find their rhythm with one another and the investment may be greater up front, diverse team culture creates greater performance, greater innovation, and greater ROI over time.

EMPLOYEE RESOURCE GROUPS: DIVERSE TEAMS PERFORMING TOGETHER

Where is this already being demonstrated in the business world? Employee resource groups (ERGs) are a powerful tool for building a culture of inclusion and demonstrating the power of diverse teams who've come together in shared purpose and are benefitting companies in real, bottom-line ways. In some larger companies, such as IBM and PG&E, they have been around for many decades.

ERGs comprise several identity- and interest-based communities, including employees from traditionally underrepresented groups (such as women, people of color, people with disabilities, members of the LGBTQ community), allies who support these groups, and people who share a common purpose, interest, or background. It can be exhausting and disheartening for employees to go through a workday constantly navigating a culture in which they are in the *minority* and have to adjust to the dominant ethos. It can also be confusing to encounter diversity-related friction with coworkers and clients, such as having a male colleague throw dollar bills at you (recalling Isis Wenger's experience), without having anyone or anyplace to turn to in order to process the experience. ERGs can offer employees that someone and that someplace when they need support, encouragement, or guidance in dealing with diversity- and inclusion-related problems.

I'll refer to ERGs often throughout this book, as they provide many

> ERGs can offer employees that someone and that someplace when they need support, encouragement, or guidance in dealing with diversity- and inclusion-related problems.

emerging solutions to persistent business problems, and I am passionate about these unique organic communities that have sprung up to support those traditionally without a voice in the corporate world. Consulting to these groups—their leaders, their members, their supporting executives—is a mainstay of our business, which also means diversity champions make up most of the people I spend my time with. And I think the reason I feel such a strong community with these brave people is because of my own diversity experience. I learned so much from time on the inside of conversations among change agents as they planned to influence their massive employers to make sweeping changes—many times, ahead of the curve. They are the kind of change agents we need.

CHAPTER FOUR

THE CHANGE HAS ALREADY BEGUN

"Knowing what must be done does away with fear."

–ROSA PARKS

All of the strongest data available, as well as our best efforts thus far to address diversity and inclusion issues in the workplace, may be superseded by the rumbling entrance of the newest generation to reach the corporate arena. Attaining a majority in the workforce as of the year 2020, the millennial migration into the workplace is causing companies to ask themselves some serious questions—not only about how to embrace this generation but also around many assumed truths about how we behave in the work context.

For their part, millennials are ushering in a new age of employee transparency and expectations, especially as they move into leadership accompanied by their unprecedentedly inclusive worldview. They are expecting the company or organization they work for to mirror that outlook, and if not, well, they're happy taking their smarts and can-do attitudes to the entrepreneurial or start-up realm instead.

According to a 2015 Deloitte University study, millennials are emphatically not interested in assimilating in order to get along in the workplace. They do not want to conceal those parts of their lives that make them different; they are inclined to celebrate those differences. That mind-set puts them at odds with baby boomers and even to some extent with Gen X'ers, in terms of the energy and expectations they bring to the workplace. To the veteran generations of corporate America, where so many women, for example, are still plucking the shards of glass ceilings from their bodies, the millennials' tenacity may appear, to some, as a glib and immature response to a decades-old problem.

But some very fundamental realities *have* shifted in those decades. For example, when asked how they define diversity, millennials consider cognitive diversity—the blending of different ideas, thoughts, opinions, backgrounds, experiences, and perspectives within a team—to be "essential for an inclusive culture that supports engagement, empowerment, and authenticity."[1]

Millennials perceive inclusion more roundly than previous generations—prizing a collaborative environment that values open participation from individuals with different ideas and perspectives, which has a positive impact on business. According to one survey respondent, "Diversity means to me your background based on your previous work experience, where you were born and raised, and any unique factors that contribute to your personality and behavior."[2]

This broader definition of diversity beyond demographics is a unique hallmark of this generation and is ushering in what we might call the era of the *ally*. Traditionally, our *human capital* strategies have focused on underrepresented affinities in the workplace and ensuring they find community, a voice, and strength in numbers. We've developed a kind of short-hand—a reduction of communities into discrete demographics such as race/ethnicity and gender—so we can identify those groups, invest in them, and encourage their progress as well as address their challenges. Law also requires it.[3]

In fact, it was that way of thinking that gave rise to the original employee resource groups. And that same way of thinking accounts for the gender- and ethnicity-based groups that still thrive today in so many organizations, especially among mid- and senior-level talent who came of professional age at a time when many were "the only and lonely." The support of single-identity groups was critical when so many were isolated and probably played an outsized role in retaining underrepresented talent in companies, serving as a stay against them walking out the door, defeated.

The support of single-identity groups was critical when so many were isolated and probably played an outsized role in retaining underrepresented talent in companies.

The impact millennials will have on single-identity groups is just now unfolding and is fascinating to observe. How will a generation that views itself as "multi" and "intersectional" (a blend of many privileged and nonprivileged identities as we discussed in an earlier chapter) reconcile their employers' individual focus on historically disadvantaged communities of talent? And if they've truly integrated or have even transcended their own diversity, what will they perceive as worth fighting for when it comes to rebalancing the workplace to make it more equal for all? Will they, in fact, be aware of disparities in opportunity and representation above them in the org chart, early in their career? Or will they not see the trouble until it has a direct impact on them personally, for example, when they start a family and struggle with balance, or when they suspect they've been passed over for the promotion, or when they begin to be "the only and lonely" at the table, as Miley at Twitter found himself to be.

Millennials' bold insistence on being seen, heard, and valued as contributors carries a critical message to older generations who have been covering relatively more of who they are at work, to survive.

Regardless of the outcomes, millennials serve as a harbinger, the bellwether of corporate culture's responsiveness and organizational flexibility. As we will discuss shortly, their bold insistence on being seen, heard, and valued as contributors carries a critical message to older generations who have been covering relatively more of who they are at work, to survive. Dismissing their message of the need for authenticity as juvenile naivety could prove fatal. For those of us who choose to listen, will it simply be to hear them out, or will we ourselves dive into the message that they're offering and apply the lessons they bring to improve the workplace for all?

THE FACTS ABOUT MILLENNIALS

While this sea of change is unfolding, we need to keep certain research in mind about these newest cohorts to enter the workplace, especially as it pertains to engaging and retaining them. For many of us who focus constantly on the business case for diversity and inclusion, it helps enormously to share with decision-makers that, according to Deloitte, 83 percent of millennials are more engaged when they are working in an inclusive environment.[4] This generation is going to shape the workplace of the future, so today's leaders that might have viewed diversity and inclusion as a "nice to have" need to begin to deepen their understanding of what constitutes an inclusive workplace environment.

Millennials place a higher value on employee well-being and employee growth and development than do baby boomers and Gen X, as generational cohorts. "Millennials also believe that an organization's treatment of its employees is the most important consideration in determining whether or not a company can be considered a leader."[5]

Millennials are referred to as generation Y, or "generation why" because one of their generational hallmarks is the need to know the reason beyond things that, perhaps, previous generations dared not question. This is a generation of interpersonal communication and transparency; these people came of age with Facebook, Twitter, and Instagram. They share a different relationship with knowledge than earlier generations did, with a perspective of "if and when I need it, I'll find it online." They are optimistic about the future and realistic about the present. They have a good work ethic and resemble the traditionalists, or "greatest generation," in this regard. The motive for working hard is different, though, than it has been for those who are closing in on retirement. Millennials do not like to take blind orders. They want to know that they made a difference in others' lives or for themselves through their labors. They prize work-life balance significantly more than they value monetary compensation. This group questions "starting at the bottom" and feels the best person for the job is the one who does it best. Seniority has to be justified, and people have to earn respect; it is not a given.

ATTRIBUTES BY GENERATION: TRAITS, TECHNOLOGY, AND TRENDS

Traditionalists (Until 1946)	Baby Boomers (1946-1964)	Generation X (1965-1976)	Generation Y/ Millennials (1977-1995)	Generation Z (1996 and later)
Major Trait: Loyal	Major Trait: Competitive	Major Trait: Self-Reliant	Major Trait: Immediate	Major Trait: Hyper-Connected
Fax Machine	Personal Computer	Mobile Phones	Google, Facebook, Twitter	Smartphone apps, Texting, Snapchat
• "Greatest" or "Silent Generation" • The Depression, WWII, and Korean War	• Divided into "Hippies" and "Yuppies" • Raised by "Silent Generation" • Civil rights, feminism, Vietnam War	• "Latchkey kids" • Raised by early Baby Boomers • 1987 stock market crash • Challenger explosion, fall of the Berlin Wall	• "Millennials" • Raised by late Baby Boomers, sometimes "helicoptor parents" • September 11th	• "Digital Natives" • Great Recession • Being raised by Generation X

All these millennial preferences are already rebalancing the work environment, which will only accelerate and transform organizational hierarchies, particularly when we consider the other demographic shifts within the workforce. According to Pew Research, 20 percent of this largest of generations has at least one immigrant parent. The foreign-born component of the population will increase by 38 percent in the next forty years.[6] Additionally, the Census Bureau predicts that the US population will increase from 319 million in 2014 to 400 million in 2051; by 2044, more than half of all Americans will identify as part of a non-white group, and we, as a country, will become what is known as a majority-minority nation. The Asian population will increase by 128 percent; the Hispanic by 115 percent. The black population will see more modest growth, by 42 percent.[7] Meanwhile, the white population is projected to comprise 46 percent of the US population by 2050, a decrease from the current level of 66 percent.[8]

Leadership that changes little to reflect these shifts will create even more profound disconnects in our institutions. While the population of those who identify with two or more races is anticipated to grow by 226 percent in the next generation, just two members of minority populations have been presidents of Ivy League institutions, and in our nation's history, just twelve Republican and fourteen Democratic senators weren't white. To date, Colin Powell has been the only black individual to serve on the Joint Chiefs of Staff.[9] There is only one non-white senior executive at a major Hollywood studio: Channing Dungey, head of ABC entertainment, became the first black television network president early in 2016.[10] While nearly 75 percent of NBA players are black, Michael Jordan remains the only black majority owner among the NBA's thirty teams.[11] There isn't one majority black owner in the NFL where, again, 70 percent of the players are black.

The population of those who identify with two or more races is anticipated to grow by 226 percent in the next generation.

There is a profound dissonance between the demographics and those who make decisions at the highest levels in this country. Companies must respond to these demographic shifts. National Public Radio noted in early 2016 that, since President Obama's election in 2008, "From race to religion, from gender to sexual orientation and beyond, marginalized groups that historically worked and waited for 'a seat at the table' increasingly demanded their share of cultural power."[12]

This demand is going to grow louder. All of our people processes, such as recruiting, development, employee engagement, and workplace culture, as well as the very essence of *how* we work, will have to evolve not merely to retain millennial and multicultural talent but also to court millennial and multicultural customers.

By identifying their behaviors, wants, and needs as these factors pertain to their work lives, we can use the available data to assist us in supporting this cohort in the most strategic way. We are smarter than ever before in understanding the make-up of cohorts—by demographic, by interest—and not only their commonalities but their unique diversity, individual to individual.

SAME . . . DIFFERENCE?

At the same time, we have to use caution when generalizing about a group; many millennials don't feel they fit their cohort's official descriptors as portrayed in the media, for example. We do meet millennials who share with us after a training, "I don't identify with any of the research on my generation," which serves as a reminder of the prevalence of stereotypes and their frequent inaccuracy. Given that developing awareness of the "diversity within the diversity" is an advanced skill, let's spend some time discussing stereotypes more broadly—beyond our current focus on millennials—considering the lasting power of such beliefs to influence behavior at work, with the ultimate goal of transcending them someday, for everyone, once and for all.

LET'S TALK ABOUT STEREOTYPES

We might all prefer to ignore this particularly unpleasant and judgmental elephant in the room, but if we are going to create a culture of inclusion, we must dive right in. We categorize ourselves and others into groups. It was once an evolutionary imperative to differentiate "us" from "them." It is profoundly less constructive in the modern world. You can take your pick of egregious and appalling stereotypical judgments, but let's name just a few so that we're all clear on what we're talking about. Sometimes, a stereotype is inherently pejorative, and sometimes, it is just a sweeping, erroneous generalization about a group or community:

- Older people are less able to learn new technology.

- Asian people are really good at math.

- Gay men of a certain generation love Judy Garland and are impeccable decorators.

- Irish people drink a lot.

- Black men are violently angry.

- Hispanic people are all in the United States illegally.

- Individuals with a disability cannot lead a productive and fulfilling life.

- All Muslims are jihadist.

I challenge you to think about one stereotype that you carry around in your head and to reexamine why you accept this simplification of a whole community of people. How did you form this impression? How true do you honestly believe it to be when you consider it deeply?

As a culture, we are still staggering under the leaden weight of ponderous gender stereotypes, as well, such as the thought that men are assertive; however, when women display the same behavior, they are thought to be aggressive. Men are ambitious; women are selfish.

Facebook COO Sheryl Sandberg and Wharton School Professor Adam Grant wrote in the *New York Times* in 2015 about the perils of "speaking while female" in the workplace:

> When a woman speaks in a professional setting, she walks a tightrope. Either she's barely heard or she's judged as too aggressive. When a man says virtually the same thing, heads nod in appreciation for his fine idea. As a result, women often decide that saying less is more.[13]

Sociologists have documented stereotype threat, which is the perception that one will be judged harshly because of a negative stereotypical expectation of a group to which one belongs. Stereotype threat has been shown, in many contexts, to compromise performance, evoke anxiety, and lead to exhaustion and burnout. According to social psychologist Claude Steele:

> People experience stereotype threat several times a day. The reason is that we have a lot of identities—our gender, our race, our age. And about each one of those identities…there are negative stereotypes. And when people are in a situation for which a negative stereotype about one of their identities is relevant to the situation, relevant to what they're doing, they know they could be possibly judged or treated in terms of that stereotype.[14]

Research has shown that, in response to these threats, individuals may choose to develop another social identity through joining a different group, disparage another group as a means of asserting themselves, or modify their behavior in order to downplay the misperception or not draw unwanted attention to themselves. Again, as mentioned above, this threat and the adjustments they make can also wear people out, leading them to disconnect or disengage.

Dr. Steele also warns, "When people are appraising identity threat, one cue can shape the interpretation of another,"[15] so if a company says it is committed to diversity but has only photographs of white employees on its website, or if all the conference rooms are named for men, as we saw in the Google example in the previous chapter, the images and the names may undermine the most carefully crafted and sincerely meant statement of intent.

After giving a presentation on the subject of diversity and employee resource groups, I have frequently been approached by a young woman or person of color seeking a confidential conversation with me about her reticence to join her company's women's network, or hesitation to get involved in related projects for fear of "being seen as a woman first, and a great performer second." I hear as well from millennials that they studiously avoid association with their age group for fear that their more mature team members will be reminded of their generation and respect them less. This is stereotype threat in action.

The flip side, of course, is embracing our identities and working from a place of alignment that does the opposite—bolstering self-confidence for the next challenge while carrying awareness that what makes us unique actually differentiates us and fuels our professional successes. From where we sit at JBC, we know those who have learned how to balance these elements in their *personal brand* (how they are seen and thought of) succeed exponentially, but millennials, especially, are hesitant, seeing their diversity more as *diversity of thought* and

> Millennials, especially, are hesitant, seeing their diversity more as diversity of thought and downplaying their gender or ethnic diversity as less relevant or less in need of support and declaration.

downplaying their gender or ethnic diversity as less relevant or less in need of support and declaration.[16] They are certainly taking cues about what's acceptable to their employer in choosing to downplay their details. We will see that their hesitation in bringing their full selves to work is shared by many and that we are a long way from building cultures that feel safe for most.

While each of us has our own diversity story that we choose to identify with, share, or play down, we have to adopt a professional persona in line with our workplace norms. This might mean we have to manage or conceal facets of our identity, culture, and work style. Assimilation into a workplace culture, to some degree, is still necessary for success; some young leaders chafe against it and prioritize self-expression from the interview process onward, while others receive the message of stigma and retreat into hiding. It depends on so many factors as to which direction they choose.

Our beliefs, religion, political affiliations, disabilities, *gender identity*, *gender expression*, and *sexual orientation* are traits we can work to disguise if we think we need to, particularly if those around us hold a negative perception of the traits or if we perceive a stereotype threat.

But all of this covering to appease false perceptions comes at a cost, particularly for those with the most to disprove or hide.

Our beliefs, religion, political affiliations, disabilities, gender identity, gender expression, and sexual orientation are traits we can work to disguise if we think we need to, particularly if those around us hold a negative perception of the traits or if we perceive a stereotype threat.

COVERING AT WORK

According to *Uncovering Talent: A New Model of Inclusion*, a study by Kenji Yoshino and Christie Smith for Deloitte University (2013), many in the workplace do something called covering, defined as "downplaying a known stigmatized identity." Employees from under-represented groups report feeling the need to cover more often, and many admit that this affects their sense of self.

Yoshino and Smith identified four main categories, known as the four axes of covering, along which people feel the need to conceal their identities:

FOUR AXES OF COVERING

- appearance: individuals change grooming, attire, and mannerisms (e.g., tattoos, dreadlocks, "black" hair).

- affiliation: individuals do not talk about meaningful relationships (e.g., motherhood).

- advocacy: individuals avoid specific topics related to identity (e.g., veteran status).

- association: individuals avoid being around specific people (e.g., lesbian, gay, bisexual, or transgender people).[17]

This is a very personal topic for me because I too felt the disconcerting need to cover at work. During my years in corporate jobs, I was also afraid I would be judged and perhaps marginalized or stigmatized because of various aspects of my identity. In retrospect, I see that I was carrying an assumption that my colleagues wouldn't be able to "handle it." Therefore, I would beat them to the punch, so to speak, by not giving them the benefit of the doubt and removing parts of myself that might be awkward or make others uncomfortable. I had a pervasive fear that they would like me less, that they might even view me with disgust. I avoided sharing personal stories; I didn't talk about what I did on the weekend. I was twisting in a terrifying and very cold wind. Eventually, I got sick of it and walked into my boss's office with a picture of my partner, Michelle. "I want you to know about this person who is so important to me," I told her. My boss looked surprised for a moment. And why wouldn't she be? Think of everything we've discussed about the assumptions we all make and stereotypes we hold in spite of our best intentions. But she smiled and asked me about Michelle. I was so relieved to come out of that dark, dark closet. We got back to work.

What aspects of you float in plain sight for all to see? What do you keep concealed beneath your waterline? Where do you set your waterline, to feel safe?

THE ICEBERG

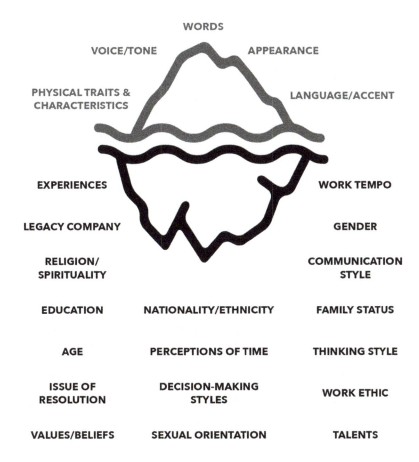

At JBC, we often utilize the metaphor of an iceberg to explore what it means to cover. Each of us has both visible and invisible aspects of diversity. What aspects of you float in plain sight for all to see? What do you keep concealed beneath your waterline? Where do you set your waterline, to feel safe? In meeting me or working with me for the first time, you might presume my race, gender, generation, but you might miss or misidentify the less observable aspects of who I am, such as my religion, educational background, or sexual orientation. I also bring diversity in terms of my cultural attitudes toward time, my extroversion, and communication style. Depending on how comfortable I am in my environment, and what behaviors or attributes are valued in my workplace, I may or may not bring more of what has shaped my experience to the workplace, effectively lowering the waterline of my personal-diversity iceberg.

Yoshino and Smith's report explored below the surface, searching for a better understanding of who was covering at work and why. What they found led to some surprising figures, revealing that LGBTQ individuals cover more than any other cohort, at 83 percent, followed by blacks (79 percent); women of color (67 percent); women (66 percent); Hispanics (63 percent); and, yes, even straight white men (45 percent).[18]

Data collected by the Human Rights Campaign and compiled in the 2014 report, *The Cost of the Closet and the Rewards of Inclusion*, disclosed an even darker picture for LGBTQ workers. Of all LGBTQ professionals surveyed nationwide, 53 percent elect to remain closeted in today's workplace, and 62 percent report hearing derogatory jokes or comments at their workplace.[19] For the LGBTQ community, numbers like these reinforce anxiety vis-à-vis historic and ongoing bullying and violence in the US and around the world.

MAKING IT SAFE TO UNCOVER

So how do we mitigate the harmful effects of covering? We first need to address where it can occur at all points in the employee life cycle. For diverse talent, the burden of representing an entire community or affinity to a larger organizational culture—and being true to self when the isolation of being an "only" is real—is exhausting, as we've already explored in depth.

As a leader, if you are trying to change the balance, you have to know that the work doesn't end with successfully recruiting someone if you can't retain them due to workplace culture issues. Losing people is expensive: experts calculate that it costs as much as 400 percent of a highly specialized employee's salary to replace her when she leaves, between the costs of recruiting and then getting the replacement up to speed.[20]

LISTEN UP: INQUIRY AND ACTIONS TO REDUCE COVERING

So you want to stop the pricey, morale-busting revolving door that long-term covering can cause? You want to start the work of building a culture of inclusion that looks like your customer base? You want to ensure that all generations feel welcomed and relish coming to work every day? You want to do the right thing? Great! Welcome!

The best first step toward designing a successful inclusion strategy for a diverse workplace is to listen to what your employees are saying. It seems obvious, but true listening is in short supply in our frenetic, hierarchical world. However afraid you are to understand the issues in your organization and bring them to light (and however much your legal team advises against it), knowledge is power, but it has to be done in a respectful and culturally competent way. Remember the *heard* in welcomed, valued, respected, and heard? At JBC, we recommend and facilitate like-affinity focus groups as a powerful tool to figure out where the pain points are within organiza-

However afraid you are to understand the issues in your organization and bring them to light (and however much your legal team advises against it), knowledge is power.

tions and certain diverse communities, while also identifying what works and what employees love about coming to work. We usually share the following tactical recommendations to get started:

- **Don't be afraid to recommend focus groups by affinity.** The safety of an exclusive conversation of employees with a shared identity is a powerful experience for participants and will yield the richest and most accurate insights. People will appreciate being asked to participate and actually get excited that they are being invited to a forum to discuss their experiences.

- **Think beyond race and gender for your affinity groupings.** Include LGBTQ, allies, disabilities if possible, millennials and other generation-specific groups, as well as white men. Ask the same, general, open-ended questions across the board, and you will be intrigued by the similarities as well as stark differences that will show up and which are critical to be aware of.

- **Organizations have to create a safe place for employees to be vulnerable and honest.** No direct-reporting relationships should be present in the room when preparing focus groups or asking for employee feedback.

- **It's also useful to engage an outside contractor to conduct focus groups for you, rather than tasking your HR team.** When employees feel they are being watched, especially by someone with any sort of relationship to performance reviews, they will be reluctant to speak candidly, and you won't get the critical information you need to move forward strategically and holistically.

Depending on an organization's history with diversity initiatives—especially failed ones—my team and I may encounter skepticism about management's intentions. In the focus-group conversations, we often hear a version of "I don't believe anything's going to change," or "Do you promise that leadership will come back to us with the results of this?" Employees are clamoring for more transparent communication with their leaders. They passionately want to be engaged, to do their best work, and to bring their whole selves to the effort, but at so many of our clients' workplaces across a variety of industries, they cannot or will not. We hear anecdote after anecdote about the ways in which individual employees have been shut down, overlooked, dismissed, or ignored. Here are just a few of the observations we heard when JBC recently conducted focus groups at a major pharmaceutical company and at an investment bank. Based on what we've discussed up to this point, some of the pain, frustration, disappointment, and paths to disengagement (and actual departure from the organization) should sound familiar:

> **Employees are clamoring for more transparent communication with their leaders.**

- "Gender is usually a barrier—not just [a] stigma of earning less. My experience on maternity leave: my supervisor left. I was not given [the] opportunity to lobby for that role. I had been mentored to take it. I was devastated when I came back. I went to [a] senior manager; he said they were looking [for] someone at a higher level. Said they thought of me. Now I am doing the role without the title."

- "My boss said, 'Oh, I didn't realize you were interested in being promoted.' Who isn't interested in that?"

- "Your job is to assimilate into a culture, and there is no room to have different points of view. You were supposed to be more 'white.'"

- "At times when I initially meet people, the first contact is uncomfortable as they assess who I am."

- "We have very few minority candidates, so I would say we are not at enough, or the right, recruiting venues. We need more minority candidates to interview; I know they're out there. Do they think we wouldn't hire them?"

- "You don't want to ask [about flex time] because you don't want to be perceived as weak. If managers give you special dispensation, it's 'Hush, hush, don't tell anyone.'"

- "Diversity as a value is not implemented consistently. Do all managers agree that it's a good thing?"

- "I've been involved in three interview processes in the last year; in two of those, I don't recall any minority candidates. That could be an issue."

Perhaps not surprisingly, focus groups can cause anxiety among employees and employers alike. They often serve as the vents where many of the suppressed emotions and pain points around diversity surface, particularly in an otherwise silent or constrained workplace. As a result, some may express concerns about the intent of the exercise or oppose it altogether. As a diversity consultant and advocate, I've heard every argument against getting like-identity groups together to talk openly. "Isn't this a case of special rights?", "Aren't we just inviting trouble by suggesting certain demographics get together to compare notes?", and my favorite, "Isn't this just another form of discrimination, or exclusion?" Once people hear the feedback, however, they realize that we've created an environment where it's safe for all participants to reveal more of who they are, be honest about their experiences, connect into a community, and get excited that the company is finally looking at their challenges with a closer eye. This is one of the easiest ways I know to boost morale, not destroy it.

While they aren't without their challenges, these first sessions with focus groups are one of my favorite aspects of developing a diversity and inclusion strategic plan with companies. We see, over and over again, that when participants get in a room with one another, they feel safe to share the observations, anecdotes, and feelings they swallowed or bit down hard on in the past. They often haven't been aware of their covering behaviors or that others shared their frustrations, and the possibly unintended organizational cues they've been receiving begin to coalesce. We look for both the patterns and the dissonances, including the outliers, in what we hear, and we work with the company to formulate a strategy to address the issues. We listen to the employees and then offer their words, their ideas, and their frustrations to the leadership team, anonymously, as a tool for substantive change. It's one of the most effective change tools we use.

When participants get in a room with one another, they feel safe to share the observations, anecdotes, and feelings they swallowed or bit down hard on in the past.

The very act of conducting focus groups can cause a seismic shift in the conversation. Gathering feedback is instructive as well as inspirational for many. Participants consider offering their name and resources, leading the charge for new initiatives and bolstering the effort—all because they've been asked and included. This is just the start of what's possible when an employee feels welcomed, valued, respected, and heard.

Focus groups serve the company tremendously well too. Leaders begin to see a more accurate, detailed picture of what employees are experiencing but probably not saying, and employees may discover a pathway to an ERG or diversity network, which can help them to discover a sense of community and belonging, as well as a mechanism for growing their network and their careers.

It can be difficult for the senior leadership team to hear what employees are saying. As I mentioned earlier, we have encountered bewilderment, finger pointing, and defensiveness from senior leaders who sincerely had no idea what the daily life of their employees comprised. If you are a leader, I encourage you to open yourself to hearing what your employees have to say through the safety of focus groups. It's better to know than to pretend that everything is fine. It only represents a failure on your part if you then choose not to act to improve conditions on the trading floor, the manufacturing floor, or in the lab at your organization.

Even at the most progressive companies, I find that there's always an opportunity to reexamine current company culture and continue to build the culture of inclusion.

If we create a safe and open environment in the room during a focus group though, it has to be felt elsewhere in the workplace to avoid provoking some potentially severe consequences. If people return to the frustrations and microinequities in their day jobs without detecting any signs of change in the larger culture, the revolving door can accelerate. When the culture around them doesn't change, employees may return to covering in order to avoid drawing the wrong kind of attention.

In order for individual employees to change, the culture around them has to begin to change. Management strategies at every level must begin to shift.[21] Good news, it doesn't have to happen all at once. But there is inevitably low-hanging fruit in the analysis of the focus groups; there are quick steps a leadership team can take to let the employee population know that they've been heard and that more changes are going to come. We specialize in helping executives to harvest that fruit and lay out the way forward.

In order for individual employees to change, the culture around them has to begin to change.

Just the mere fact that a company is undertaking a hard look at its culture and levels of engagement goes a long way in engaging the millennial talent we described earlier. If they like what they see, they may stay a while—a long while.

TRANSLATORS OF CHANGE: THE BENEFIT OF BEING IN THE KNOW

Former President Bill Clinton said, "Profound and powerful forces are shaking and remaking our world. And the urgent question of our time is whether we can make change our friend and not our enemy."[22] Former President Woodrow Wilson said, "If you want to make enemies, try to change something."[23] Did I mention that change is hard?

But the degree of difficulty related to change can often depend on how we perceive it. If we see the opportunity to use the various sets of our advantages to effect positive change around us, then change, while hard, can also be incredibly rewarding. For example, if a large swath of younger talent has differing expectations of the workplace experience, they can also serve as an idea-generation and innovation asset that can inform how the organization might shift to resonate more broadly.

Young talent can serve as an idea-generation and innovation asset that can inform how the organization might shift to resonate more broadly.

Julie Battilana and Tiziana Casciaro wrote an article in the *Harvard Business Review* in 2013 on the topic of the power of change agents within an organization. They studied the UK's National Health Service as it worked to effect constructive change to its bloated and sclerotic bureaucracy, delayed appointments, and lousy customer service. The following were among their findings:

1. Change agents who were central in the organization's informal network had a clear advantage, regardless of their position in the formal hierarchy.

2. People who bridged disconnected groups and individuals were more effective at implementing dramatic reforms, while those with cohesive networks were better at instituting minor changes.

3. Being close to "fence-sitters," who were ambivalent about a change, was always beneficial.[24]

What do they mean by *informal network*? Suppose you task a newly appointed or recently hired executive to lead an initiative. She will likely encounter all the resistance to change that's so common among most human beings. Change is scary and, even if a situation stinks, lots of us are more comfortable with a familiar discomfort than with the unknown risks that accompany change. While that new executive may have the imprimatur of the CEO and may even have a zeal to implement the initiative, if she isn't able to leverage the support of those around her, she may fail. But perhaps her administrative assistant has been with the company for twelve years. He's worked in a few different departments over the years and knows people throughout the organization, from the loading dock to the CEO's assistant. Perhaps people rely on his advice to navigate the company's processes; people trust him and are connected to one another through him. As Battilana and Tiziana wrote, "Those who are harder to convince will be pressured by others in the network to cooperate and will probably give in."[25] If the executive is willing to share the effort, as well as the credit, with her connected assistant, the enterprise might thrive much more broadly.

Don't confuse formal authority with the ability to effect change.

There are also, already, people within your organization who are doing things in a better way. There are likely pockets of greater inclusion

Don't confuse formal authority with the ability to effect change.

which can provide a kind of template to follow for company-wide inclusion strategies. There may be, as mentioned earlier, executives who refuse to conduct any interviews until they are presented with a diverse pool of candidates. By insisting on diversity, they are driving culture change and don't need to be held accountable to do so. There are managers who conduct their morning stand-up with their team in a more inclusive way. Find those people. Sometimes, you find them through the comments you hear in focus groups, but you may have to launch a search for them and then harness their forward-thinking brains and passionate hearts to help your company pivot. Cultivate evangelists; talk about what works.

If we can start to see difference as an inspiration to lead in a constructive new way rather than as a hurdle over which we need to leap, we can approach the work with enthusiasm and determination rather than with dread and resentment.

Cultivate evangelists; talk about what works.

DIFFERENCE IS A CAUSE FOR CELEBRATION

It is a great time to have grown up and weathered a challenge, of any kind. Challenge is a great teacher. I am going to share six experiences specific to my LGBTQ identity that have driven my skill development and some of my current and key leadership competencies. Authenticity around my difference, for me personally, has meant in part evolving to a place where I can work and live from a more aligned, truthful version of myself—and in doing this, I have noticed how my professional profile morphed and finally shaped more accurately around my gifts, passions, and talents. As you review the following list, notice what resonates for you, what surprises you, and what, from your challenges and the change you've navigated in yourself or for your organization, has helped you to grow as a leader.

1. Outsider Experience

Might there be an invisible reward for spending some time on the-margins, on the outside of a larger group? While we might wish to have learned the lessons in less threatening circumstances and desired an easier path, can we celebrate the discoveries we've made from the outside? Does the outside lead to courage, to creativity, to resilience? Can we reconsider our differentiators and our challenges as tools that enable us to be more innovative problem solvers, as agents of diversity of thought? One builds certain kinds of skills in order to survive. It can sometimes be a life-or-death situation to survive, much less to thrive, if one is stereotyped, stigmatized, marginalized, and ignored. Most people have felt the sting of exclusion at some moment in their lives, even those who appear to have privilege. I am an insider and the beneficiary of tremendous privilege based on my ethnicity, socioeconomic status, educational back-

Can we reconsider our differentiators and our challenges as tools that enable us to be more innovative problem solvers, as agents of diversity of thought?

ground, and nationality. Yet I also belong to a stigmatized community (LGBTQ), and I am a woman business owner working with the C-suite, where women are grossly outnumbered and from where they have been, traditionally, silently barred. Leading from the intersection of these seemingly opposing inclusion/exclusion experiences can create exponential power to connect and understand experiences on both sides of the equation. I am grateful every day to have learned, and continue to learn, how to navigate that line.

2. Inclusive Leadership

We can't assume that anyone who has outsider experience of any kind is automatically going to beautifully practice inclusion; diverse communities may have some challenging diversity dynamics themselves. As I mentioned earlier, this can be called the diversity within the diversity. For example, at LGBTQ fundraising and networking events, I am often just one of a very few women in the room, and no one on the planning committee for the event noticed or worked to balance the guest list for gender. These men ask me, "Jennifer, can you bring more women to us?" The irony is striking. A community traditionally marginalized has a blind spot toward inclusion because it's been so inwardly focused, which in itself is a survival mechanism and one that I have great compassion for. In organizations, however, and as leaders, we must increase our vigilance for inclusion and our insistence that more voices participate.

3. The Three Rs: Resilience, Resourcefulness, Risk-Taking

When I think of the challenges of bringing my full self to work over the years, and specific to my identity as an LGBTQ individual, it has involved overcoming my fear about acceptance while still being productive (resilience), the scramble to decide to come out over and over again while calculating the risks (resourcefulness), and actually having to come out again over and over (risk-taking). I have cultivated nimbleness and flexibility. My flexibility has grown out of adjusting to what others assume I should be or what they need me to be or their comfort level, while simultaneously challenging myself toward authenticity and holding that truth. I'm doing all this while I'm building the relationship and establishing myself as a trusted friend or advisor. It's not an accident that some of us might exhibit the celebrated leadership skill sets of resilience, resourcefulness, and risk-taking given this balancing act.

4. Intrapreneurial Thinking

In 1984, Gifford Pinchot coined the term *intrapreneurial*, connoting, "Dreamers who do. Those who take hands-on responsibility for creating innovation of any kind, within a business."[26] When people are born with an outsider status and have experienced not fitting in and feeling unwelcome, the impulse to create and to own their destiny, much like an entrepreneur, is often particularly strong, even if they work in a full-time job at an organization where conformity is demanded.

The need to author our lives and control our destinies can be especially acute in communities of difference and is actually an asset for the companies who do a good job of investing in relationships with these internal communities. What a company doesn't want is the exit of talented individuals who feel they can't create within the four walls of that company. When it's clear that all kinds of people and contributions are welcome, the company is the beneficiary of diversity of thought.

The need to author our lives and control our destinies can be especially acute in communities of difference and is actually an asset for the companies who do a good job of investing in relationships with these internal communities.

5. The Power of Community

I find validation and a sense of belonging when I consider how organized and strategic my several communities are, from the LGBTQ community to my tribes of woman entrepreneurs and ally change agents. Seth Godin describes this:

> Successful heretics create their own religions…You can recognize the need for faith in your idea, you can find the tribe you need to support you, and yes, you can create a new religion around your faith.[27]

From the ever-increasing buying power of diverse communities to the diverse talent that's entering organizations and demanding support, change, and progress, I imagine that I am fortified with an army—several armies—by my side. It is an honor to be seen and heard deeply by them; it has fortified me to journey beyond safety and beyond my comfort zone, to forge new pathways of understanding in less-familiar territory.

6. Drive to Perform

Researchers as well as generations of black parents, Jewish parents, and parents of daughters have documented, all in their own way, that their sons and daughters might feel a particular need to overcompensate, to overperform. First Lady Michelle Obama articulated this imperative in a commencement address at Tuskegee University when she said that people might not recognize the accomplishments of the graduates because they would, instead, "make assumptions about who they think you are based on their limited notion of the world."[28] President Obama himself, in an address at Morehouse College, said, "Every one of you has a grandma or an uncle or a parent who's told you at some point in life, as an African American, you have to work twice as hard as anyone else if you want to get by."[29]

Ernest Owens wrote in the *Huffington Post* that "minorities have been taught and raised to be humble of our accomplishments,"[30] and to feel lucky rather than proud. As a result of the stereotype threats we discussed earlier, many find greater safety in perfectionism, achievement, and conforming to a traditional workplace norm. This could include everything from a person of color dressing more formally at work to withholding personal details to silently tolerating offensive comments to staying in the office every night until the last colleague leaves.

Covering, combating *microaggressions*, and compensating for imaginary inadequacies takes energy, time, and focus away from our confidence, our contributions, our careers, and ultimately, from the company's productivity. The millennials, for one, will not have a high tolerance for these real and perceived dynamics; they are bringing an expectation that organizations *are already good at this*. This is a generation that has no earthly idea why a diversity strategy is even necessary, as the benefits of diversity should be so obvious.

To summarize, organizational leaders who want their organizations to pivot successfully to welcome this generation—and the next generation following them—will need to not only come to terms with covering behaviors in themselves and others but also understand the value of any definition of "outsider" to their business, and empower those voices to drive change with a relentless focus on the goal from the top. This is the only way we can create the organizational shifts we so desperately need. The work culture must adapt to properly welcome and emphatically support the whole employee, and the employee needs to stay motivated to meet that effort.

When employees can work as themselves, fully and confidently, highlighting the new age of employee transparency and expectations we opened this chapter with, they're empowered to contribute in equal measure, and the business ultimately benefits.

> Covering, combating microaggressions, and compensating for imaginary inadequacies takes energy, time, and focus away from our confidence, our contributions, our careers, and ultimately, from the company's productivity.

CHAPTER FIVE

GENDER AT WORK

It's Not a Woman's Problem

"Because I am a woman, I must make unusual efforts to succeed. If I fail, no one will say, 'She doesn't have what it takes.' They will say, 'Women don't have what it takes.'"

—CLARE BOOTHE LUCE

In 2012, Ellen Pao, who later became Reddit's CEO, filed a gender discrimination lawsuit against her former employer, Kleiner Perkins, a Silicon Valley venture capital firm. In the suit, Pao alleged that she was hired as a junior partner and promised opportunities to move forward. Instead, she was repeatedly passed over for promotion, was on the receiving end of retaliation within the company because she was vocal in her protest, and was, ultimately, fired as a result. Amongst other colorful language to emerge during the trial, jurors heard that John Doerr, Ms. Pao's supervisor, said Pao had a "female chip on her shoulder." *The New York Times* reported that ChiHua Chien, a partner, said women should not be invited to a dinner with former Vice President Al Gore because they "kill the buzz" and that

Ray Lane, then a senior partner, joked with a junior partner that Pao should be "flattered" that a colleague had shown up at her hotel room door wearing only a bathrobe. This might remind our readers of Isis Wenger, a female engineer, and the story we shared involving dollar bills.

In 2015, Pao wrote that, in addition to the difficulties of proving discrimination under California law, "I saw how hard it was going to be to win when every potential juror who expressed a belief that sexism exists in tech—a belief that is widely recognized and documented—was not allowed to serve on the jury."[1] Juror Marshalette Ramsey told *The Times* she believed Ms. Pao was discriminated against and that the male junior partners at Kleiner "had those same character flaws that Ellen was cited with," but they were promoted.[2]

Pao did not win, but her determination to bring the case to the public and media ensured that the national press highlighted the dismal gender diversity statistics in the tech industry. As she departed the courthouse after the jury's verdict, she said, "If I've helped to level the playing field for women and minorities in venture capital, then the battle was worth it."[3] In addition, Pao has also taken multiple, concrete steps to address the systemic problems that hold women back, including the hiring of a diversity and inclusion expert at Reddit. Delineating the variety of ways in which she was outgunned and outstaffed by Kleiner during the trial, Pao urged,

> I have a request for all companies: Please don't try to silence employees who raise discrimination and harassment concerns. Instead allow balanced and complete perspectives to come out publicly so we can all learn and improve. I and many others are eager to hear more stories being shared by women and minorities. I turned down offers to settle so I can keep telling mine. We need to keep

telling our stories and educating people on how it can be that women and minorities form such a small fraction of our investor base, our tech workforce and our leadership.[4]

Of Silicon Valley as a whole, in response to the verdict in the suit, *The New York Times* wrote,

> Episodes of men behaving badly make the news frequently here, whether it is sexism or harassment in the workplace or just derogatory attitudes toward women. Critics are increasingly drawing a straight line between such behavior and the small percentage of women who are engineers and executives, and the even smaller percentage of women who are venture capitalists.[5]

Pao's experience speaks to multiple important aspects of today's dialogue about gender in the workplace. For one, I believe there is a lack of awareness of the statistics on gender equality, which we'll help with in a moment. I spend a lot of time working with executives sharing how the problem has been documented, focusing on the research that clearly shows disparities. Believe it or not, this is not information they are already fluent in; the good news is that, once learned, many feel catalyzed to take action.

But there is, as *The Times* points out, especially a connection that's also poorly understood between behaviors in the workplace and those statistics. By now, the theme should be very clear: toxic workplace cultures prevent diversity numbers from improving—in subtle and pernicious ways, as well as obvious ones. We will not shift the diversity mix only by hiring more aggressively but by changing everyday behaviors and obstacles that stem from unconscious, and perhaps conscious (as in Pao's story), bias.

There are bright spots, however. For example, we have reached a point where Americans overwhelmingly believe that women are just as capable as men. The Pew Research Center told us that, in 2015, "Most Americans find women indistinguishable from men on key leadership traits such as intelligence and capacity for innovation,"[6] with possibly deeper reserves of compassion and organizational skills.

When it comes to the need for change, there is a perception gap: 75 percent of millennial women report that society has to do more to advance workplace equality; only 57 percent of millennial men agree.[7]

Just as there is a lack of understanding of the data, this perception gap is alive and well in the conversations I have; it takes the form of discussions about how wise the invisible hand of meritocracy is, that the best talent rises to the top naturally, and that it would be insane not to hire "the best person for the job," however subjective that value judgment might be. In the spring of 2016, Stefanie K. Johnson and David R. Hekman wrote in the *Harvard Business Review*, "Roughly 85 percent of corporate executives and board members are white men. This number hasn't budged for decades, which suggests that white men are continuing to select and promote other white men."[8]

There is another disturbing aspect to the research findings on the perception gap. The study was done with millennial men and women; to see the gap play out along gender lines is puzzling, to say the least. Millennial men would, presumably, have had a front-row seat to the ascension and challenges of their career moms. Maybe their dads worked for a woman. If the data is correct about their predisposition to inclusion and equality as a generation, we have to wonder if they haven't yet seen or grasped the magnitude of dysfunctional gender dynamics in the workplace—or felt called to apply their efforts toward change. This will become evident in the years to come, and much is riding on whether they know the facts, grasp that change is needed, and apply themselves to the problem.

KNOW THE FACTS

In any conversation about gender parity, it's important to back up and know the facts. So what is the current state of the labor force and equal pay? Let's look more at the numbers.

- Today women comprise 19 percent of our representatives in Congress, despite comprising 50.8 percent of the population.[9]

- Women hold 19.2 percent of board seats at US Stock Index companies.[10]

- A scant twenty-three women are CEOs of Fortune 500 companies.[11] According to CNNMoney, "[O]nly 14.2 percent of the top five leadership positions at the companies in the S&P 500 are held by women."[12] That includes CFOs and COOs, as well as CEOs.

- Seventy-nine percent of all mid-level or senior-level women say they have the desire to reach a top-management position over the course of their careers, compared with 81 percent of mid-level or senior-level men, according to McKinsey research,[13] and two-thirds of both men and women say they are prepared to make personal sacrifices in order to move forward at work.

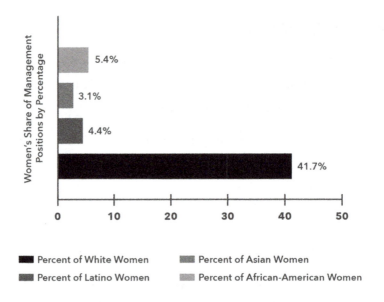

WOMEN'S SHARE OF MANAGEMENT, PROFESSIONAL, AND RELATED OCCUPATIONS BY RACE/ETHNICITY, U.S.

Source: Current Population Survey, Bureau of Labor Statistics, "Table 1: Employed and Experienced Unemployed Persons by Detailed Occupation, sex, Race, and Hispanic or Latino Ethnicity, 2012," *Annual Averages 2012*, Unpublished Tabulations (2013).

Women in professional specialty occupations earn 72.7 percent of what men in the same position earn. Women in upper-level executive, administrative, and managerial occupations earn even less at 72.3 percent. The pay gap is wider for Hispanic, black, American Indian, and Native Hawaiian women than for white and Asian American women. Black women earned 64¢, and Latina women earned 56¢ for every dollar earned by a white man in 2014. The pay gap gets wider when we consider benefits packages. In a 2015 report, the White House noted:

Women are less likely to have an offer of health insurance from their employer. Overall, women are also less likely to have retirement savings plans, however this gender gap is concentrated among lower income women. Prime-age women with college degrees are about as likely as their male counterparts to be covered by their employer's pension plan, while less-educated women are less likely to have an employer-based retirement plan.[14]

In speaking about women as a cohort, we must bear in mind the diversity *amongst* women, as those statistics show the stark differences. Women of color share gender challenges with white women, but at the same time have different experiences from those of white women, who have different experiences from those of transgender women, and so on. It doesn't serve anyone to lump all women together without discernment and targeted efforts to address particular disparities. We will take time later in this chapter to share specific research on what is unique amongst women of color in ascending the ladder.

Returning to the pay gap, Rich Henson, writing for ResourcefulManager.com, calculated that "[b]y age 65, the average working woman will have lost more than $430,000 over her working lifetime vs. men, because of the wage gap."[15] That's the cost of college tuition for two children or a pretty nice house in most of the USA, and this can also be the difference between a stable retirement and a precarious one. The bottom line is that all of this adds up, for *all* women.

By age 65, the average working woman will have lost more than $430,000 over her working lifetime vs. men, because of the wage gap.

In late 2014, I witnessed a firestorm in real time on Twitter that elucidates the real and perceived gender gaps, and reasons for them. I was, via hashtag, "attending" the Grace Hopper conference, listening in to the feed as hundreds of women were sharing their insights and experiences, virtually. A CEO panel was invited onto the stage. When the question of how women should navigate their careers arose, Microsoft CEO Satya Nadella advised this all-female audience not to ask for a raise: "It's not really about asking for a raise, but knowing and having faith that the system will give you the right raise…That might be one of the initial 'super powers' that quite frankly, women [who] don't ask for a raise have. It's good karma. It will come back."[16] You can imagine that Nadella found himself having to retreat from his "have-faith" stance in the face of confusion, disappointment, and righteous viral anger. Twitter absolutely blew up. The next day, there was an emergency panel called for these same executives, except this time, they were in the audience, listening to women leaders speak about their experiences and challenges in a workplace that seems to put obstacles in their path. It was a powerful correction.

DIVERSITY OF THOUGHT EQUALS BETTER RESULTS

Nadella's ill-conceived statements were tone-deaf, certainly. He seemed unaware of the need for women to feel valued and financially remunerated in equal parts, in order that they remain in organizations and ascend up the ladder, and he seemed to downplay the challenges to this. But gender equality has been proven to be great for business. *Women Matter: Gender Diversity, a Corporate Performance Driver*, a report on the findings of a study by McKinsey & Company, found that the eighty-nine European-listed companies with the highest proportions of women in senior leadership positions and at least two women on their boards outperformed industry averages for the Stoxx Europe 600, with a 10 percent higher return on equity, a

48 percent higher EBIT (operating result), and 1.7 times the stock price growth.[17] In their research on women's participation in IT patents for the National Center for Women & Information Technology, Catherine Ashcraft and Anthony Breitzman found that mixed-gender teams in the United States produced patents that were cited 26–42 percent more frequently than the average.[18]

Analyzing S&P firms, researchers René B. Adams and Daniel Ferreira found that gender-diverse boards have higher levels of boardroom involvement and corporate oversight:

- Boards with women on them have better member-attendance records.

- Women directors were tougher monitors than men directors and were more likely to be assigned to monitoring-related committees.[19]

Catalyst has noted that companies with woman CEOs experience a 50 percent increase in stock and a 25 percent increase in the S&P 500. *Fast Company* documented that companies with at least three women directors have experienced a 66 percent return on capital investment, a 42 percent increase in return on sales, and a 53 percent increase in return on equity. *Fortune's* most desirable employers for women outperform industry medians on profits as a percentage of revenue (55 percent higher), profits as a percentage of assets (50 percent higher), and profits as percentage of equity (59 percent higher).[20]

The benefits from a diversity-of-thought approach to decision making haven't just been observed in the business sector. MIT, Carnegie Mellon University, and Union College have all found that collective intelligence surpassed the cognitive abilities of the individual members of the group. Groups in which one person dominated—which should sound familiar to anyone who has spent time in the corporate paradigm—were less collectively intelligent. The researchers found that a major factor in creating a group with the right internal dynamics for collective intelligence to emerge is the number of women. Because women tend to have higher levels of social sensitivity, the analysis revealed that the number of women in a group significantly predicts the effective problem-solving abilities of the group overall.[21]

AMBITION VERSUS REALITY

Similarly to the perception gap we saw earlier among millennials, in its 2014 study, *Moving Mind-Sets on Gender Diversity,* McKinsey found that "[F]emale executives are ambitious and sure of their own abilities to become top managers, though they are much less confident that their companies' cultures can support their rise." Respondents cited structural and cultural obstacles at work as a primary factor for why their aspirations didn't often reflect their reality.[22] Deborah Gillis, CEO of Catalyst, says, "When we close our eyes and picture what a CEO looks like, too often the picture that comes to mind is that of a white man."[23] And, as I mentioned, largely white-male leadership teams continue to develop and promote white men. This, ladies and gentlemen, is our collective unconscious bias at work.

> Female executives are ambitious and sure of their own abilities to become top managers, though they are much less confident that their companies' cultures can support their rise.

In an earlier study, McKinsey measured the "organizational excellence" of companies in Europe, North America, and Asia by evaluating them on nine organizational criteria. When McKinsey examined the senior management teams of these companies, it found that those with three or more women had higher scores, on average, than teams with no women. McKinsey found that the score increased significantly once critical mass was reached: about one-third women.[24]

The kinds of assignments women are given as they prepare for advancement matter a lot. For example, "We need to give women more full P&L experience and the task of managing brands—the nuts and bolts of the corporations. There is a disproportionate number of women in staff roles. It's on the backs of both women and the corporations to fix this problem," says Denise Morrison, CEO of Campbell Soup.[25]

Americans, though, don't think that the obstacle is management chops, or other commonly referenced challenges such as parenting and work-life balance. While career interruptions for family do make it harder for women to advance, Pew found that about four in ten Americans believe that there is also a double standard that demands that women do more than their male colleagues to prove their worth in the workplace.[26] And again, this finding is profoundly skewed by gender. Men

Men generally do not agree that women face additional challenges in moving up the corporate ladder.

generally do not agree that women face additional challenges in moving up the corporate ladder, and McKinsey reports that white men also are slower to acknowledge the value of diversity initiatives. While 75 percent of men agree that "diverse leadership teams with significant numbers of women generate better company performance," only 19 percent of men believe that reaching the C-suite is more difficult for women.[27]

In the face of a preponderance of evidence of the value women add to their organizations, we return to the structural resistance to change. A palpable lack of support often resonates throughout the organization from the C-suite because its current occupants cannot always see the land mines and microinequities hidden on women's career paths, and either don't know how to, or aren't prepared to, do the introspective work of examining their role in the current state and locating their desire to change that state.

Many decision makers fail to acknowledge, much less empathize with, the experiences of diverse talent. This is why the asking of questions in the form of focus groups and having the courage to honestly consider the feedback, as we discussed in the last chapter, is paramount. I cannot count the number of times I have heard otherwise well-intentioned executives say, "I hire the best person for the job. I don't think about gender or race when I do that." This can also sound like the very well-meaning and heartfelt statement, "I don't see gender" or "I don't see color." Of course, we want to see ourselves as inclusive and fair; many of my clients consider themselves very progressive and committed to doing the right thing and to equality. A well-intended reassurance that gender and color and difference are not seen or considered, however, rings hollow for many, rendering them and their challenges invisible. Meritocracy only works if everyone

> A well-intended reassurance that gender and color and difference are not seen or considered, however, rings hollow for many, rendering them and their challenges invisible.

has a legitimate shot at the target. These senior leaders are precisely the ones with the most leverage to create cultural change within an organization. And as we've seen, companies can no longer afford the luxury of this particular unconscious bias; it is literally preventing progress.

WALLS IN THE CORPORATE STRUCTURE

Corporate America has a "leaky" talent pipeline: at each transition up the management ranks, more women get washed away. According to a report from Catalyst, averaging a four-year data investigation of women in Fortune 500 companies from 2001 to 2004, women represent 53 percent of new hires, yet Catalyst estimates that at the very first step in career advancement—when individual contributors are promoted to managers—the number drops to 37 percent. Up a rung, only 26 percent of vice presidents and senior executives are female, and only 14 percent of the executive committee, on average, are women.[28] At this point, women are doubly disadvantaged because, as McKinsey's research of the largest US corporations shows, 62 percent are in staff jobs that rarely lead to a CEO role. In contrast, 65 percent of men on executive committees hold line jobs.[29]

This helps explain why the number of women CEOs in Fortune 500 companies appears stuck at 2–3 percent.

If companies could raise the number of middle-management women who make it to the next level by 25 percent, it would significantly increase the flow through the pipeline.

In 2014, McKinsey researchers Joanna Barsh and Lareina Yee identified several of the structural obstacles confronting women, including lack of access to informal networks where they can make important connections, lack of female role models higher up in the organization, and lack of sponsors to provide opportunities, which many male colleagues have. Nadine Augusta, director of diversity and inclusion and corporate social responsibility at the Depository Trust & Clearing Corporation (DTCC), reinforces this: "Women and people of color have let us know that they find it difficult to advance in the organization and that they are hindered by the unwritten rules for getting ahead and being seen as future leaders."[30] The McKinsey team also identified lifestyle and institutional mind-set issues, including the fact that half of fathers with one child say they will not accept a new job that reduces work-life balance; 55 percent of women *without* children say the same thing.[31] While women remain highly confident of their qualifications throughout their careers, they are, on average, less satisfied than men are with their chosen professions and jobs.

WHO NEEDS WHAT KINDS OF SUPPORT?

Sylvia Hewlett, from the Center for Talent Innovation, recently wrote in *Inc.* that,

> Women tend to be viewed as a monolithic talent pool, without taking into account the differing cultural, histori-cal, and socio-economic factors steering women of color along a career path marked by a very particular set of chal-lenges…Black women have always leaned in; they're more likely than any other ethnic group to be employed…Yet their leadership experience often goes unrecognized by white male management. And their distinctly differenti-ated motivators and misgivings are frequently amalgam-ated into a generalized "women" mash-up.[32]

While we are being mindful of the diversity among women of different identities and backgrounds, we need to consider what roles effective ***sponsorship*** and strong personal branding play in their advancement. Sponsorship doesn't mean just mentoring someone, although that is a good start. Sponsorship means actively advocating for another, facilitating introductions, funneling opportunities, issuing invitations into the room where decisions are made. Fewer than 11 percent of black women have sponsors. "Executive sponsorship is critical," says Rosalind Hudnell, vice president of human resources at Intel, "as it can result in accelerated promotions and highly visible positions of strategic value to the company."[33]

Among its benefits, when leadership prioritizes high-potential women specifically—especially in technical disciplines—the return on the investment can be substantial and lasting.

We recently worked with a multinational technology company's supply-chain organization to design and deliver leadership development coaching for high-potential women at the director and manager levels. We cultivated safe, confidential relationships and established a forum in which we supported and coached these high-potential women on developing their voices, brands, networks, and strengths. We advised that the care and development of high potentials must be a shared responsibility among senior leaders, and we engaged the level above them in what participation and support looks like. Tangible benefits from this work included increased sales, cost reductions, and improved productivity. Some of the initiative's intangible benefits included reduced conflict, better working relationships, and better customer service. During the course of our six-month engagement with this tech giant, JBC also consulted on structural changes in recruiting and talent management to deepen the pool of women leaders.

Hewlett reinforces the significance of cultivating high-potential women of color:

Programs aimed at developing black women's leadership skills and fomenting sponsorship must absolutely include their managers and line-of-sight leaders. Because women of color struggle to be their authentic selves at work, they're not inclined to share details of their life outside work, such as leadership positions they embrace in their church or community with their managers.[34]

"That makes it hard for managers to know enough about them to represent them as talented people to their own superiors," says Trevor Gandy, head of diversity at Chubb Group of Insurance Companies. "Successful outcomes depend on [managers] being involved in the initial discussion, on having a role so that they're vested in these women's advancement."[35]

Employee resource groups also offer multiple value propositions for diverse talent, and this is certainly the case for female leaders because the groups can provide professional development opportunities that can be missing from a day job, such as

- gaining exposure and visibility within broader networks;

- working across business units with colleagues the employees might not otherwise encounter;

- learning a broader set of skills by collaborating on ERG projects and initiatives;

- seizing leadership opportunities within ERGs that employees may not otherwise realize in their day jobs; and

- contributing to the company's cultural competency through participation in sales, market, and product development.

In our consulting work, we encourage women to take advantage of and leverage these networks, to grow their careers and also demonstrate the value of female and diverse talent and markets. ERG leadership opportunities are significant development opportunities for building careers. We believe these networks are a unique opportunity for women, as well as all other kinds of talent, to supercharge their professional development. In cutting-edge companies, those functions that drive development for high-potential talent are utilizing ERG leadership positions as development opportunities, enabling a broader cross section of leaders to display their broader skill sets, and facilitating their personal and professional platform as emerging and future leaders.

These networks are a unique opportunity for women, as well as all other kinds of talent, to supercharge their professional development.

Comedian George Carlin is reputed to have once said, "Men are from Earth. Women are from Earth. Deal with it." In the end, gender equality really is just that simple. Women have an enormous contribution to make to our world and to our workplaces; it is well past time that we clear the obstacles, reconsider what we take for granted, and cultivate gender parity at work, in the marketplace, and at home.

CHANGE STARTS WITH US?

The book *Lean In* by Sheryl Sandberg, COO of Facebook, made tremendous waves when it was published in 2013. It was a clear call from a successful woman to other women mainly about managing their careers more intentionally, more boldly, and paying attention differently to the rules of the game. I appreciated Sandberg's call to step up, not to play small, and not to hesitate in negotiating salary or moves up the ladder.

In her *TED Talk*, Sandberg described how women unintentionally hold themselves back in their careers and urges them to be fearless and bold.[36] She expanded upon these ideas in *Lean In:* "Women need to shift from thinking, *I'm not ready to do that,* to thinking, *I want to do that—and I'll learn by doing it.*" I would define the restraint or "I'm-not-ready-ness" as the collateral impact of stories we tell ourselves about our worth, our value, and our ability to lead, as well as the messages we receive from the wider culture; it's connected to the stereotype threat we have grown up with as girls, and now women trying to make it in the business world. Sandberg laid a tremendous amount of responsibility for women's slow advancement on women themselves, and while the book was widely lauded, there was also a backlash from women who did not share Sandberg's relative privileges as a starting point. It's a lot easier to lean in to the discussion if you are already at the table, if you are already in the room, and if you enjoy relative privilege in terms of your ethnicity, your education, and your socio-economic background.

Women do need training and mentoring in order to rewrite their narratives so that they can move forward with intention, but as I hope I have made clear by now, organizations must equally participate in and prioritize inclusion and opportunity from the top. Women showing up differently can have adverse effects if those like her, and her senior leadership, aren't ready to provide steadfast support.

Women showing up differently can have adverse effects if those like her, and her senior leadership, aren't ready to provide steadfast support.

Sandberg herself acknowledges the structural inequities and bias when she writes, "Success and likeability are positively correlated for men and negatively for women. When a man is successful, he is liked by both men and women. When a woman is successful, people of both genders like her less."[37] While the onus is on all of us to rewrite this narrative—a tall order—there is a critical part for top leadership to play in elevating female role models up the hierarchy, lauding their successes, and providing air cover for them to show up powerfully without being subject to a double standard.

ENGAGING THE MAJORITY

The ancillary work stream to the message for women to modify their approach is, of course, to call for change in the system affecting women. It is fascinating to me that we've assumed all of our business cases, our data, our case studies, our *HBR* articles, and so on, will be enough to convince our organizations and their leadership that change is needed—without enlisting those very leaders as real *partners*. Successful movements for equality have often turned a critical corner when those *outside the demographic who need the most support* step forward to learn more, to challenge their assumptions, and to advocate and push forward on the behalf of that demographic. In the diversity context, a largely white and male executive suite in so many companies is precisely the audience we need to proactively include.

There are—and I know some of them—male champions in our midst, hailing from that majority whose participation we so badly need. We must focus on arming our early adopters in the majority with the facts to understand the problem, help them over the hurdle of the inalienable fact that they haven't experienced the same headwinds, and then lay out a plan for action with them as full partners.

There is no single way to make change happen; companies need a whole ecosystem of measures. But shifting our mind-set to focus on those who haven't, traditionally, participated in the dialogue would certainly get us further, faster. We can't afford to leave such a powerful resource on the table.

MEN'S ALLIES COMMUNITIES ON THE RISE

What is an ally, exactly?

It's an important question and one we must understand before moving forward. An ally in the workplace is any member of a "majority" group who uses that position to further equality for non-majority populations. When diverse people tire of the constant need to educate others, allies can step in to relieve them. The purpose of allies is not that they should speak for others or claim they've walked in anyone else's shoes but their own. Rather, their purpose is to educate on behalf of those who are less represented or less understood, and they should use their relative privilege to accomplish this, whether that privilege is defined by platform, social capital, ethnicity, socioeconomic background, or otherwise.

> An ally in the workplace is any member of a "majority" group who uses that position to further equality for non-majority populations.

As a consulting partner to the founding members of a male allies effort at a Fortune 50 technology company, my team and I had an incredible opportunity to witness some of these champions in action. It would be the company's first-ever, male-executive community dedicated to increasing the number of visible male-executive allies of diverse talent. We spent time dissecting the data available to the public, the company data, and exploring their diversity story—in a safe place where they could learn together as senior male peers. The closed-door nature of our work was critical in creating a sense of safety and, for that moment, a judgment-free zone. I learned so much about this important cohort, including the following:

- More education is needed on the current state of our gender gaps in the workplace to match the particular passion of groups like this. I mentioned the need for basic education earlier. They need to be armed and comfortable with the problem statement, articulating it to other executives and connecting the dots back to the business impact. In my experience, everyone has a vague understanding that something is wrong but is unfamiliar with all the available research findings with which to make a case.

- They are hesitant to ask questions to build their knowledge and to understand where they might help. Adam Grant writes about this in his article entitled "Why So Many Men Don't Stand Up for Their Female Colleagues."[38] Research has shown there are real or perceived penalties for allies who stand up, which works as a disincentive for action.

- They don't believe they have a diversity story that would be compelling enough to share. This is a coaching opportunity. If you have access to executives and can provide a framework and encouragement to these leaders to share their story widely and communicate how powerful and needed such sharing is to all those in the organization, we will accelerate change.

As a member of the LGBTQ community, I felt so convinced of the power of straight allies in the workplace, I wrote one of our first white papers on the topic *Allies Come Out*. I wanted to document the tremendous passion, courage, and conviction being shown by allies in several industries and by clients I knew well—from banking to technology to industrial manufacturing—and help them literally find each other, compare notes across the company, and show the strength and momentum of the movement. Now, six years later, the ally concept has taken hold firmly and far beyond its original LGBTQ birthplace, into programs that encourage allies for inclusion more broadly. We are now discussing male allies, white allies, allies for people with disabilities, and the list goes on. Many companies today have LGBTQ employee resource groups that are made up of a majority of allies—80–90 percent, in some cases, and I foresee this trend continuing and growing, especially with eager millennials hopping into the mix.

But it's not stopping at the LGBTQ community. I had the pleasure of giving a presentation with Shavondalyn Givens of NASA on their powerful Allies for Inclusion program, which has brought a new audience to the agency's table to discuss how wider, deeper, and faster cultural change might occur if they're "all in." It's critical to their ability to attract, retain, and develop the best and the brightest.

WHAT'S NEXT?

As one of the first and largest diverse affinities to be identified as a priority by many companies, female talent has stepped forward in large numbers in their efforts to seek community, support, and to identify their unique value proposition to the business. When there are women's networks at established companies, these networks have thousands of members and regard themselves very much as intact organizations—businesses "within the business." Their successes and challenges provided (and continue to provide) valuable lessons for women trying to get ahead in a workplace where there are overt and shadow challenges all around. We still have a long way to go based on the number of organizations who scarcely track their workforce statistics by gender, let alone other characteristics.

On the flip side, however, women's networks are setting the pace for inclusion, mindful of their own internal diversity and proactively seeking out their male allies for the unique support they can give. These are some of the most stunning success stories in the workplace today. They have set a high bar for subsequent generations of diverse talent to shoot for and have already left a remarkable legacy, with an incredible amount of potential remaining to create change. As we've shown, the battle isn't over yet, but we can play it smarter now.

CHAPTER SIX

■ ■ ■

WHAT'S YOUR PURPOSE?

"No one changes the world who isn't obsessed."

–BILLIE JEAN KING

How do you view work in your life? Is it a fulfilling experience that enriches your life, or is work simply a grueling financial obligation? Is it just a means to an end? As we expand our understanding of what difference looks like, beyond the traditional classifications like race, ethnicity, and gender, I suggest that one's stance toward work—we could call this a "work orientation"—represents another dimension of diversity. To borrow from Robert Bellah, who first articulated the concept of work orientation in the mid-1980s: Do you have a job, a career, or a calling?

I have become intrigued with our relationship to our work and believe there is so much untapped and underutilized potential in legions of employees who have not connected into their own deeper professional purpose—or who have but cannot connect to their employer's purpose and therefore live their purpose *outside the office walls*. Perhaps you know someone who's a researcher by day and a Shakespeare director by night, and when you talk to them, they truly come alive when they talk about their artistic endeavors. You know right away where their passions align with their work and where they would spend every moment of every day, if they could.

Many of us have become comfortable living this dichotomy between our jobs and our passions and resigned ourselves to these parts of us *not* being part of our work selves. Employers need a job to be done and a body to fill the seat. Employees need that paycheck. This is the straightforward equation of it, for many.

Employers, for their part, underestimate (if they think about it at all) the importance of purpose and therefore, most often don't excel at defining and sharing a purpose their people can get behind. When we do look for purpose-driven statements in company communications, we see language about driving revenue, pleasing shareholders, or increasingly these days, "attracting the best talent." This last one feels a little bit more personal to the average employee but is still too high level and corporate driven to really take root in people's hearts and minds and awaken a shared purpose in them. It's a value proposition for the company but not for the individual. It's certainly not an effective rallying cry to the incoming generation of talent, who highly value not only connecting to their employer's purpose but also letting their personal values drive their career.[1] In our inability to align work experience to purposes that resonate, we are leaving the gifts and passions of many outside the four walls of the office. This is yet another disconnect that hurts any organization's ability to attract and retain talent—another crack in the armor of the relationship.

> In our inability to align work experience to purposes that resonate, we are leaving the gifts and passions of many outside the four walls of the office.

A few notable consultancies are conducting innovative and deep research on where and to what degree purpose exists in organizations. Aaron Hurst, founder of the Taproot Foundation and author of *The Purpose Economy,* partnered with Arthur Woods to create Imperative, which is a **B Corp** that has built the first talent assessment platform to measure and grow purpose within organizations. I was introduced to Aaron's team to explore collaboration in 2015, and I was immediately struck—really, encouraged—by what their recent study showed. I began to consider the connections between purpose orientation, as they defined it, and our knowledge of the role that diversity and inclusion plays in people being able to bring their full selves to work.

Imperative surveyed 6,332 adults—employed either full time or part time, across industries, age groups, and occupational and educational levels—and found that, from baristas to CEOs,

> 28 percent of the 150 million-member US workforce defines the role of work in their lives primarily as a source of personal fulfillment and a way to help others. These Purpose-Oriented Workers, roughly 42 million strong, not only seek out purpose in their work, they create it and as a result, outperform the rest of the workforce.[2]

The numbers also show that approximately 108 million people view their relationship with work as transactional. In other words, their job is a means to an extrinsic end.

Can one's work orientation change? This research shares that it tends to remain fairly fixed, as a "trait, not a state." We can think of it as an aspect of who we are, meaning that in order to change the way we think about work, we must change the way we think about the purpose of our work. And as organizational architects leading change, we need to get much more skilled at locating our purpose-driven workforce.

> As organizational architects leading change, we need to get much more skilled at locating our purpose-driven workforce.

HARNESSING WORK PURPOSE

The best leaders and companies know how to capture people's imagination and awaken their purpose. This is how we capture so-called *discretionary* effort—that extra energy and passion that people either give or don't give, depending on how they are being treated. And make no mistake, *it is* about how they are being treated—in diversity parlance, it comes down to "Am I feeling welcomed, valued, respected, and heard in this organization?" The answer to that question determines for many whether they contribute all of their ideas, thoughts, energy, and heart.

Knowing one's ultimate purpose in relation to the company's mission gives people something they can take pride in, offering a powerful source of personal motivation for when challenges begin to take their toll. It's estimated that purpose-oriented workers will stay with a company 20 percent longer than other employees, are 60 percent more likely to be in or pursue leadership roles, are 47 percent more likely to advocate for and promote their employers to others, becoming de facto corporate ambassadors, and are 64 percent more likely to be fulfilled, or engaged, at work. Purpose-oriented workers report having more significant connections to coworkers and clients alike; they are also more likely to speak up for themselves and others.[3] Sounds like they might be great diversity champions, given these characteristics!

Work orientation can help predict future behavior in a way that engagement, while critically important, cannot. One's level of engagement can change, can be impacted by coworkers, by supervisors, by soul-sucking tasks and mind-numbing bureaucracy, whereas one's work orientation, one's view of the role of work in one's life, is stable.

PURPOSE ORIENTATION BY INDUSTRY

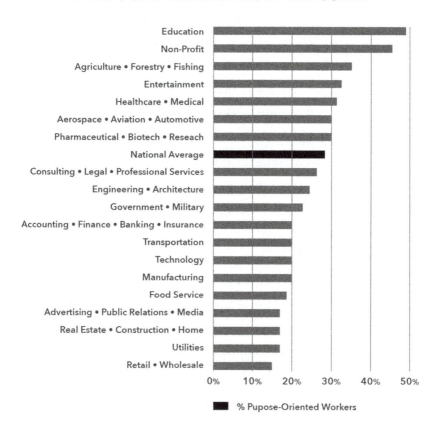

Source: Aaron Hurst and Anna Tavis, *2015 Workforce Purpose Index*, Imperative, 2015, https://www.imperative.com/index2015.

Purpose orientation is not the province of millennials, either, as one might think. Women and people over the age of fifty-five are more likely to be purpose oriented. And it does not follow class or ethnicity lines; the researchers found that neither income nor race was correlated with purpose orientation. Hurst and Woods conclude that "Purpose-Driven Workers are the foundation for successful organizations, a thriving economy, and a healthy society overall."[4]

To transform this hope-y, change-y purpose stuff into a management strategy, we might consider the words attributed to French writer Antoine de Saint-Exupéry: "If you want to build a ship, don't drum up people to collect wood, and don't assign them tasks and work, but rather teach them to long for the endless immensity of the sea." Purpose-oriented leaders are especially talented at this—at sharing the "sea" in such a way that will drive followership. They are aware of the core role of purpose for themselves, and therefore others, and go to great lengths to try to understand how they can enlist as many purpose-driven audience members in the task with them as possible. They know their success depends on awakening common purpose in others, who will then pass it along—speeding everyone's way toward success.

I, for one, am absolutely a purpose-oriented worker—and employer. Alignment with this concept has always been at the top of my list, but it hasn't always been my professional reality. In my years in nonprofits, and then as a stage performer, I felt very aligned to furthering my purpose: improving the world, expressing myself, moving and shifting people's thoughts and feelings. I had a short but tough couple of years in corporate environments, far away from my purpose and disconnected from the "why." These were lonely years, but I am grateful that the urgent need to escape provided the impetus to start my company, and purpose returned as I architected how I would make my next contribution. As a business owner, I had full authority to do just that.

What I was surprised to learn, however, as I was exposed to more and more corporate environments as a consultant, is that purpose lives all around us—in every industry. It needn't be the case that only non-profits or careers in the arts can fuel one's sense of purpose. Based on the many change agents I know person-ally who are employed at some of the biggest corporations in the world, I would agree with Hurst's and Woods' finding that there are purpose-ori-ented workers in every industry.

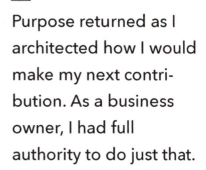

Purpose returned as I architected how I would make my next contri-bution. As a business owner, I had full authority to do just that.

Every job type, from artist to professional to assistant to laborer, is comprised of at least 13 percent purpose-oriented workers. And these folks are paid the same as their peers across industries. I want to reinforce that they don't suffer a financial penalty for their focus on purpose, even by comparison with those workers for whom the paycheck is the whole point.

I founded my company because I felt called to build more inclusive workplaces, where all kinds of people can bring their full, their whole, their "best" selves to work. That means they bring their talent, curiosity, insight, perspective, experience, communication styles and, yes, even their work orientation, to work every day. In the most healthy work environments, they know that it is safe to do so, and the quality of their work reflects that.

Many of my clients are purpose oriented as well. They know there are gaps and challenges, but they want JBC's help to sift through the sedimentary layers of their corporate processes, proce-dures, implicit biases, and "we've-always-done-it-this-way" thinking in order to create workplaces of greater inclusion and more equitable opportunities. And if you are reading this book, the odds are good that you too are a purpose-oriented worker. You are seeking better answers, for yourself and others, and you want work to matter.

Purpose-oriented people volunteer for cause-oriented charities; they lead philanthropic organizations and initiatives. They raise their hands to participate in diversity efforts. And they may find that they are voices in the wilderness if they don't get encouragement and support from a manager or leader. In a way, they are a high-risk species of colleague, as the stakes are higher for them. Remaining in a job, at a company, involves significance—of themselves, of others, of the product or service they are delivering—every day. This is in direct opposition to so many of our management practices, which ignore the individual in favor of the system, of efficiency, of the supposed bottom line.

> Remaining in a job, at a company, involves significance—of themselves, of others, of the product or service they are delivering—every day.

Another way the purpose discussion challenges the status quo is the research finding that purpose-oriented workers exist at all levels of the organization, and this, of course, includes the midlevel and entry level. When we have assumed for so long that the most knowledge and the "best" leaders sit at the top of the organizational pyramid, we may need to rethink our approach. We have a disconnect between the resources, kudos, and accolades given to those with the highest salaries and biggest titles, and our purpose-oriented workers whom we are not habituated to identify, recognize, and galvanize.

What we do know fairly certainly is that all American workers have labored in stratified structures with increasingly irrelevant systems of evaluation and a disconnect between those in the C-suite and those on the trading floor, in the mailroom, behind the retail counter, and on the loading dock. The command-and-control leadership strategy can be painfully slow to respond to the needs of workers and even to the needs of the business. In the misalignment, we are not sustaining our most precious resource, the human one, even as corporations tout their commitments to social responsibility and sustainability in fancy annual reports. The purpose-oriented among us are the first to jump ship.

We've already talked about how the millennials, as a cohort, want a much more clearly articulated purpose in their working lives, and they seek employment with companies that have already prioritized this alignment—internally and externally. When we consider that millennials are soon to be the largest generation in the workforce today, alongside the cohort of purpose-oriented workers, then the critical mass gathering to light the fuse of profound corporate fission should be obvious. With today's record-low unemployment, smart companies know they need to offer more than good salaries to engage the best employees across demographics, and a lived corporate mission that resonates can be a compelling recruiting tool as well as an effective way to engage the employees who are already onboard. In the words of Hurst and Tavis, "Employers that attract and empower this exceptional talent will have a significant competitive advantage."[5]

ORGANIZATIONAL PURPOSE

It turns out that attracting purpose-oriented workers is great for business too. Who knew? In *Firms of Endearment*, Rajendra S. Sisodia, David B. Wolfe, and Jagdish N. Sheth profile companies that foreground purpose. They looked at IKEA, Commerce Bank, Whole

Foods, Southwest Airlines, Nordstrom, Costco, Patagonia, Trader Joe's, TOMS, Virgin, and Starbucks, among others, and found that these companies outperformed the S&P 500 by 83 percent in three years and by more than 1,500 percent after fifteen years. The authors contend that these companies are creating all kinds of value, from financial to experiential, which breeds customer loyalty.[6] I contend that it also breeds productivity and engagement among employees, which can fuel innovation and impact, which then bulwarks purpose, creating a glorious feedback loop.

Patagonia's mission statement reads: "Build the best product, cause no unnecessary harm, use business to inspire and implement solutions to the environmental crisis."[7] It speaks to corporate social responsibility, to sustainability, and also to creating products that will reward the company in the marketplace. The company, which makes outdoor clothing and gear, donates time and services as well as at least 1 percent of its sales to environmental causes, for which they lobby. On their website, they declare:

> Patagonia supports candidates who push hard for clean, renewable energy, restore clean water and air and turn away from risky, carbon-intensive fuels. We support leaders who will act on behalf of the future and the planet.[8]

That last sentence is a powerful call to action for anyone who shares Patagonia's purpose. Patagonia's mission statement combines both the values that bring them market success (building safe, high-quality products) and the values that contribute to a better world (philanthropic efforts to help the environment). They are clearly calling out to those who share their purpose; for them, "a love of wild and beautiful places demands participation in the fight to save them."[9]

It is also inspirational to read about the company's detailed and multifaceted commitment to becoming ever more responsible, as well as the difficulty of realizing their mission, or "failing forward." Patagonia founder Yvon Chouinard has said, "Living the examined life is a pain in the ass." On its website, the company says, "In the end, Patagonia may never be completely responsible. We have a long way to go and we don't have a map—but we do have a way to read the terrain and to take the next step."[10] The admission that the "examined life" of a company may compromise sales, revenue, and results, in the short term, and that the company has a long way to go, is commendable for its transparency and its authenticity. This wins the hearts and minds of many proud Patagonia employees, as well as the customers who've bolstered the brand.

At IKEA, the company vision is "to create a better everyday life for the many people."[11] The company creates good designs at a price that is low enough to make products affordable to as many people as possible. The Swedish company also partners with social entrepreneurs locally and globally in order to work toward ever-greater sustainability. According to Glassdoor, a website where employees and former employees anonymously review companies and their management, employees love working for IKEA because they are inspired, they are proud, and there are tremendous opportunities for lateral moves into different parts of the business as well as for promotions. IKEA's workers are stimulated by purpose and by new challenges. Eighty percent of them would recommend the company to a friend as a great place to work, and 90 percent give an enthusiastic report on CEO Peter Agnefjall.[12] As we move into a world where we're not just rating the products we buy on Amazon or the trips we take on TripAdvisor but are also considering a CEO's scorecard as judged by those who work for him or her, I foresee greater accountability flowing from the workforce to C-suite leaders, regarding their behaviors and their relative ability to "walk the talk."

An intriguing question on this topic does arise for small or start-up companies: What happens to an original purpose orientation as an organization grows? Does it become difficult to maintain as a core commitment? In a 2015 Pulse post, LinkedIn co-founder Reid Hoffman wrote,

> In a start-up environment, when teams are small and most everyone who's involved is, by nature, a risk-taker with a desire to create something that will potentially have outsized impact, it's relatively easy to find purpose-driven individuals…But to become the company we wanted to become, we knew that we'd eventually need more employees, with different skill sets and different temperaments. And inevitably our culture would change.

> Still, my co-founders and I were determined to preserve our shared sense of purpose as a core value, even as we grew. In job interviews, and then again, in new hire orientations, we always emphasized our guiding value: Individual LinkedIn members always come first. In emphasizing our philosophy so persistently, we inevitably dissuaded some talented potential hires for whom it did not resonate. But we also attracted individuals who did connect with it, and thus ensured our ongoing cohesiveness even as we started to expand beyond our core team.[13]

While focusing on their purpose, LinkedIn has begun to consciously craft a culture of inclusion. The company has implanted unconscious bias training across the organization. It has designed and implemented a Women's Initiative for the Global Sales team, and a

Women in Technology initiative in the Engineering and Product lines of the organization to hire, retain, develop, and advance women. The company has also formed an array of partnerships designed to flood the STEM pipeline.[14] As part of its inclusion strategy, the company supports six employee resource groups that serve women, black, Hispanic/Latino, LGBTQ, veteran, and employees with disabilities. Fortune found, in 2015, that LinkedIn is one of the most gender-diverse companies among high-tech firms, and nearly half its employees are nonwhite.[15]

LinkedIn's Reid Hoffman clearly connects the dots on organizational purpose, purpose-oriented workers, engagement, and productivity, while prioritizing a diverse workforce and the importance of an inclusive workplace culture where all kinds of talent feel energized to contribute and connected to a larger effort.

We are fortunate that so many of the leaders we partner with are tasked every day to awaken the specific purpose of inclusion at their companies. Our consulting work with employee resource groups means that we spend our time supporting these existing purpose-oriented communities within the many organizations that have them. Many people take their purpose-oriented energy outside their employer's four walls, volunteering or working on personal projects and ventures because they don't perceive a connection to what their companies are doing. Employee resource groups are not only about enabling safety and support for underrepresented groups; their greatest function is helping

Employee resource groups are not only about enabling safety and support for underrepresented groups; their greatest function is helping employees and leaders discover and harness a shared sense of purpose.

employees and leaders discover and harness a shared sense of purpose. This is why they come together and why they grow in such a unique, organic, and powerful way. Leaders and members of these groups work well past their regular work hours. They represent the company with pride at community events, and they find their own opportunities for growth. This is purpose "at work."

PIVOTING TOWARD PURPOSE: EXECUTIVE LEADERSHIP ON DIVERSITY AND INCLUSION

While all clients tell me how unique and special their company is, respectfully I point out that there are well-worn paths and patterns in the resistance to organizational change, as well as to the gradual adoption of inclusion as an organizational value. Organizations, and the individuals in them, have differing capacities and appetites for change, but one thing is true: change requires consistent, strategic effort in many forms before we see acceptance and commitment. One of the most powerful tools is a committed executive who is purpose oriented on the topic of diversity—who has been awakened to the need for change and who is passionate about gathering others around this purpose. No one can do it alone.

Executives who do this well not only articulate a strong vision and hold others accountable for behaviors and outcomes but also build messages and actions into their everyday to-do list.

For an organization to orient, or reorient, itself to purpose—especially the purpose of building a more inclusive workplace where all can thrive, which is a fairly personal and complex purpose—the first step has to come from the C-suite. *Executive sponsorship*, starting with the CEO, is critical to effecting organizational change in terms of defining purpose and realigning with it. Executives who do this well not only articulate a strong vision and hold others accountable for behaviors and outcomes but also build messages and actions into their everyday to-do list: regularly talking about what inclusion means to them in a variety of forums, such as town halls and leadership meetings, and follow-ups to discussions, and by checking in, attending events, showing their support of the conversation, and so on. This is top-to-bottom, visible support, and while it's rarer than I'd like to see, it truly works.

There is a difference here between quantity and quality. A busy calendar of attending diversity-related events is a solid first step, but we might call it table stakes at this point for anyone who works and leads in today's world. However, if an executive speaks from core organizational or personal purpose, fluently and authentically, connecting the dots in a way only an executive can, that imbues all programmatic efforts with a special weight, and many sit up in a different way and pay attention. There is such a craving to hear leadership speak in this way and utilize their platform to connect.

The ability to speak earnestly about big ideas in small detail is a rare skill in the C-suite, and often, it is the missing heartbeat of an entire initiative. All eyes look upward when diversity is discussed as a company priority. Employees are watching and listening to ascertain the veracity

All eyes look upward when diversity is discussed as a company priority. Employees are watching and listening to ascertain the veracity of the commitment, judging for themselves how deep it goes by assessing personal conviction.

of the commitment, judging for themselves how deep it goes by assessing personal conviction. They know too that change is hard, and they ultimately want to know if you really mean it and if it's a commitment for the long haul. With all of our millennial research, we know they are also asking, "Who are you, really?"

In conversation with executives, I ensure they move into the often-uncomfortable place of finding their own diversity story and telling it as the powerful agents of change that they are—helping them appreciate and utilize their influential platforms (we'll talk about how to do self-guided work on storytelling later). In these conversations, I am often armed with focus group data we've collected throughout the organization, which helps to refine the discussion (and can be rather uncomfortable in and of itself, as we've described). We review the cry for help embedded in the results, rather than deliver criticism for what these executives and the organization have not yet done, and then we move from awareness building to action.

Where do we get the most compelling data to awaken purpose in leaders and to incite change and commitment? There is nothing like organizational demographics, enhanced with personal quotes. We start with quantitative data on representation, recruiting, retention, and promotion, as well as qualitative information on workplace culture and employee engagement, often from surveys. Through focus groups and interviews, we gather answers to many questions that give us a sense of the gap to be closed and where the company is missing an opportunity to locate and align with those purpose-oriented employees who will be so critical for transformation. We ask questions such as the following:

- "What is great about working for this company?"

- "What is painful or uncomfortable within your organization's current culture?"

- "Do you dread coming to work, or do you look forward to it?"

- "What delights you?"

- "Where do you hit a wall?"

- "What role does your identity play in your answers to these questions?"

Once we are grounded in the current state, we ask both employees and executives the following questions:

- What would success look like?

- How would the company culture be different?

- Who would work here in the future who isn't here now?

- Who's missing from the conversation?

- What are you working toward, and how will you know when you've arrived?

- Are we ready to get started, and how do we begin?

In our debrief of the data, we point out the quick wins that create not just good visual impressions of diversity and inclusion efforts but also near-term change while we design and implement longer-term initiatives. Working the short term

Working the short term and the long term simultaneously is a change-management best practice that creates some early momentum.

and the long term simultaneously is a change-management best practice that creates some early momentum.

It's also important to step back and view the organizational journey of purpose in historical context. Have there been failed or aborted diversity and inclusion efforts in the past? Are employees going to be skeptical of new proposals because once or twice or even three times before, the company has made a big initial push, only to lose its way? Where is the impetus for change coming from now, and will it be lasting? Is a new CEO, market, product, competitor, or pressure from the board of directors fueling the work? None of these factors is empirically good or bad, but if you want to win your organization's trust, you are going to have to clean up the garden before you can begin to grow inclusion in fertile ground.

Once we are in the coaching conversations with executives, some important guidance we provide includes

- being transparent with communication about the organization's focus on diversity and why it is critical to the business;

- addressing any fears about the motivation behind the efforts by underscoring how critical inclusion is, and how it has to be an intentional effort;

- meeting resistance head-on; and

- emphasizing what's in it for multiple stakeholder groups— articulating the value proposition for change to the individual as well as to the whole employee population.

People cannot be afraid of what they don't know if you make sure that they actually do know; they cannot worry about how it's going to affect them negatively if you continually point out how it will benefit them. Tell them at the outset. Tell them often.

More often than not, by the end of the dialogue, executive leaders are very stirred by newly awakened purpose to fix what's not right and to leave a legacy they are prouder of.

For us as consultants, finding that sense of clarity, affirmation, and deeper purpose is what diversity and inclusion training should look like. We help our clients to ask these questions and to discern the answers. We help them navigate the fear, anger, and suspicion that, perhaps, as leaders, they didn't know were simmering in the culture. Then we work with them to design diversity and inclusion strategies that are aligned to their corporate vision, often facilitating discussions about revising that vision to be bolder and to speak more to all aspects of their workforce. We help them to anticipate the challenges to success, to engage the employee population in the programs, to coach and support team members throughout the change, and to create a new or retooled corporate culture that is more inclusive as well as more sensitive to the diverse and changing marketplace.

People cannot be afraid of what they don't know if you make sure that they actually do know; they cannot worry about how it's going to affect them negatively if you continually point out how it will benefit them.

The ability to discover and attain the core purpose of yourself within your workplace is real culture-changing work. We recommend the passion for diversity and commitment to inclusion as a great shared purpose to address and harness. Many will resonate with it— and most importantly, the most at-risk and underrepresented talent will connect and engage in an unprecedented way. If done right, where that purpose can take you will only be determined by where you want to go.

CHAPTER SEVEN

THE WORKPLACE
OF THE FUTURE

Breaking the Mold, Letting Everyone In

*"Do not go where the path may lead; go instead
where there is no path and leave a trail."*

–EMERSON

Career consultant Kathy Caprino, in an issue of *Forbes*, poses a simple question to organizational leaders: "When you look around your office, do you see a positive organization that fosters growth, expansion, and engagement, or the opposite?"[1]

Caprino raises a good point: Is what you can see around you representative of people's actual experience? As we've explored, it's much easier to create our narratives and success stories based on what we want to see, or what we see through our own lens, versus what is true for others.

When my team and I walk into workplaces all across this country, we see the literal, or "above-the-line" environment first.

Organizations have icebergs, just like people do. We notice whether the company has prioritized the meshing of public and private spaces—the colors, the amount of natural light, the buzz and energy you can feel immediately (or not). These are our first indications of the tone of the workplace. Of course, we immediately hone in on— you guessed it—the visible demographic mix we see as we walk through the hallways, including gender, assumed ethnicity, and generational diversity. In other words, we notice who's in and not in the room as best we can, given there are visible and invisible aspects of diversity, of course.

We've grown acutely sensitive to the feedback so many of our clients have received from *their* customers about the lack of diversity they see, literally, in sales meetings, in the hallways, and in the company's collateral.

Why have we trained ourselves to notice all of this? First, because we've grown acutely sensitive to the feedback so many of our clients have received from *their* customers about the lack of diversity they see, literally, in sales meetings, in the hallways, and in the company's collateral. We, of course, put ourselves in those customers' shoes, as outsiders looking in, so we can assist our clients in understanding how they are perceived, whether it's serving them, and if desired, changing that picture.

But we have also come to learn that the office designs with the latest bells and whistles are only one piece of the culture puzzle. The culture and its relative "health" underlying all that's shiny and new might be a totally different story. If we're facilitating focus groups in a company, we hear about the less-appetizing aspects of what might look like a progressive, hip environment on the surface. It may look like a workplace of the future, but we discover just as many parallel but very different experiences based on identity, cultural background, or style. In other words, the culture of a place still underlies everything—and still needs constant tending.

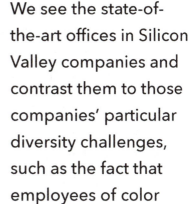

We see the state-of-the-art offices in Silicon Valley companies and contrast them to those companies' particular diversity challenges, such as the fact that employees of color represent less than 5 percent of their workforce...

Workspace design doesn't necessarily address inclusion dynamics unless the designers are very mindful of inclusion and the clients have made it a priority; it might actually portray a false sense of confidence, of a culture having figured it out, of collaborative space where people are working together more effectively than ever before—when many still feel challenged by the same old biases. We see the state-of-the-art offices in Silicon Valley companies and contrast them to those companies' particular diversity challenges, such as the fact that employees of color represent less than 5 percent of their workforce, or less-than-flattering focus-group feedback, and realize the disconnect between intended inclusion, and real inclusion.

Angelica Coleman, a young African American woman, walked into the offices of Dropbox for a job interview in October 2013, and one of the first things she noticed was that nobody there looked like her. When she decided to leave a year or two later, one of the last things she was told by her direct manager was that if she wanted to keep climbing the Silicon Valley corporate ladder, "you need to go somewhere else."

Coleman told *International Business Times*:

> It's disheartening to look around you when you walk into a tech company of the size and caliber of a Dropbox, Facebook or Google: You know they're making big impacts on everyday life for tons of people, they have money and they are a good company with good products, but you look around, as a black person, and the only people who look like you are the help. That's really hard."[2]

It's not enough to check the boxes of inclusion; we must become students of company culture, dismantling past structures and building a flexible model that speaks to the way today's workforce wants to work and wants to be seen, heard, and engaged. As a Gen X'er speaking for my generation and on behalf of baby boomers, especially, we need to acknowledge that the very definition of being included at work has changed dramatically since we first learned about the role of work and the workplace in our lives and, in the process, conceived our sense of self in that context. Coleman's honest insights remind us that the need to "see it to be it" is very human; the struggle that many face when trying to envision a career for those who look like them at certain employers is real, and the hurtful consequence and conclusion is too often that they must go elsewhere to find those opportunities. The promised visions of a thriving and profitable future of innovation and flexibility can only exist in a culture where the maximum number of people feel comfortable and confident contributing their fullest selves to the work.

The hurtful consequence and conclusion is too often that they must go elsewhere to find those opportunities.

Regardless of what we believe about our progress in these areas, or how well intended we are, engagement numbers, according to Gallup, are still stuck at 13 percent for workers worldwide.[3] I believe building more inclusive cultures would finally change those numbers, but we have much work to do before then.

The opportunity in front of us now, as the designers of work and the workplace, is to start connecting employee engagement, diversity and inclusion, and economic value. They are all intertwined.

If people are companies' dearest assets, as companies often proclaim, then it is time to look at them as invaluable resources that should be carefully nurtured. We need to understand how employees flourish, as well as when they are at risk. We haven't done a great job of this, and while each of us suffers from the missed opportunities, diverse talent is most at risk because they, like Coleman, have many doubts about their future prospects, based on what they observe, hear, and see. As they should.

As we discussed earlier, the solution some organizations have implemented includes open office plans and flexible work arrangements. This is a good step toward retaining the talent they've worked so hard and spent so much on to recruit. There is a growing understanding that strategies that encompass the whole person are not only good for those individuals but also good for the organization that employs them.

Diverse talent is most at risk because they, like Coleman, have many doubts about their future prospects, based on what they observe, hear, and see.

Part of embracing the whole person as a retention vehicle includes our health, in the broadest definition of the word. Employee health and wellness, including mindfulness, are being added to company benefits, such as health screenings and financial-acumen training. Mark Bertolini, CEO of Aetna, is well known as a chief executive who has made employee wellness a priority. "If we're going to invest in our people to get them engaged every day," he says, "we have to reduce their stress levels, we have to pay them fairly, we have to allow them to live their lives fully so that when they're taking care of other people, they don't have all that other baggage with them." He practices mindfulness and yoga in his own life, as he lives with pain on a daily basis due to an accident he suffered many years ago, and through the provision of those services to his employees, Aetna's workforce reports a 28 percent decrease in stress levels, a 20 percent improvement in sleep quality, and a 19 percent reduction in pain. For an investment of under $2,500 per employee, Bertolini says,

> We've saved people's marriages; they've lost weight. We had people come back and say, "You know what? You saved my life." And it cost us $197,000 to do the first program. If that saved one life, I think that's like a huge return on investment.[4]

We spend the vast majority of our lives in a workplace of some kind and have to begin quantifying the cost of working, every day, in an environment that, when originally designed, didn't consider, let alone prioritize, our health.

Here are some more radical ideas and experiments that have the potential to move us in the right direction and, more importantly, that incorporate diversity and inclusion fundamentals at every step along the way.

THE GREAT FLATTENING

Traditional hierarchies in organizations—those structures built in another era that drive top-down, command-and-control behaviors— had a valid rationale at one time. Jacob Morgan, author of *The Future of Work: Attract New Talent, Build Better Leaders, and Create a Competitive Organization*, reminds us that "linear work where no brain power is required and where the people . . . are treated like expendable cogs"[5] was a hallmark of the mid- to late-twentieth century. But as we have discussed throughout this book, that cog strategy is not churning away as it once did. Communication, collaboration, innovation, and employee satisfaction all take significant hits under a traditional hierarchy; agility is limited, and the whole person is truly beside the point.

A flatter structure begins to open the lines of communication and peel away some of the layers of management. Morgan maintains that this model requires "an understanding by executives and managers that employees don't need to work at your company; they should want to work there and as a result, everything should be designed around that principle," and that "managers exist to support the employees and not vice versa."[6]

As a CEO, I believe I work for the people in my company and focus on being of service to them. Without them, I cannot accomplish the vision I committed to when I founded my company. I avoid pulling the "CEO card" as much as possible and encourage them to solve problems as flat, empowered teams in which the solution is just as likely to arise from the most inexperienced member as from the most senior member. We are virtual, flexible, collaborative, and nonhierarchical in our approach.

This is relatively easier, of course, for smaller companies that are more nimble and quicker to shift. But these days, most large companies committed to progress are acknowledging that the way we work needs to change. A quick scan shows that companies as diverse as Cisco, Whirlpool, and Pandora are beginning to flatten their structures through flextime, telecommuting, and elimination of traditional job titles, as well as focusing heavily on the overall employee experience and work environment.

A completely *flat organization* is rare, but it's a fascinating experiment—one with no titles, no managers, and no executives. Valve, a Washington-based video-game development and distribution company, ensures that all of its employees can see what projects are in the pipeline and that they can choose where to commit their time. If any employees want to start a new project, they need only build a team and secure funding in order to do so. Admittedly, this is an extreme example, but extreme examples are useful in stimulating our imagination around what could be and in laying out small and doable steps toward change that can be initiated in larger organizations—first in limited cases and then more broadly.

Old habits are hard to break. Morgan does observe that while flat approaches can work well at a smaller enterprise, they can be difficult to sustain. "Informal hierarchies automatically get created based on seniority; people who are at the company longer just tend to be viewed as being more senior. The lack of structure can also make accountability and reliability a bit of an issue as well."[7] The advice might be to proceed with caution, but make sure you do proceed.

Bill Gore was ahead of his time on the concept of flat organizational management. He left DuPont in 1958 to start a new business, and he wanted to create and implement a new style of management to go with it. Of his ideology's origins, business strategy expert Gary Hamel wrote,

He wasn't simply interested in inventing new materials or selling products, he was bent on creating an entirely new kind of company—one that unleashed and inspired every person in it, one that put as much energy into finding the next big thing as milking the last big thing.

Gore's core business values included believing in the individual to do what's right for the company, providing freedom for associates to make their own decisions, fairness, and collaboration. His company, W. L. Gore & Associates, went on to develop Gore-Tex, a waterproof, breathable fabric membrane, among other products, and remains steadfast in its pursuit of Gore's founding principles. On the company's website, corporate social responsibility is touted, as well as the company's commitment to its team: "Acting responsibly is a natural outgrowth of Gore's culture. We respect the environment and treat our associates and partners fairly."[9]

I believe that businesses must stop treating employees as if they were felons waiting to pilfer resources or children waiting to throw paper airplanes at the substitute teacher. If we want the best results and the most engaged employees, Gore's fundamental faith in his employees' desire to do right by the company is a worthy place to begin.

Businesses must stop treating employees as if they were felons waiting to pilfer resources or children waiting to throw paper airplanes at the substitute teacher.

DISMANTLING HIERARCHY

Cross-hierarchy dialogue is limited in many of the companies we work with. One focus group attendee shared her frustrations: "If they could only flatten the hierarchy . . . it feels you are not allowed to go beyond your manager, whether he/she listens to you or not. If you go to your manager's manager, it's a scandal. It's very closed."

Zappos has experimented with creating greater employee autonomy through its implementation of *holacracy*, a concept that dismantles traditional hierarchies in favor of greater employee autonomy in the processes and the running of the business.[10] To empower all of its 1,500 employees, Zappos has organized itself into roughly four hundred different circles in which employees can have multiple roles, creating company-wide transparency and more personal accountability. Company founder Tony Hsieh believes that, free from management control, the organization can be more agile and adaptable to the changes he sees as necessary to create a better workplace within a profitable business.

Zappos has a goal of radical transparency. However, some people misconstrue holacracy as anarchy. As Hsieh explained, in January 2016, "It's easy…to just read the headline of 'No managers' and assume that that means no hierarchy. It's actually a hierarchy of purpose."[11] There's that theme of purpose, again.

Holacracy hasn't been an easy system for staff to learn at Zappos. Hsieh recently likened it to learning a new language, and it can take a long time to become fluent, but it has also transformed working life for those who embraced it. For those who didn't, there was a severance deal—a minimum of three months of salary, or one month for every year worked. Just over two hundred people took the deal, however, which resulted in a 14 percent reduction in the workforce. This made some headlines as evidence of failure, but only a third said they had based their decision on the implementation of holacracy.[12]

HOLACRACY VS. HIERARCHY

HOLACRACY takes powers traditionally reserved for executive and managers and spreads them across all employees.

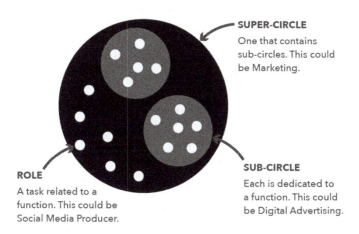

SUPER-CIRCLE
One that contains sub-circles. This could be Marketing.

ROLE
A task related to a function. This could be Social Media Producer.

SUB-CIRCLE
Each is dedicated to a function. This could be Digital Advertising.

In a **TRADITIONAL HIERARCHY** layers of management establish how products are approved and monitored.

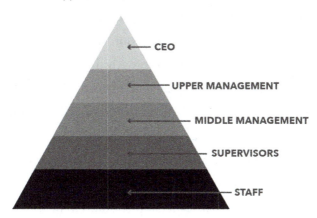

CEO

UPPER MANAGEMENT

MIDDLE MANAGEMENT

SUPERVISORS

STAFF

Source: Samantha Lee/*Business Insider*

Hsieh believes the new culture is working because giving workers more power is effective for employees who have the company's back. In the *Harvard Business Review*, Tim Kastelle recently observed that "there is a growing body of evidence that shows organizations with flat structures outperform those with more traditional hierarchies in most situations."[13]

Zappos employee Tyler Williams loves the new opportunities he has found to help shift the culture through the new system:

> Employees who desire control find Holacracy makes their lives so difficult that they leave. The people who are thriving here have a service mindset, and by that I mean they view themselves as a service to an organization. I can offer my knowledge and skills and create something of value with them. It's like lots of little entrepreneurs being innovative within one big enterprise. I couldn't go back to the old way of working.[14]

In their book *Why Should Anyone Be Led by You?* Robert Goffee and Gareth Jones, both professors at the London School of Economics, suggest a less radical approach that employs some of the holacracy principles. They argue that instead of using hierarchies as crutches to establish social distance in companies where radical rethinking isn't yet possible, senior executives should work to get closer to their employees, and more importantly, in my opinion, that they should be authentic with their employees. Rather than bringing a predigested idea of what leadership should entail if it is to work, executives should bring their real selves to their interactions with their team.[15]

SHEDDING LAYERS

Whether they know they are writing about the tenets of diversity and inclusion or not, I would argue that appreciation for and the active seeking of diversity is core to this approach and its eventual success. One concrete way leaders can shift how they resonate with others is to build relationships through authenticity and, in some cases, vulnerability by sharing their stories and willingly admitting challenges.

While distance can have value for strategic planning, fewer layers can provide senior executives with the flexibility to adapt when necessary in order to serve their teams better. This also fosters direct communication, which builds trust and speeds up decision making. Goffee and Jones talk in detail about striking that critical balance between vulnerability and distance.

Jason Fried, cofounder of 37Signals, now known as Basecamp, a web-application developer, recently wrote in *Inc.*:

One concrete way leaders can shift how they resonate with others is to build relationships through authenticity and, in some cases, vulnerability by sharing their stories and willingly admitting challenges.

> We revere "horizontal" ambition—in which employees who love what they do are encouraged to dig deeper, expand their knowledge, and become better at it. We always try to hire people who yearn to be master craftspeople, that is, designers who want to be great designers, not managers of designers; developers who want to master the art of programming, not management.[16]

While the company isn't as concerned with hierarchy-signaling elements like titles and promotions through ever-higher layers of management, they do include above-market salaries, generous benefits, four-day summer workweeks, and tremendous autonomy in arranging one's paid time off, or PTO. Fried observed,

> One thing we've found is that groups that manage themselves are often better off than groups that are managed by a single person. So when groups do require structure, we get them to manage themselves. Management responsibilities rotate regularly. It frees us from the often-toxic labor-versus-management dynamic, in which neither party truly understands what it's like to be on the other side.
>
> Because we rotate management duties weekly, everyone is more empathetic toward one another. When you'll be management soon, you respect management more. Same with labor.[17]

Fried is effectively cultivating and harnessing another dimension of diversity: diversity of thought. "We would rather everyone work together in an environment in which everyone has a chance to move proudly and thoroughly sideways." Everyone is welcome; everyone gets heard; and the "us-versus-them" binary is shattered, opening everyone's access to the same sense of place and purpose.

We consult for some extremely large companies, with three hundred thousand employees or more. One would not be crazy to lose any hope for change, considering such an insurmountable number and size and the intense bureaucracy seemingly required to manage it. It is overwhelming to consider how we can ever make a difference to a system of that size. But we persist, and the key is to identify those early adopters, those current or newly awakened change agents. If they are well placed and passionate, their impact is felt by tens of thousands, vertically and horizontally. They are often the purpose-oriented workers we have described, who, with some careful support, can influence the many. People who are passionate about culture change might be few in number, but they make up their own community of ambassadors and recruiters who can be very effective in furthering the inclusion cause.

People who are passionate about culture change might be few in number, but they make up their own community of ambassadors and recruiters who can be very effective in furthering the inclusion cause.

DOES SIZE MATTER?

Smaller or less-represented communities in the workplace are often strengthened by dismantling hierarchies. Bigger is not always better, as we know, and large companies are already waking up to the law of diminishing returns when it comes to size. Huge, immobile, bureaucratic—they cannot pivot effectively to seize market opportunities or to mobilize their workforce around opportunities. Start-ups and early-stage companies, on the other hand, have the opposite problem of preserving the magic energy of the early team against dilution as growth accelerates.

In massive organizations, people have a hard time connecting not only to the organizational mission but also to a meaningful sense of community. What is, then, the ideal size for workplace communities? Something called "Dunbar's number" posits that social structure and behavior can be related to group size. Through a study of the number of holiday cards a household sent, British anthropologist Robin Dunbar discovered that an individual can hold about 150 meaningful connections before the number of connections becomes overwhelming and unmanageable.[18] This same number has been found in other social scenarios including companies, hunter-gatherer societies, and military units. Considering this limit of 150, no wonder we all feel overwhelmed with the number of connections we imagine we need to maintain on Facebook and LinkedIn, let alone in our professional and personal lives. I know mine far exceed 150 (and that the situation often feels unmanageable).

We have mentioned employee resource groups as team members who come together organically because of a shared identity and passion and have improbably found each other in the midst of massive, anonymous institutions. Employees are deriving tremendous strength and actualization through their participation in, and leadership of, these flat communities built not around seniority but around doing what's best for that community, as well as for the company. Is there a broader lesson on workplace design to be learned from the power of these connections? We will explore this and a myriad of other benefits to these groups, later on in the book.

DO OPEN PLANS EQUAL GREATER OPENNESS?

Some of the most radical commitments to office-plan experimentation are being undertaken by our country's oldest companies. General Motors, for instance, is in the early stages of a $1 billion renovation of its Warren Technical Center campus in Michigan. Among its many plans, the corporation is creating new design studios and renovating existing research facilities in the hopes of luring engineers who are accustomed to the wide-open and stimulating environments at companies such as Pixar and Google.

The open-plan office space was intended to foster communication, spark innovation, and display transparency, although it is also a cost-effective way to house one's employees and reduce real-estate costs. The infusion of the multitasking millennial generation into the workforce has played a role in ushering in this new way of thinking.[19]

Company by company, employee by employee, the reviews are mixed on how well this is working. A new study based on a survey of over forty thousand US office workers in 303 office buildings finds no evidence to substantiate the supposition that these plans support communication and innovation. The study found that workers in enclosed private offices were the most satisfied with their workspace, followed by those in shared offices. Those in open-plan offices were, reportedly, the least satisfied with their workspace.[20]

A 2009 review article published in *Asia-Pacific Journal of Health Management* found that 90 percent of studies of open-plan offices linked them to health problems such as stress and high blood pressure. A 2009 study in Sweden found that occupants of private offices were most happy with their environment, while most dissatisfaction was registered in medium and large open-plan offices. Noise, distractions, and loss of privacy top the list of employees' workspace miseries.[21]

After surveying sixty-five thousand people over the past decade in North America, Europe, Africa, and Australia, researchers at the University of California, Berkeley, report that more than half of office workers are dissatisfied with the level of "speech privacy," making it the leading complaint in offices everywhere.[22]

Anne-Laure Fayard, a professor of management at the Polytechnic Institute of New York University who has studied open offices, reports "many studies show that people have shorter and more superficial conversations in open offices because they're self-conscious about being overheard."[23]

Although there is still much experimentation with balancing collaboration and privacy, there is also a strong, positive sense of how open-plan offices democratize the workspace. Former New York City Mayor Michael Bloomberg famously eschewed a private office in favor of occupying a bullpen with his staff for greater transparency, ease of access, and communication.[24] He effectively flattened the hierarchy of his very hierarchical elected office.

Among the complaints about loss of privacy and distraction that arose in the studies I mentioned earlier, there are both diversity challenges and opportunities. All of us have our own working and communication styles; some of us are introverts, while more of us are extroverts. Introverts can demonstrate extroverted behaviors in the service of an issue or project about which they are passionate, but they may be drained by the effort, whereas their extroverted counterparts may be energized.[25] (To learn more about the power of introverts and introversion in business, read Susan Cain's work on the topic at http://www.quietrev.com/.) Introverted, but purpose-oriented employees may be better served by an open-plan space that has, here and there, conference rooms, reading nooks, or even a restaurant-style booth in which they can seek refuge to focus on their work. Beyond personality and style, there are functional diversity issues at play; programmers are in a role where they often code with their headphones on as a way to drown out the incidental noise of the office or a coworker's lively discussion of the most recent episode of *Game of Thrones*.

You'd expect Google to be pushing the boundaries of workplace configuration, and you'd be right. Engineers can build their own desks at the company's sprawling Manhattan location, and there are labyrinths of both quiet reading and play areas. Large open spaces are balanced with private nooks.

Benefits include classes on-site, discounted massages, and a culture that expects you to check out on the weekend rather than obsessively checking in.

Teresa Amabile, a business administration professor at Harvard Business School and coauthor of *The Progress Principle*, has said the following about the broader relationship between the workplace and creativity,

> There's some evidence that great physical space enhances creativity. The theory is that open spaces that are fun, where people want to be, facilitate idea exchange. I've watched people interact at Google and you see a cross-fertilization of ideas.

However, Amabile added, "There isn't a lot of research to support this. And none of this matters unless people feel they have meaningful work and are making progress at it. In over 30 years of research, I've found that people do their most creative work when they're motivated by the work itself."[26]

BRINGING OUR FULL SELVES TO (VIRTUAL) WORK

Taking it beyond the office space, though, how do we bring our full selves to the ever-growing virtual workplace? Are there other diversity issues at play? As many companies contract with increasing numbers of freelancers who work remotely, diversity issues may, interestingly, get a boost. Conformity and assimilation take on a different hue when employees aren't physically colocated, which allows greater control of the terms of their working relationships. Not being seen but, rather, assessed on work product and output can open up some powerful possibilities for people who suffer disproportionally from stereotypes, assumptions, and unconscious bias.

Not being seen but, rather, assessed on work product and output can open up some powerful possibilities for people who suffer disproportionally from stereotypes, assumptions, and unconscious bias.

Consider the famous example of blind auditions: as late as 1970, the top five orchestras in the US had fewer than 5 percent of women musicians. It wasn't until 1980 that any of these top orchestras had an increased representation of women at 10 percent. But by 1997, they were up to 25 percent, and today some of them have more than 30 percent.[27] Although the original impetus for blind auditions was, anecdotally, to root out biases for and against students of certain well-known teachers, the results of installing a curtain, laying down carpet to avoid the hearing of footsteps, and anonymizing details from resumes also led to a dramatic rise in the number of female players accepted into major orchestras.

Theoretically, the same technique should work in business. Many experiments have been done on the presence of bias in recruitment, and the findings are startling, as we'll see shortly.

AN UNUSUAL COST

Virtual or not, how do we peer into complex, large employee populations and accurately perceive how and where bias exists? And how do we avoid assuming one person's story and experience speaks for an entire community when we have limited data? Lastly, how do we calculate the cost to the individual or the organization of allowing bias to take its toll, over time?

In chapter 1, we discussed how often social groups are explained by a small number of representatives, for better and for worse. For members of any social group in the minority, individuality is often replaced with how a majority generally views their respective group.

Until recently, there's been little data to put a number on the economic cost of bias, whether conscious or unconscious. That lack of quantitative research caught the attention of Dr. Vivienne Ming, a neuroscientist and founder of the educational technology and data-mining company Socos. What followed was an eye-opening report on how bias can impact the recruiting and hiring process. She called it the "tax on being different" and focused on data pertaining to the names of applicants and their employment potential.[28]

Given identical resumes, Dr. Ming found a preference for male names over female names in response frequency, white names over black and Hispanic names, with bias present in common e-mail introductions and even for matching gender and ethnicity. "Given this large and growing body of research, the classic claim, 'I had to work twice as hard to get where I am' is believable. Is it possible, though, to actually quantify this difference? What does it cost José to achieve the same career outcomes as Joe for the same work?" Dr. Ming has written.

To find out, Dr. Ming turned to a data pile of 122 million professional profiles collected by the HR technology-company Gild. By isolating her analysis to every "José" and "Joe," Dr. Ming found 151,604 Joes and 103,011 Josés. The numbers began spelling out some intriguing questions, such as why someone named José is more likely to become an MD than someone named Joe, and why Joe is four times more likely to be found in the C-suite than José.[29]

To help examine the differences, Dr. Ming presented the concept of signaling cost through the lens of a peacock's tail. As Dr. Ming stated, a male peacock's tail affords it no real survival advantage; it is a signal of the male's fitness to the female. The fittest males are able to waste energy on the biggest tails, a symbol of genetic strength, which influences how the female predicts the survival of their offspring, and therefore her preference for a mate. Dr. Ming compared the assessment of a male's tail by the female to how many recruiters rely on Ivy League degrees to determine the value of a candidate. By using the signaling-cost concept, Dr. Ming wanted to know what it would cost José to "achieve the same career outcomes as Joe."

Her analysis began by collecting data on all the Joes and Josés working as software developers. She found thousands of both names working under the title of "software engineer" in her data and decided to follow the data to find the probability that each was promoted from "software engineer" to "senior software engineer." To start, Dr. Ming isolated the "signals" required for José to be equally likely to be promoted as Joe, starting with college degrees.[30]

Dr. Ming's analysis found that for José to be equally likely to get the same promotion as Joe, José would need a master's degree or higher, while no degree at all was required of Joe. Accounting for tuition, living expenses, student loan interest, and "the opportunity costs that education entails" over a six-year period, José's "tax" on being different would be somewhere between $500,000 and $1,000,000 over his lifetime.

José's "tax" on being different would be somewhere between $500,000 and $1,000,000 over his lifetime.

Dr. Ming went on to analyze data to see what female software engineers needed to compete with male software engineers, finding that a female would need a master's degree to compare equally with a male's bachelor's degree. While not as steep as José's tax, women would still need to pay a tax of $100,000–$300,000 for a chance at the same career outcomes.

Her research also found that the tax is superlinear in that a black woman would have to pay more than a white woman and a black man combined.[31] A study abstract, reprinted in *Psychological Science*, found that this bias is firmly established in academia as well as in the board room: in a study, inquiries from prospective male graduate students with white-sounding names were granted access to faculty members 26 percent more often than were women and minorities; also, compared with women and minorities, white males received more and faster responses.[32]

The giant cost of something as simple as a name tells us that the magnitude of bias and discrimination, in economic terms alone, on someone deemed "different," is seismic. Otherwise qualified candidates are being asked, often indirectly, to pay extra in exchange for the differences they may bring into the workplace. The National Bureau of Economic Research (NBER) has validated Dr. Ming's findings through its own study. Half of the research fellows sent resumes to recruiters with names that are "remarkably common" in the black population. The other half of the research fellows sent resumes with white-sounding names (such as Emily Walsh or Greg Baker) in response to more than 1,300 employment ads in the sales, administrative support, clerical, and customer-services job categories. Nearly five thousand resumes were sent out. The researchers observed that "job applicants with white names needed to send about ten resumes to get one callback; those with African-American names needed to send around fifteen resumes to get one callback." This would suggest either employer prejudice or employer perception that race signals lower productivity. That's a 50 percent difference in the response rate to the exact same resume.[33] Applying this back to Dr. Ming's work—thousands of Josés likely gave up when faced with the enormous cost, and because any of those thousands of Josés may have been a top asset, the company ends up paying a large tax too, in squandered potential for a strong employee. Concluding her report, Dr. Ming put the cost of bias bluntly: "Companies and communities that fail to recognize and elicit the full potential of their workforce will not remain competitive."[34]

FLEXTIME/FAMILY LEAVE

Another way in which companies can engage their employees, paradoxically, is by letting them go. Or at least, by letting them work from home when they need to, and letting them craft their own paid time off in a less structured, less rigid way than has been the case for decades in many organizations. Just as so many other aspects of diversity may be hidden below the waterline, so is one's need for personal time. While one employee may have small children, another may have an aging and infirm parent. Millennials want a different work-life balance and may prefer to work only thirty hours a week rather than the traditional forty (which, according to the Bureau of Labor Statistics in 2015, was more like fifty-hour to sixty-hour weeks for over 20 percent of the workforce.)[35] Gen X'ers may want to teach a class each semester in addition to their regular workload. Maybe the traffic is so congested during regular office hours that employees' ability to adjust their schedule is a true blessing and relief.

> Thousands of Josés likely gave up when faced with the enormous cost, and because any of those thousands of Josés may have been a top asset, the company ends up paying a large tax too, in squandered potential for a strong employee.

In a traditional corporate environment, employees often perceive that they will be judged harshly if they are not seen at their desks until well past five o'clock. In companies that have begun to understand that their employees are truly their richest assets, flexibility is a tool that facilitates trust and greater engagement.

As Dr. David G. Javitch points out in *Entrepreneur*, however, "It can also be problematic to coordinate people, tasks and productivity when your employees aren't at work at the same time."[36]

That's one reason why we at JBC spend a tremendous amount of energy coordinating people's schedules and priorities. It is critical for me that each team member feels we respect the dynamics in their lives and what's important to them. We want to provide them the autonomy to get their work done when, where, and how they choose. It is my job to work around these constraints, to check in often on how they are experiencing our work together and, most importantly, to ensure they are doing work they want to be doing. If these needs are met, engagement flows more organically, and they will want to stay. This is our lifeblood.

And it's not just the province of small consultancies to embrace these shifts. Large organizations are trying to flex more than ever, challenging themselves to think beyond the traditional policies of leave and working remotely. In his 2014 *Harvard Business Review* article, "Flex Time Doesn't Need to Be an HR Policy," Scott Behson observed that while formal parental leave and telecommuting policies are important, "the ability to carve out small, informal flex solutions can be really important for employee well-being, engagement, and retention."[37] These, in particular, resonate with millennial employees, who want to dial-up and dial-down on an ongoing basis.

One of the newest groups to take advantage of flexible arrangements is working men. In its recent study entitled *How Men Flex*, the Working Mother Research Institute found that while only 29 percent of working men had regularly scheduled flextime/flexplace arrangements, 66 percent stated they can use flex when they need to. This "as-needed" flexibility is actually the preferred work schedule of a plurality of the study respondents (as opposed to formal work-from-home days or full-time work-from-home careers). The study also found the following:

- Seventy-three percent of working men were happy with the extent to which they were able to work from home.

- Seventy-eight percent stated that they were at least somewhat comfortable using flexibility.

- Sixty-two percent said their employers encourage the use of flexibility to at least some extent.

- Men who said their employers encouraged flexibility stated that they were happier, healthier, and more fulfilled at work.

- By huge margins, men respondents believed that work flexibility helped them be more productive, happier, less stressed, more motivated at work, more effective at home, and more committed to their employers.[38]

Policies and practices are often not aligned, however. Men are much less likely than women to take advantage of family leave, paid or otherwise. In a study for the Boston College Center for Work and Family, researchers Brad Harrington, Fred

Men are much less likely than women to take advantage of family leave, paid or otherwise.

Van Deusen, and Beth Humberd found that only one in ten fathers took more than two weeks off after their most recent child was born.[39] Only an estimated 14 percent of US companies currently offer some kind of paid paternity leave, a margin that has stayed about the same since 2005, according to Kenneth Matos, senior director of research for the Families and Work Institute.[40]

Men perceive that they are stigmatized at work for prioritizing family, even immediately after the birth or adoption of a child. We discussed covering in a previous chapter; this is a strong example of feeling compelled to cover parenting status, and flexibility needs related to this, especially amongst men who are more likely to be stigmatized for desiring that flexibility. *Forbes* profiled a Kansas City corporate accountant who said of his paternity leave experience,

> I could have taken the whole week off after my son, Lyle, was born, but they said they really needed me, and they did, because it was the end of the fiscal year. I could tell they weren't going to look kindly on my taking the whole week, so I didn't. But the truth is, they could have hired a temp without taking too much of a loss, and I would have been happy to put in some extra time when I got back.[41]

In his article for the *New York Times* last year, sociologist Scott Coltrane agreed that the family-man stigma is real, and he used the case of Major League Baseball player Daniel Murphy to illustrate it.

> Daniel Murphy, a second baseman for the New York Mets, was criticized when he took the three days of paternity leave allowed by Major League Baseball. "I would have said, 'C-section before the season starts. I need to be at opening day,'" Boomer Esiason, a radio talk-show host and former professional football player,

said on his program. (He would later apologize for the remarks.) Mike Francesa, another radio talk show host, added, "You're a Major League Baseball player; you can hire a nurse."[42]

The motherhood penalty for women is well documented, but we rarely discuss the fatherhood stigma. At a time when dual-income households are more common than ever, parenthood is kind of a three-legged race when it comes to navigating work schedules and constraints. Without policies that enable both men and women to shoulder parenting responsibilities, young families are often left choosing between costly child-care options and a change of employment.

Of course, many organizations have stepped up to this challenge too, rolling out innovative work-schedule solutions for their employees with the intent of reducing the strain at home. IBM, for example, has a flexible leave policy that is incumbent upon employees getting their work done. As long as that happens, they can come in late and leave early, as they need. State Street Corp has a formalized, flexible work program with five different alternative work arrangements, including flextime, compressed schedules, reduced schedules, job sharing, and flex place (working at home or remotely); line managers have the authority to engage with individual employees about what is possible, given their specific roles within the company, without having to consult with HR. Flex work is a part of the company's design rather than an afterthought that employees may not feel safe to utilize. This increased adoption of the policies across the enterprise

Flex work is a part of the company's design rather than an afterthought that employees may not feel safe to utilize.

created greater management buy-in, destigmatized flex, and ensured greater alignment with the business.

LoadSpring Solutions not only approves time off but actively encourages employees to broaden their horizons by going overseas. The company offers employees who want to travel an extra week of vacation and up to $5,000 toward their travel expenses—all because they recognize the value this returns to the company in the form of rested, restored, engaged, and committed employees. Netflix has famously abandoned rationing out vacation days to its employees. Cofounder Reed Hastings, speaking about the company's "freedom and responsibility" culture, said, "Keeping vacation unlimited requires mature, responsible employees who care about high-quality work." Netflix doesn't stop at allowing employees to take however many vacation days they choose, though. The company also has an ongoing, day-to-day flextime policy so that employees may respond to more immediate issues outside work.[43]

This kind of flexibility may be even more important to most employees than unlimited vacation days. We all have our own set of personal issues, whether they include child care, elder care, medical concerns, teaching a class, coaching a softball team, volunteering with an organization, or something else. Employees may or may not wish to discuss these issues with a supervisor or a manager, and they should be allowed to retain that choice as long as they are able to manage their work responsibilities and effectively communicate their schedules to their colleagues.

In a video for Makers.com, Sheryl Sandberg, COO of Facebook, talks about her decision to leave the office promptly each afternoon:

> I walk out of this office every day at five thirty so I'm home for dinner with my kids at six, and interestingly, I've been doing that since I had kids. I did that when I was

at Google, I did that here, and I would say it's not until the last year—two years—that I'm brave enough to talk about it publicly. Now I certainly wouldn't lie, but I wasn't running around giving speeches on it.[43]

To combat the stigma of slackerdom, Sandberg said that, for years, she sent e-mails late at night and early in the morning as a way of demonstrating that she was still hard at work even though she had left "early."

Can we destigmatize leaving the office after eight or nine hours? Can we begin to trust our employees rather than perpetually judging, criticizing, and suspecting? An employee may choose to keep her role as primary caregiver to an elderly or ill parent under her waterline at work, but a flexible policy that doesn't punish her for not sitting at her desk until the middle of the evening so she can *be seen to be working* allows her to create her own balance among her personal and professional responsibilities. The company trusting her to get her work done, and working with her to facilitate that, reinforces that she is respected and valued within the organization.

Companies that empower their employees to take responsibility while also offering them the freedom to determine their schedules reap tremendous benefits in terms of retention, commitment, and engagement.

Companies that empower their employees to take responsibility while also offering them the freedom to determine their schedules reap tremendous benefits in terms of retention, commitment, and engagement. Again, this is a diversity and inclusion issue. A transparent and equitably applied flextime or vacation policy allows all employees to create their own work-life balance.

SUPPORT DIVERSE TALENT IN A VIRTUALIZED WORK WORLD

We now live in an age when you can be virtually whoever you want to be online. It's a kind of "choose-your-own-identity/identities" mentality that exists in the online world and that carries over into how we work as well. Technological advances and cost-saving measures have enabled virtual workplaces. The skill set of working in and managing virtual teams is fairly new to many leaders but can be a rich opportunity that enables all of us to focus on the work itself and on building relationships that may be less biased by what we perceive, what is perceived about us, and the stereotypes we tend to apply to others.

The physical office has long enabled connection points for employees to, literally, find each other, and for many of us, it is a rare opportunity to interact with colleagues who don't share our identity—be that race, ethnicity, sexual orientation, or disability.

Of course, the flip side is that relationships might be much more difficult to build in the virtual work world. The tendency toward superficiality is real. Employees' ability to connect to communities of affinity and interest may decrease. The physical office has long enabled connection points for employees to, literally, find each other, and for many of us, it is a rare opportunity to interact with colleagues who don't share our identity—be that race, ethnicity, sexual orientation, or disability. Many programs and initia-

186

tives assume the presence of conference rooms in which to meet, hallways in which to greet, senior executives with whom to converse in an elevator, and so on. They assume hierarchies are in place for mentoring programs, for executive leadership to have an outsized span of control, and responsibility to match. Radical experiments like holacracy challenge the very existence of these roles.

Not to be nostalgic, but we have predicated so many of our human-capital strategies on that physical proximity inherent in the baby boomer-built workplace; more traditional workplaces provided a place to find each other, to find community, to gain strength, and perhaps even to take on the challenge of building more inclusive workplaces where incoming and future talent would feel more welcomed, valued, respected, and heard than previous generations did. It was easy to wrap our arms around a headquarters location and an org chart that showed us the hierarchy there.

As we've explored, there is much to be gained from thinking outside the box—literally, the four walls of the office and the sharp corners of the org chart—in building environments more conducive to collaboration, which should overall open up a greater appreciation of diversity. With the virtualization of our work world happening in parallel to office-plan redesign and dismantling the hierarchy, building momentum for diversity and inclusion will take on a different hue. Individuals like Angelica Coleman and many of those who come after her won't ever walk into a physical office; instead of not seeing anyone that looks like her, she will experience her virtual work team—likely a global collection of associates with exponentially more diversity than many of us have ever experienced in our lives. Her career role models may not be apparent from an org chart; rather, in her flat organization, her community will be multiple teams with horizontal career journeys and rotating leadership.

If bias is triggered by stereotypes and assumptions, but the amount and kind of data we share about ourselves and we know about others shifts or decreases, will this be an improvement to workplace cultures and solve some of our long-standing challenges? Regardless of the impact, it will be an exciting exploration of new levels of freedom, which will certainly come with more opportunities to learn and grow.

■ ◼ ◢

CHAPTER EIGHT

THE CHANGING MARKETPLACE AND OUR DIVERSE CUSTOMERS

"Every business needs a leader that does not forget the massive impact business can have on the world. All business leaders should be thinking, 'How can I be a force for good?'"

–RICHARD BRANSON, FOUNDER, VIRGIN GROUP

Economists at the Federal Reserve Bank of Dallas conservatively estimate that 40 to 90 percent of one year's output ($6 trillion to $14 trillion, the equivalent of $50,000 to $120,000 for every US household) was foregone due to the 2007–09 recession. Economists at the Federal Reserve Bank of Dallas also calculated that including losses ranging from output to skill atrophy to unemployment to government interventions, the recession cost every American at least $20,000—a total price tag of nearly $30 trillion for the country.[1]

Between 2008 and 2010, just shy of 40 percent of American households experienced unemployment and negative equity in their home, or they fell behind on rent or mortgage payments. Even in

2016, as I write this, American workers have higher expectations of near-term unemployment than they did in 2007 and remain guarded about the stock market.[2]

Black workers and Hispanic/Latino workers lost their jobs at higher rates during the Great Recession than did their white and Asian American counterparts, according to the US Bureau of Labor Statistics. Millennial women are also much less likely to have as many children as women of previous generations, a speculation researchers attribute, in part, to the economic decline stalling planned pregnancies. Sociologist Philip Cohen, PhD, writing for *The Conversation* in 2014, reported that "[w]omen who were in their early twenties during the Great Recession are projected to have some 400,000 fewer lifetime births and an additional 1.5 percent of them will never have a birth."[3]

The career trajectories of many millennial workers will, likely, never fully recover from having begun in the midst of this crisis. Baby boomers, who thought they were close to retirement, lost a huge percentage of their savings in the crisis and have retooled their careers. This, in turn, leaves Gen X ready to step into senior leadership positions; however, they are not opening up, because fewer are retiring. The global markets had become so intertwined that a kind of international domino effect ravaged most of the major economies that the US market depends upon in times of economic calamity. The 2008 recession was the biggest economic catastrophe and cultural upheaval since the Great Depression cast thirteen million workers into the unemployment line, redistributed populations from rural to urban centers, and battered domestic commodity production for a generation.

Want a little upside to the 2008 catastrophe? Well, a new consumer has emerged from the scramble too, one who is committed to saving, shops more deliberately, and demands greater social responsibility from the businesses with which she interacts as well as from the employers for whom she works. As Paul Flatters and Michael Willmott noted in the *Harvard Business Review*,

> ...pre-recession consumer behavior was the product of more than 15 years of uninterrupted prosperity... Consumers could afford to be curious about gadgets and technology, shell out for enriching (or just fun) experiences, and indulge themselves with premium products.[4]

The days of supersized consuming ended unceremoniously as millions of Americans confronted debt, joblessness, homelessness, and uncertainty in nearly every aspect of their lives, including at the workplaces they had, until recently, seen as a safety net. Many downsized, spending less, conserving and living more sustainably when it came to food, home size, and community sharing. Drivers kept their cars longer than ever before,[5] credit-card debt dropped to record lows, and shoppers began listening to other consumers much more than any marketing campaign.

The Great Recession ushered in additional paradigm shifts. Workers grew more wary at work. Sites such as Indeed.com, as well as Glassdoor, which saw 111 percent growth in a year's time, increased in popularity as millions searched not just for a job but for an employer whose fair treatment and ethical behavior was a core value and whose practices they could verify through their peers' endorsements.[6]

With the founding of the B Lab in 2007, hundreds of for-profit companies with social and environmental missions (B Corps) came to life. *Inc.* magazine has called B Corp certification "the highest standard for socially responsible businesses,"[7] and the *New York Times* has said, "B Corp provides what is lacking elsewhere: proof."[8] Like Aaron Hurst's Imperative—which we discussed earlier and which advocates that purpose-oriented workers are critical to the workforce, the workplace, and to business results—B Corp classification (certified by B Labs) is to for-profit companies what Fair Trade certification is to coffee or USDA Organic certification is to milk: credibility.[9] Ryan Honeyman in the *Stanford Social Innovation Review* cited the rapid global rise of this new kind of entity: "Ben & Jerry's, Dansko, Etsy, Method, New Belgium Brewery, Patagonia, Plum Organics, and Seventh Generation are just a few of the more than 1,100 certified B Corporations (distinct from benefit corporations) now established across eighty industries and thirty-five countries, including Afghanistan, Australia, Brazil, Chile, Kenya, and Mongolia."[10]

Authors, pundits, and executives began to talk about **corporate social responsibility** (CSR) and sustainable business practices; it wasn't just consumers who wanted a new market. Corporate leaders from around the world took to the mission of raising consciousness about a business's impact on the communities it depends upon. CSR continues to evolve, but the **triple bottom line** centers on three main components: people, planet, and profits.[11]

As the talent landscape shifts to favor millennials and their expectations of "radical transparency" at work, which extends to greater transparency of business dealings generally, companies are right to examine their business ethics, both in the way they treat their people, as well as how they behave in the marketplace.[12] Let's look a bit deeper

> Companies are right to examine their business ethics, both in the way they treat their people, as well as how they behave in the marketplace.

into corporate social responsibility and continue to make the links between it and talent strategy.

CORPORATE SOCIAL RESPONSIBILITY

As we discussed earlier, CSR is all about sustainability, but it's probably best understood as a way to create shared value for the company, for its employees, and for the greater society. At its best, it demonstrates a company's commitment to contribute to the community and the society of which it is a part. CSR can look like the funding of community activities and grants to organizations that are already working on a particular issue, but it can also include a stated and lived commitment to environmental sustainability, educational opportunities, or some other social good that is connected to a company's business goals.

And guess what? Consumers like ethical companies. A 2013 CSR RepTrak® 100 study found that 73 percent of the 55,000 consumers surveyed were willing to recommend companies perceived to be delivering on corporate social responsibility. Only 17 percent of consumers are willing to recommend a company perceived as poorly delivering on its CSR.[13]

About the driving concept behind CSR, Kasper Ulf Nielsen, executive partner at Reputation Institute, had this to say:

> CSR speaks to who the company is, what it believes in and how it is doing business. It's a core element of reputation and can be used to help establish trust and goodwill amongst stakeholders. [Almost half] of people's willingness to trust, admire, and feel good about a company is based on their perceptions of the corporate social responsibility of the company, so this is a key tool for companies to

use to improve support from stakeholders like consumers, regulators, the financial community, and employees.[14]

We've already talked about how the millennials, as a cohort, are much more interested in working for and doing business with companies that they perceive to be doing good in the community, however that's defined, as well as doing good business.

In a Harvard Business School study, Kash Rangan, Lisa A. Chase, and Sohel Karim identified PNC Bank's Grow Up Great® program as an example of strategic corporate social responsibility. This early childhood education program offers school-readiness resources to underserved populations in communities where PNC operates, which creates a stronger community and brand loyalty, not to mention potential future employees. PNC has incorporated the program into its management-training and employee-volunteer programs, cementing its commitment and creating support across multiple business lines. Both CEO Jim Rohr and many employees wanted to get directly involved in a local cause, and through Grow Up Great®, they are. According to PNC's website, the bank has spent $105 million on the initiative since 2004, and "PNC employees have volunteered more than 575,000 hours and donated more than 825,000 classroom items to help make our vision a reality."[15] The bank has partnered with the Sesame Workshop to create new digital storybooks for children, has devised a Mobile Learning Adventure, and also shares teaching resources on its site. ***Corporate philanthropy*** has been good for the bank, good for the larger community, and it unites many employees who can take pride in the company's efforts and perceive their shared commitment to a good cause. Beneficial all around.

As an example of a symbiotic connection between CSR and diversity, let's look at Standard Chartered Bank, in Kolkata, India, which has created several "all women" branches. At these branches, the entire staff is comprised of women, from the tellers to the security guards to the managers; even the artwork is created by female customers. The bank commissioned a formal survey of its current female customers, who longed not only for a more personal touch in financial interactions but also for shorter lines, friendlier faces, and more compassionate service personnel. Women don't dislike banks, they conclude, but they do dislike bankers, whom they have found to be "difficult" and "standoffish." The first two all-women's branches drove net sales up for the bank by 127 percent and 75 percent, respectively, from 2009 to 2010, compared to a 48 percent average among the bank's other ninety-plus Indian branches. They also held decidedly unbank-like seminars and events, including a health camp on International Women's Day. The staff are engaged and perceive that they have a kind of ownership and personal responsibility to their customers, which offers a tangible and specific purpose for them all to rally around. The clients are also more comfortable discussing their financial concerns with other women, so they actually have those conversations now instead of avoiding them and, ultimately, conduct more business with the bank. That's the very embodiment of good business intersecting with good corporate citizenship.[16]

Management structures began to dissolve and reinvent themselves too, hoping to engage the evolving mindsets of a post-recession workforce. John Mackey, CEO of Whole Foods, contends in his book ***Conscious Capitalism*** that capitalism is inherently good and that the strongest organizations create value for all their stakeholders—including customers, employees, suppliers, investors, society, and the environment.[17] Hurst's book *The Purpose Economy* detailed his vision to better serve people and the world while doing business through employees who crave purpose in their day job.[18]

The economic crisis also catalyzed positive social changes across the country. A 2014 survey from the Corporation for National and Community Service (CNCS) and the National Conference on Citizenship (NCoC) found that roughly one in four Americans volunteered with an organization, more than ever before. The survey also revealed that roughly three out of every five Americans engage in some form of informal volunteering by helping neighbors with such tasks as child care, shopping, or house-sitting. And since 2002, Americans have donated 104.9 billion hours of help to others, a number the NCoC values at approximately $2.1 trillion in labor costs.[19]

Millenials are the first generation in a century that won't likely do better, financially, than their parents.

For all the bad brought on by the 2008 recession, the millennials, having somewhat come of age in the crisis, are, perhaps, most changed by the financial struggle's unifying aftermath. They are the first generation in a century that won't likely do better, financially, than their parents. While they are the best-educated cohort of young adults in American history, they also have significantly higher levels of student-loan debt, poverty, and unemployment. They are, financially, risk averse, and they value sustainability.

Deloitte's *Millennial Survey 2016* aligns with what we shared previously, about the role of purpose for this generation. Millennials are drawn to mission-driven institutions, both as employees and as customers, and they are particularly adamant about connecting social purpose to their purchases and to how they allocate their working hours.[20] If we consider all of these findings together, a portrait begins to emerge of a generation more concerned with community, social responsibility, the environment, and a business purpose that aligns more with those concerns than achieving high amounts of personal wealth or the corner office.

The phoenix of greater social responsibility and more mindful consumption has risen out of the ashes of the Great Recession, and companies have to embrace the priorities of the communities upon which they rely: the consumer, the employee, and the supplier.

CULTURE TRADE: REACHING A TRIBE OF TRIBES

The American marketplace now finds itself in a kind of accelerated evolution. Corporations need to regain customers' trust as well as that of employees, as both groups are more informed and discerning than ever before, thanks to the self-empowerment social media facilitates as well as the experience of surviving the profound economic betrayals engendered by the Great Recession. Some corporations are meeting these demands in boldly innovative ways, paving the way for unprecedented advancement and transparency in organization management, marketing techniques, and business strategies overall, such as Dove's Real Beauty campaign and McDonald's Our Food, Your Questions campaign. Patagonia maintains a *Worn Wear* blog and gives away literally tons of gently worn clothing. Tide sent a mobile fleet of washers and dryers to Louisiana, post-Katrina, and to other areas hit by natural disasters. The UK supermarket chain Tesco has healthy competitions among its different stores to see who can reduce electricity expenses and food waste in the most sustainable ways. This type of action helps communities in need, first and foremost, but it also boosts the brand's image as one that cares about its customers while remaining aligned to the brand's goals.

B Corp understood the relationship to the workforce from the beginning. In the *Stanford Social Innovation Review*, Ryan Honeyman wrote:

Becoming a Certified B Corporation can unleash the passion, initiative, and imagination of employees by connecting them with the larger purpose behind their work. Ryan Martens, founder and CTO of Rally Software (the first publicly traded Certified B Corporation) says that the certification has made a "huge difference" to Rally's 530 employees: "Our B Corp certification gives us a way to differentiate ourselves from Google or the latest tech startup in a marketplace that has negative unemployment."[21]

If a corporation wants to sell itself to the people, it must represent the people to which it sells.

If a corporation wants to sell itself to the people, it must represent the people to which it sells.

ECONOMICS OF CHANGE: THE DIVERSIFYING BUYING POWER IN AMERICA

External changes in consumer buying power and preferences are increasingly influencing what companies are doing on the inside with their workplace cultures. There is an ever-closer relationship between the two, with a growing expectation that they reflect each other. A correct assumption is that in order to resonate with the external market, we need organizations that reflect those markets internally, in terms of their employees and their demographics. There must be congruence.

And the demographics are certainly shifting. According to Nielsen, US multicultural buying power is growing at an exponential rate compared to the average, increasing from $661 billion in 1990 to $3.4 trillion in 2014. Nielsen observes that, "this is more than double the growth of total US buying power."[22] African Americans,

Asian Americans, and Hispanics now have a combined spending power of $3.4 trillion.[23] The global LGBTQ community's buying power was recently estimated at $3.7 trillion dollars by *Harvard Business Review*.[24]

THE REFLECTION MISMATCH

Perhaps the most relevant finding in the Nielsen report involves the observation that multicultural consumers gravitate toward brands and products that reinforce their cultural roots and heritage. More than ever before, being "different" is normal, even desirable, particularly from a millennial's point of view. Companies such as Apple and Nike have invested heavily in presenting a business ethos that affirms how *different* drives innovation and relevance.

> Companies such as Apple and Nike have invested heavily in presenting a business ethos that affirms how *different* drives innovation and relevance.

As we've noted, inside companies, diversity is beginning to be widely understood as necessary for innovation as well. What was once reduced to the idea of meeting some vague demographic quota, and little more, has seen a tremendous metamorphosis in the decades since. Today the notion of bringing diverse talent into the workforce has begun to realize its own purpose, revealing to company leaders that it isn't just about the diversity of workers; it's the diversity of thought that makes the difference.

The ROI on harnessing diversity of thought has been studied extensively but is not yet so widely practiced. In an October 2013 survey, *The Economist's* Intelligence Unit found that 79 percent of CEOs believe that "diverse teams can produce better, more creative ideas because of a synergy among contrasting approaches."[25] In November 2013, Cathy Gallagher, a Canadian diversity and inclusion and CSR expert, wrote that diversity's benefits include "increased market share among diverse communities, increased ability to serve the diverse population, access to a deeper pool of talent, higher levels of employee engagement, and lower turnover rates among under-represented groups of employees."[26] Deloitte observes that the American workforce has undergone "a shift from improving employee engagement to a focus on building an irresistible organization."[27] Engaging employees is critical, and cultivating a diverse community of colleagues is essential in order to compete in the new economy.

How can organizations that are predominantly white and often mostly male at the top, and at several levels down in some cases, appeal to diverse recruits and customers and retain their current talent when the incoming workforce and customer base looks little like them?

So, how can organizations that are predominantly white and often mostly male at the top, and at several levels down in some cases, appeal to diverse recruits and customers and retain their current talent when the incoming workforce and customer base looks little like them?

One way is to engage with diverse-owned businesses. Major corporations are examining their supplier base and seeking diversity among vendors in light of today's growing, socially conscious marketplace. At JBC, we are proud to be certified as a woman-owned and LGBT-owned business by the certifying bodies WBENC (Women Business Enterprise National Council) and the NGLCC

(National Gay and Lesbian Chamber of Commerce). I am often asked if we maintain our certification and share it publicly because we believe we should be entitled to special treatment. For anyone who's bid on an RFP, you know this difficult experience hardly qualifies as "special treatment." In all seriousness, we believe corporations have an opportunity to cultivate a competitive advantage by partnering with key stakeholders in less-represented communities. Large entities are not only required to allocate a certain percentage of their spend to women-owned and minority-owned businesses if they are government contractors but are also awakening to the fact that bringing in the diversity of perspective that comes with a more diverse supplier base is good for their ability to innovate and be responsive to a dynamically changing marketplace. Choosing to do business with a diverse supplier is also an opportunity for companies to invest in the economic viability of diverse communities and to communicate their commitment to inclusion, even while they are slowly building their diverse talent pipelines internally. It all circles back to the purpose orientation we discussed earlier—revealing itself this time to be a very marketable strategy that will endear customer, client, vendor, and employee to any institution that prioritizes them.

We believe corporations have an opportunity to cultivate a competitive advantage by partnering with key stakeholders in less-represented communities.

DIVERSITY IN MARKETING

For marketing and sales strategies of the future to succeed, workplace culture will need to reflect its consumer culture, as a company inevitably absorbs its creativity, direction, and sense of purpose from the culture within the workplace and then radiates it outward.

When companies fail to grasp the subtleties of reaching across cultures, they are held quickly and publicly accountable for any missteps by both mass media and social media. In a matter of minutes, a company that unwittingly demonstrates its ignorance of its diverse consumer base finds itself vilified and shamed. Employees are watching, too, and are impacted by these decisions from a moral point of view.

> **In a matter of minutes, a company that unwittingly demonstrates its ignorance of its diverse consumer base finds itself vilified and shamed.**

The disconnect between company culture and consumer culture is not always blatantly offensive and widely publicized, though. Sometimes, it just reduces an ad's effectiveness and results in a loss of investment. In his book *Diversity & Inclusion: The Big Six Formula for Success*, diversity executive D. A. Abrams tells the story of a billboard purchased by a Fortune 500 children's clothing company in central Los Angeles a few years ago. A driver noticed that the ad featured "two adorable white babies dressed in white outfits lolling on a white blanket," yet fewer than 20 percent of the drivers passing it daily were white. The billboard's target customer was 17 percent white, 62 percent Hispanic/Latino, and 21 percent Asian or black. Abrams asks, "[W]hy did a big company decide to target only 17 percent of the population with its key images and marketing spend?"[28] The company didn't notice its own unconscious bias: by neglecting to include any diversity at all, the ad failed to engage its audiences in a community that was overwhelmingly black and brown. If audiences don't "see" themselves in an ad, they're less likely to feel connected to, or respected by, the product's purpose and much less likely to spend their money on a product whose ad didn't bother including them.

In 2015, Cheerios released a commercial featuring an interracial couple and their daughter that incited dialogue both constructive and destructive as it went viral. YouTube ultimately closed the comments section on the ad because of the vitriolic and racist comments, but at the same time, people flooded the Cheerios Facebook and Twitter streams with enthusiastic gratitude at finally seeing their own families represented. "Consumers have responded positively to our new Cheerios ad. At Cheerios, we know there are many kinds of families and we celebrate them all," said Cheerios Vice President of Marketing Camille Gibson.[29]

Later, we will more fully explore the growing role that diverse employees, under the auspices of ERGs, are playing in helping guide organizations to approach both consumer and talent markets in a culturally competent way and advising their employers on corporate social responsibility as it pertains to their communities. Internal diverse talent is increasingly invited to the decision-making table in order to teach internal stakeholders what is meaningful and what will resonate with the external audiences they know best. Not only does this save companies

> Playing the role of adviser to their employer on topics of CSR and diversity in the marketplace provides a developmental and networking opportunity for the organization's internal talent as they interact with business leaders and other functions in a way that's not possible in most day jobs.

from mortifying and costly public missteps, as mentioned previously, but it also provides a developmental and networking opportunity for the organization's internal talent as they interact with business leaders and other functions in a way that's not possible in most day jobs. In 2010, I solicited case studies from leading companies who were pushing the envelope with their networks and produced our ERG Benchmarking Report, a document that has remained an evergreen resource on this topic. We'll take a deeper dive into that research in the next chapter.

Companies have an exciting opportunity to communicate their values in a variety of ways, and increasingly, the most appealing values are ones that respect a diversifying world, from consumers to new recruits. Markets and talent are listening closely for ***cultural competency***, and there is no shortage of resources with which to make the right decisions. Those who don't will be speedily left behind.

CHAPTER NINE

ERGs

Change Can Be Tribal

"A tribe is a group of people connected to one another, connected to a leader, and connected to an idea. For millions of years, human beings have been part of one tribe or another. A group needs only two things to be a tribe: a shared interest and a way to communicate."

–SETH GODIN

At the same time that I was coming out as a member of the LGBTQ community in my professional life, at a friend's suggestion, I investigated my local Out & Equal Workplace Advocates (www.outandequal.org) chapter in New York City. The board was full of representatives from corporate America—from large banks, consulting, and technology companies, mainly—who were leading their companies' LGBTQ employee resource groups as volunteers, while managing their day jobs as lawyers, consultants, and bankers.

I had never realized that these groups existed and was inspired by my fellow chapter members' passion to create more equitable workplaces for themselves and others. I noticed quickly how strategic they were and that they had the ear of management. Back then, in 2003, many had already been successful, advising on a bank's first-ever LGBTQ-inclusive marketing materials or working for an actual business development team whose sole purpose was to cultivate the company's LGBTQ customer base. If the corporate stereotype I had was of bureaucratic, homogenous, and hierarchical environments, this unexpected and potent grassroots advocacy gave me hope not just for marginalized communities but for corporate America as a whole. My interest in partnering with the for-profit world as an advocate for better and more inclusive leadership was kindled in those days. I believed I could contribute to the conversation and do my part. I began to make the link between my purpose and the work I'd be able to do with these large companies.

Diverse communities could speak with a potent voice to influence the direction of corporate policies.

These early ERGs demonstrated to me that being seen and heard at work was not only possible but empowering. Diverse communities could speak with a potent voice to influence the direction of corporate policies, simultaneously furthering the progress of their respective communities and companies. I have remained active with Out & Equal, giving more than twenty-five presentations at their annual Workplace Summits, and many, many supporters of my consulting company, from employees to partners to clients, have emerged from this collaboration. The extended Out & Equal community is a deep part of our fabric.

I was so struck by the potential power and opportunity inherent in ERGs that my consulting company evolved, over time, into an expert resource on these powerful networks; we published a myriad of white papers and research and have partnered with dozens of clients in a variety of industries on their consulting and strategic needs. I have shared our thought leadership at many conferences over the past decade and served as a channel for stories of success and impact to emerge and have a platform. We developed compelling tools by which employee resource groups could assess their progress and measure their success, as they are, these days, being asked to step up as true business partners, signaling the rise of the *business resource group* (BRG) in recent years. I am proud of the role we've played in fueling this progress and shining a light on what's possible.

A LITTLE ERG HISTORY

The first ERG was born in 1964. Joseph Wilson, CEO of the Xerox Corporation, and his black employees formed the first alliance in order to address the issue of discrimination and to help create a fair corporate environment after violent race riots in Rochester, New York, in 1964. Xerox launched the National Black Employees Caucus in 1970. Ten years later, the Black Women's Leadership Caucus (BWLC) was born. In 1969, at Pacific Bell, the Community NETwork was formed to respond to what members perceived to be discriminatory hiring practices. Other groups followed in rapid succession.[1]

The early affinity groups acted as a support system and social outlet for their members, and they lobbied for more equitable pay, more equal opportunities, and policy changes. The first participants in these networks were often apprehensive or even fearful about speaking up to management about their minority identities and the challenges they encountered; they didn't want to be judged troublemakers, but they also found that they could not remain silent. We learned about stereotype threat earlier; those were risky days to highlight one's difference from the norm.

We tend not to talk about affinity groups very much anymore; the nomenclature has shifted to employee resource groups or even business resource groups, a term I mentioned earlier, which is increasingly in vogue due to its clear priority on driving business. For our purposes, we'll refer to the networks as ERGs.

ERGs, these days, tend to be more closely aligned to the larger enterprise's mission and vision than they were in the early days, but they still, typically, organize around a shared characteristic or life experience. The most common networks are for women, blacks, LGBTQ, veterans, people with disabilities, Hispanics/Latinos, Asians, working parents, specific generations (especially millennials), and new employees, but some companies also have groups organized around particular skills, environmental issues, or religious beliefs. In some of the larger companies we consult to, the memberships of these groups are in the thousands.

Nearly 90 percent of Fortune 500 companies now have ERGs, and they regularly host events in collaboration with strategic partners and focus their efforts on generating business value throughout an organization. They are often required to implement a business plan or strategy that includes objectives, goals, strategies, initiatives, and metrics. Each ERG is tracked and monitored against its own self-described objectives, and increasingly, their funding is connected to their compliance with these reporting requirements, as well as what they accomplish.

What's next for ERGs, as they grow in number, membership, and influence? I want to share a few essential practices as well as some "next" practices for more experienced or evolved companies and groups.

RAISING THE CHANGE YOU NEED

We work with many clients just embarking on their diversity and inclusion journey. When the topic of whether or not to create single-affinity networks—such as women's or ethnicity-based groups—arises, we sometimes hear anxiety, fear, discomfort, and resistance to change in all sorts of ways (sound familiar?). Some very large companies have actually made the decision that the groups are counterproductive and should not be created. As I mentioned when discussing focus groups in an earlier chapter, we hear statements such as the following:

- "It's going to make the problem worse."

- "Will people just feel singled out?"

- "It's going to give people license to agitate."

- "It will fracture company interest to the point of stagnation."

- "Someone will be offended."

- "Are we sure this isn't going to just be a gripe session?"

- "Isn't this just exclusion in its purest form?"

- "Well, if 'they' get groups, do the white men get their own group too?"

There are clearly a lot of issues going on here. The first thing I always say is that same-affinity folks are already gathering, informally, and likely discussing their workplace experience, while providing support to each other. If leadership thinks they're not, they're sorely mistaken. In some workplaces, you can count on one hand the number of women or people of color in a certain area. The seeking of likeness and community is a survival mechanism. It's important to acknowledge that they are seeking support, unofficially, and the world hasn't come to an end yet. In fact, finding each other is likely helping those individuals to feel less like "the only and lonely."

The next point that's critical to acknowledge is the fear imagined that, somehow, by encouraging honest dialogue and acknowledging that two people working in the same company can be having radically different experiences based on their gender, race, ethnicity, sexual orientation, or ability, we are opening up Pandora's Box. There is a fear we have of being inundated with complaints, or worse, having formal legal action brought about by certain groups; we'll have to acknowledge our dirty laundry. Maybe we've heard in exit interviews that a disproportionate number of women and people of color felt they had less opportunity at the company. Maybe the company's representation numbers for diverse talent are way out of alignment with the general population, but we don't talk about it publicly, or even internally. Maybe we don't have the HR systems to even identify the problem in the first place, but we sense, anecdotally, that we have a problem.

> Maybe the company's representation numbers for diverse talent are way out of alignment with the general population, but we don't talk about it publicly, or even internally.

And then there is always the question of power. We have the assumption that empowering one group means the disempowerment of another—that those who have dominated the upper levels of organizations somehow have something to lose from proactively listening to, considering, and yes, empowering those at all levels of the company—that something will be taken away from them, rather than being added.

Although I am a Gen X practitioner, I have heard enough stories about how previous generations talked about diversity in the workplace. When I come across CEOs who are hesitant to bless a proactive diversity strategy or affinity networks, I have to remember they are imagining the old days of diversity, before we talked about it in terms of business value and back in the era when diversity was compliance driven and involved painful multiday trainings that discredited one group in favor of another, a.k.a. the "shame-and-blame" era. If they were on the receiving end of the criticism, as those with relatively more privilege were, those experiences were not pleasant. Although very eye-opening for many on both sides of the conversation, they were, perhaps, more painful than they needed to be and certainly weren't built on the assumption that, as we say now, everyone has a diversity story, even those with relatively more privilege.

The previous questions and concerns are just some of the resistance points to inclusion, but I'm happy to say that companies are continuing to support and encourage ERGs anyway, pushing through the resistance because having them is an acknowledged best practice.

Thankfully, we now have a new way to talk about diversity, one that celebrates voices not in spite of their input but because of it, as we know diversity of experience and thought builds stronger organizations. When

Having ERGs is now an acknowledged best practice.

we decide not to have the conversation at all, we miss out on the positive benefits of engaging in dialogue about what a healthy and welcoming culture looks like that could concretely impact business metrics such as recruitment, retention, and sales. What business leader doesn't want that?

IMPORTANT THINGS TO KEEP IN MIND BEFORE FOUNDING AN ERG

Once we are able to move past hurdles such as fear and resistance, we can begin to explore how to initiate an ERG strategy. At JBC, we keep three main concepts top of mind when launching and maximizing ERGs.

THREE PILLARS OF SOUND ERG STRATEGY

1. ERGs should be chartered clearly with the purpose of driving the three pillars of workforce, workplace, and marketplace—key business imperatives that translate across most companies.

2. Their creation is intended to honor a community that is valued by the company; these communities tend to be those that are underrepresented or less understood.

3. The point should be made that everyone, from employees to senior leaders to customers to the business itself, will benefit from getting involved in the effort. Everyone is welcomed to participate, as a member of the affinity or as an ally. Any employee supporting the mission is welcomed and encouraged to participate in any network; they are not exclusive.

One important recent evolution for forward-thinking groups is the value proposition for allies. ERGs provide a forum for employees who are not part of the marginalized or minority community to learn about cultural or experiential differences in a nonthreatening environment.

Throughout this book, we have discussed the costs, financial and human, of continuing to stumble forward without hearing, respecting, and addressing employees' needs. Employee resource groups have the potential to clarify and then relieve that distress within an organization. Functioning as mini-communities within the larger organization, they provide a sense of belonging and connection, and if run effectively and strategically, can blossom into a "business within the business" offering real products, services, and advisory help back to the business.

Allyship

All ERGs should look for opportunities to identify, influence, build alliances, and cultivate allies. While this wasn't the predominant thinking when ERGs were first formed in organizations, it has become a priority for groups that strive to be perceived as strategic business partners across their organizations. Allies, as we have discussed, help to amplify an ERG's message and also enhance cultural understanding across the larger organization.

Senior leaders, and middle management too, need to release their fear that connected employees will stage some kind of corporate coup. Engaged and empowered employees who participate in resource groups can become vocal canaries in the coal mine, alerting the C-suite to pockets of suffocation as well as to pools of rich oxygen within the company's ecosystem. It's nearly impossible to gauge employees' authentic feelings and workplace experiences from surveys and interviews; many people do not feel safe in answering with complete candor. ERGs are a powerful tool to create a space where workers can speak freely about what they're encountering in the workplace. We can generate more authentic communication and candid understanding between workers and management through healthy, supported resource groups and help individual employees connect their personal purpose into the larger organizational mission.

> ERGs can become vocal canaries in the coal mine, alerting the C-suite to pockets of suffocation as well as to pools of rich oxygen within the company's ecosystem. It's nearly impossible to gauge employees' authentic feelings and workplace experiences from surveys and interviews; many people do not feel safe in answering with complete candor.

Priority Drivers

How ERGs are utilized to drive priorities, such as workforce development, is another important benefit of their existence. Research shows that 94 percent of Diversity Inc.'s *Top 50 Companies for Diversity* rely on ERGs for talent development. They utilize ERGs and their multiple aspects of diversity (such as experience, function, and geographic location) as models for how to use diversity of thought to service innovation. They have seen that ERGs create increased opportunities to develop leadership competencies in a safe environment. ERGs also help to create a competitive advantage because diversity of thought can lead to innovation through collaboration, and employees can share perspectives on small efficiencies and policy improvements from recruiting to benefits.

Testing the Marketplace

ERGs must make the case for how their efforts align with company goals. Some ERGs do this by becoming a strategic resource. Like those early LGBTQ groups I encountered years ago at Out & Equal, members may serve as a kind of in-house test market or focus group to ensure that the language, tone, and visuals used in company marketing materials are appropriate and resonant for target audiences. In this way, the ERG contributes invaluable cultural competency to any organization marketing to an increasingly diverse customer base. (And that should be just about every organization, as we've seen already.)

Most ERGs still begin their lives primarily as networking groups for specific races, genders, or affinities, rather than as potential contributors to revenue generation. Given that the most effective groups grow organically rather than being implemented by executive fiat, the members decide on the initial degree of involvement and purpose for each ERG. The company will, ultimately, decide which groups meet its criteria to become official ERGs and how much funding they will therefore receive. Innovative companies are inviting their ERGs to participate in an increasing number of critical tasks and projects, while strategic ERGs continue to assert themselves as subject-matter experts and workplace leaders. On its website, Goldman Sachs reports that its networks "offer training and educational programs, create networking forums, host leader-

> Members may serve as a kind of in-house test market or focus group to ensure that the language, tone, and visuals used in company and marketing materials are appropriate and resonant for target audiences.

ship conferences, and sponsor client events. We have developed and support over 80 affinity networks and interest forums globally."[2]

THE ERG PROGRESSION MODEL[SM]

At JBC, through our many years of providing strategic consulting and guidance to ERGs, we've developed a strategic framework to utilize with the groups called the ERG Progression Model. As companies have begun to appreciate the business value of a more diverse workforce and building more inclusive cultures, they have started to see ERGs as potential drivers of these business goals. The groups have often formed organically with cultural, social, and community-focused activities at their core, and many today are maintaining that core DNA while layering in a new business focus, formalizing their structure to play a bigger, more strategic business-partner role. This evolution is great news for all involved.

We saw an opportunity to build a model that captures this growth and evolution and that honors the social, the community, and the business aspects of ERGs: the Progression Model. The model demonstrates what healthy growth looks like for an ERG; it provides examples of how the groups could expand their thinking, enhance how they present their value, measure their success, rebrand themselves as they grow if needed, and continue to provide that all-important safety and human connection that so many individuals need, given the statistics on covering that we shared earlier. Their span of influence is expanding rapidly.

Our model describes a set of development stages for ERGs and creates a road map that ERG leadership and members can use to

- assess their current capabilities;

- define best practices for ERG success;

- inform the setting of goals and objectives;

- articulate the value proposition (the "what's in it for me" or WIIFM) for individual members, leaders, and the organization; and

- build metrics and measurements.

In JBC's Progression Model, we think of ERG development in terms of five levels. We'll describe Foundational Level 1 and Dynamic Level 5, to illustrate the span of the journey:

- Foundational Level 1 usually starts with a small group that may, initially, come together to talk about a particular pain point that seems unique to their experience, or to celebrate a cultural event, such as Diwali or Chinese New Year. Members work without clear accountabilities and with a focus on building their internal community. Groups may declare an event a success if fifty people show up.

- Dynamic Level 5 is seldom achieved, but the road there includes leadership changes, real business results, and a network positioned to provide expertise not just inside the company but also to community and other corporate stakeholders and colleagues. By the time an ERG reaches Dynamic Level 5, it is known and leveraged as a versatile resource, and its efforts and activities are fully and strategically aligned with those of the organization. Success looks very different and involves tracking not only attendance but also a host of other measures.

The Asian ERG at one of our manufacturing clients decided to participate in a Dragon Boat race several years ago. This began as, principally, a cultural celebration and a way for members of the

ERG to get to know one another while inviting the larger workplace community to attend, cheer them on, and row along, if they chose. This is a great example of a Level 1 activity. This past year, six executives also participated, and rank-and-file employees staffed the volunteer booth and race teams alongside senior leaders, cultivating relationships that will extend back into the work environment. The ERG's outreach has inspired non-Asian ERGs to create two new teams at other company locations. This is cultural education, horizon expansion, team building, professional networking, brand enhancement, and community engagement all at once; it's a bonus that it's also a lot of fun. The ERG is maturing beyond Level 1 as it grows and enhances its value proposition.

Many of our clients are metric driven and competitive. When we conduct focus groups or map their ERGs to the Progression Model, they want to know whether they get a grade of A. The Progression Model does help us to evaluate the current state of an ERG and to determine the best next steps for the group to take, but it is not about hanging a gold star or a scarlet letter on the group. Our goal with the model is to help groups grow in the most constructive, deliberate ways possible, not to shame anyone. A group has to be Foundational Level 1 at the start, almost by definition, and there is no shortcut from Foundational to Dynamic. At Dynamic Level 5, an ERG may continue to plan and implement some of its Foundational Level 1 activities, although it will measure the success of its efforts in a more robust way, such as the amount of media coverage, other corporate participants, regional attendees, and external sponsorships. At Dynamic Level 5, an ERG has established an internal structure, synchronized its voice, partnered with business stakeholders, and successfully engaged executive sponsors to sit at the table in order to influence brand awareness at the highest levels.

In our ERG benchmarking report, formally titled *Employee Resource Groups That Drive Business*,[3] we profiled twenty best-in-class examples that demonstrated the certainty and speed of this evolution. We were surprised and delighted to discover that ERGs weren't stopping at offering safety and community to those who felt isolated and underrepresented; they were actually bringing the workplace together as a whole, helping to restore long-missing connection and significance to employees.

Given the latest research on purpose-oriented employees, it is my belief that these groups contain a disproportionate number of purpose-oriented people. At a well-attended ERG conference in the midst of the Great Recession, the conversation in a large debriefing session turned to ERG budget cuts. I asked the group, "How many of you would do the work you do for your ERG, even without a budget?" Almost everyone's hands went up in the air. Many employees are getting, through ERGs, leadership development and networking opportunities that are not available in their jobs, and in a competitive market, these opportunities encourage employees to stay rather than look around for the next job at the next company.

'How many of you would do the work you do for your ERG, even without a budget?" Almost everyone's hands went up in the air.

This includes the wanderlust-driven and purpose-seeking millennials. Through participation in ERGs, we found that employees are able to find common purpose with one other, connect to and learn about the business, access senior leadership in rare ways, and create a vibrant sense of community that is in such short supply in today's environment. ERGs become another critical ambassador and retention mechanism for companies that are beginning to retool long-held but outdated structures and policies, with multiple generations in mind. The overwhelmingly multicultural millennials bring a new kind of diversity to the corporate doorstep, and ERGs are poised to fling wide the door to harness millennials' longing for purpose in the most constructive and business-aligned ways.

HOW ERGs WORK

While an ERG's focus varies from company to company, and sometimes from chapter to chapter within a company, at JBC, we consistently see ERGs expend their efforts and resources in one or more of the following functional areas:

- community outreach

- cultural education

- marketing to employees as customers

- marketing to external customers

- product development

- professional development

- recruitment and retention

- supplier diversity

Not all ERGs will engage the same areas, and even if they do, they won't always tackle them in the same way. Depending on the ERG, unique challenges will arise within each category, and their customized solutions will require executive-level flexibility and accommodation. The leader of a black ERG at a Fortune 50 company, for instance, recently asked me, "Is it okay that we're stuck on education?" Given the current state within his corporation, and candidly, within our larger society, I told him that not only was it okay, but actually, they weren't stuck. They were addressing a critical set of misperceptions about inequities, microaggressions, and structural racism within our culture. There is so much understanding that still needs to be built. Through a series of lunch-and-learns, book clubs, film screenings, and guest speakers, they were inviting their colleagues across the enterprise to increase their cultural acumen and to participate in a bigger conversation about race in America. This isn't stuck; this is mighty!

We often see Foundational Level 1 ERGs participate in charitable activities in their communities. This is a great way to come together. A veterans group might partner with a local charity to honor fallen heroes on Veterans Day or to prepare care packages for soldiers on active duty. A women's network might create a team to participate in the local Race for the Cure or partner with Dress for Success to help other women prepare for job interviews and new work opportunities. The activities give participants that essential opportunity to connect with one another while—you might notice a theme here—fulfilling their sense of purpose. They may also begin to build the company's identity in the community as a socially responsible enterprise, although it is rare that ERGs are thinking about that alignment when they are at Foundational Level 1.

Charitable activities and community engagement will likely continue to be a component of an ERG's portfolio of activities as it evolves beyond Level 1, but the activities and the ways in which the ERG defines success may change. Instead of documenting that "we prepared fifty backpacks for the first day of school," the group might record that it created a cross-ERG coalition and collaborated with their counterpart ERG at another company or partnered with a regional foundation in order to establish a mentoring program at the same school where they used to simply deliver backpacks. Now they also measure how many of those kids graduate, go on to college, and perhaps, even come to work for the company. They might also communicate success stories through local media and work with community relations as a trusted adviser. As ERGs see their value proposition expanding and tackle greater and more significant things, they begin to engage with the business in new ways, attracting positive attention.

From charitable work and cultural education, ERGs often begin to align to the business through their unique cultural expertise. As I mentioned earlier, this might start as providing an internal focus group on what will best resonate with their particular community in terms of marketing strategies; it could grow into consultation on, or innovation of, new products. A few years ago, Macy's Pride Network partnered with its multicultural marketing team to create a national identity and a marketing strategy to reach LGBTQ markets nationwide. At Pride events through the USA, the network launched a full-blown ad campaign including branded T-shirts for all Macy's employees who volunteered at Pride parades. The campaign included Pride kiosks from which people could access Macy's online Pride registry for wedding and commitment ceremonies. Macy's even created coupons that were coded to track back to the ERG in order to measure the impact of the program so they could report a return on investment.

ERGs also provide their members with professional development opportunities in the form of skill-development workshops, lunch-and-learns, and guest speakers, which might start with an executive from within the company and might, eventually, include a celebrity with particular insights, such as Sheryl Sandberg, Donna

Brazile, or Juan Williams. Over time, an ERG might send representatives to conferences or off-site training initiatives with the blessings and support of the human resources and talent development departments. Our good friends at Wells Fargo, for example, have a unique ERG leadership structure that is defined internally as a "stretch assignment." It demands a high level of motivation and skill, often exceeding what is required in a standard functional role. ERG leaders are selected through a talent-identification process, and Wells Fargo encourages high-potential employees to take on these stretch assignments.

An ERG can be a powerful recruiting tool, too. Members can serve both as ambassadors to help woo more diverse talent into the company and also as detectives to help the company locate that diverse talent. ERG leaders and members will know about events in addition to job fairs that might also be valuable sources of qualified new talent,

ERG leaders and members will know about events in addition to job fairs that might also be valuable sources of qualified new talent.

such as local Meet-Up groups with a particular interest or area of knowledge. At Prudential, the Disabilities ERG turned its attention to building a talent pipeline for employees with disabilities, and the company developed a structure allowing individual business lines to hire students or adults with disabilities for summer or interim positions that would, ultimately, evolve into full-time jobs. The ERG worked with hiring teams to enable them to best attract and serve candidates with disabilities. Your ERG members are subject-matter experts. Ask them for help.

At the same time, ERG leaders can band together with the leaders of other ERGs and lobby human-resource administrators, diversity and inclusion, and the executives in the C-suite to recruit differently, suggesting the importance of diverse slates—that is to say, a robustly diverse set of candidates to consider in any interviewing, hiring, or promotion process.[4] ERGs can consult with HR colleagues about how to rewrite the language in job descriptions to create more inclusion. Rajat Taneja, executive vice president of technology at Visa, wrote,

> A diverse workforce is good for business. There are no two ways about that. The more a workforce represents the general population and the customers we serve, the better it will allow us to perform. At the end of the day we are solving problems every day at work and a diverse workforce helps us solve these problems better by bringing different perspectives and experiences to bear on the issues . . . It is therefore incumbent upon hiring managers to demand more diverse slates of candidates and be open to hiring people with different backgrounds and perspectives.[5]

Diverse talent knows other diverse talent, and *if* they feel engaged in their workplace and proud to reach out into their various communities, the benefits are many.

As ERGs affiliate themselves with a company's talent management strategy, they collaborate with human resources professionals and recruiters to help attract, retain, and develop diverse talent. This is one of their greatest gifts to organizations. Diverse talent knows other diverse talent, and *if* they feel engaged in their workplace and proud to reach out into their various communities, the benefits are many. Not only does direct intercommunity recruitment save an organization time and effort; it also provides the developmental opportunity to diverse talent to be passionate brand ambassadors to external talent markets while showing those markets the diverse faces of the company itself.

As they move through the Progression Model, ERGs continue to grow from being internally, member-focused groups to serving as strategic partners for a range of business units throughout an organization. At the upper ends of the model, such as Dynamic Level 5, they represent a large network of internal talent connected with external ERGs at partner and competitor companies, as well as community stakeholders, addressing multiple aspects of their employer's ecosystem. They seek and secure new business relationships, serve as company ambassadors, collaborate with senior leadership, and receive financial support once they demonstrate they are achieving business-related goals.

By the final stage of maturity, the network is connected to the business at all rungs along the corporate ladder. Employees are empowered by their accomplishments and connected by their teamwork. They have that all-important purpose. They're increasing productivity and sales for the company, and the company is clearly benefitting.

Don't get me wrong. ERGs struggle with certain challenges, as well. While a charismatic and passionate founder may be able to rally the troops and painstakingly build the membership person by person in the Foundational Level 1 phase, when the group begins to pivot toward greater alignment with the larger business goals, the ERG may find it needs a different kind of leader. Perhaps it needs a leader with more seniority. Maybe its leader has the ability to think and plan strategically and demonstrate the business value of diversity but lacks the executive presence to not only get that seat at the table but also engage the other leaders while there. ERGs struggle with a few people doing a lot of the work in the early stages; groups that mature must effectively establish their own organizational and leadership structures, delegate work to subleads, and build strategic relationships across the business. They may also struggle to engage and sustain membership, particularly in an environment in which they lack executive support and recognition for their endeavors. I won't sugarcoat it: Raising an ERG is hard work, as is change in general. It requires thinking strategically about what a group wants to contribute, how it can grow sustainably, and where it can implement more standardized processes. Considering these aspects simultaneously is the only way they can grow sustainably. All this, in addition to people's day jobs!

In order for the ERG leadership to make a significant impact, the company leadership must walk the talk and visibly support the groups, demonstrating consistently that they have important business value to add. "I have to be the champion of diversity and inclusion," said L'Oréal Americas Executive VP Frédéric Rozé. "It is my job to be a role model and show how important this is to our company. It is part of my responsibility to set objectives and monitor progress within our teams."[6] If the C-suite doesn't advocate for, engage with, and show up at ERG events, the groups can linger in the more grass-

> **ERGs struggle with a few people doing a lot of the work in the early stages; groups that mature must effectively establish their own organizational and leadership structures.**

roots, social mode of Foundational Level 1, which, while still beneficial to employees, doesn't leverage the full potential of the group.

EXECUTIVE SPONSORS

As we've consistently discussed so far, change occurs from the top. For ERGs, there is a senior-level champion assigned to provide a variety of support functions, and this role is critical. It's that of the *executive sponsor.*

ERG executive sponsors are usually highly accomplished, respected, and influential leaders assigned to mentor and advocate for specific ERGs. Sometimes, these leaders share the same diversity identity as the ERG's members, and sometimes they do not, instead serving as an ally. Given the lack of diversity at corporate executive levels, the latter is more frequently the case—more on that in a moment.

Executive sponsors ensure ERGs undertake a broader, more influential vision for contributions and ensure the ERG has the organizational capital to make that vision a reality. As chief strategic advisor and mentor for her ERG, an executive sponsor often has an eye on maintaining long-term viability for the network. Creating a sustainable ERG means the group is also successful at navigating challenges such as growing and broadening membership, demonstrating value to the organization, securing a more diverse funding base, and monetizing social and intellectual capital.

In our travels throughout the diversity landscape, the responsibilities of the executive sponsor remain elusive to many of our clients, both for the sponsors themselves and ERG leaders they are there to support. We are all moving so fast, and sometimes we don't provide adequate explanation or direction to these important resources. Several years ago, struck by the chasm between the many inspiring and authentically supportive executives I knew personally and the bewildered, befuddled, or frankly inept sponsors I'd encountered elsewhere, I decided to conduct my own research and lay out a vision for the role. These leaders are charged with giving ERG members broader access to leadership, offering a greater understanding of the corporate structure and business goals at higher levels, and providing mentorship and sponsorship to the ERG leaders themselves, but sometimes, no one ever tells them what that entails or how to go about accomplishing it.

> Executives are charged with giving ERG members broader access to leadership, offering a greater understanding of the corporate structure and business goals at higher levels, and providing mentorship and sponsorship to the ERG leaders themselves.

After we wrote our popular *Employee Resource Groups That Drive Business* white paper it became apparent that a similar format would be helpful to expand on the role of sponsor, answering such common questions as the following:

- Who are they?

- How are they chosen?

- What do they contribute?

- What do they get out of the experience?

- What is their vision for change?

Although I had a deep sense of the answers already, it was important for those of us who architect inclusion programs of all kinds to have a detailed exposition on the topic, as a learning tool for new sponsors, a refresher for more seasoned sponsors, and as a model for those of us who support these change agents.

Often, when key roles in organizations are studied, we begin by looking at best-practice examples. We seek role models who are enacting the desired behaviors and having an outsized impact on their teams and organizations. In this case, I worked closely with our thought-leader partner, Cisco, and Sandy Hoffman, the company's diversity officer at the time, as well as with many chief diversity officers in the Fortune 500 to locate that one "star" in their executive sponsor firmament. We ensured we had a good cross section of diversity of identity, function, and industry among our interviewees, and then we were off to the races. In 2015, we released our white paper, *Executive Sponsors Fuel High-Performing ERGs*,[7] which has been received enthusiastically.

The paper describes many facets of the executive sponsor experience. For instance, we documented that executive sponsors learned from ERG members about the challenges faced by people who are different in some way from the workplace majority around them. Even executive sponsors who are diverse themselves, in ethnicity, gender, disability, and sexual orientation, found it "grounding" to learn more about the headwinds faced by those *like them* in their community, at different levels of seniority, and in various parts of the organization, or of a different generation. A female executive, for example, shared that she hadn't really focused before on the specific challenges faced by more junior women in her organization, in terms of their advancement. She admitted to not being knowledgeable about the well-documented challenges for women in the workforce. Occasionally, leaders will share that they don't feel they've faced any barriers due to their diversity. For all of these folks, stepping outside their own experience and acknowledging that others are experiencing the same company very differently is a real growth opportunity.

Sponsors who show up for their ERGs gain new perspectives on their own work environments, as well as on the social or cultural issues that ERG members may encounter. "This has opened my eyes to how much the person sitting across the table from me might be struggling with bringing their full self to work," said one sponsor.

> "This has opened my eyes to how much the person sitting across the table from me might be struggling with bringing their full self to work," said one sponsor.

They may also see the company's products with new clarity or from a new point of view, and they can then bring a new resource to the larger company as they advocate and connect the growing ERG across business lines. "I get to drive rebranding our company to a customer base who's felt unwelcome," said another sponsor, in response to such an experience.

Executive sponsors can be game changers in the diversity and inclusion space by doing precisely what exceptional leaders do:

- Challenge teams with a much bolder vision of what is possible.

- Collaborate to establish the goals, standards, and metrics that generate action and movement toward realizing the vision.

- Coach and motivate the team, especially as obstacles arise.

- Leverage their clout and influence to help achieve outstanding results.

- Deepen their sense of purpose and connection to diversity efforts generally.

THE FIVE KEY ROLES

In our research for the *Executive Sponsors Fuel High-Performing ERGs* white paper, we found that executive sponsors have essentially five key roles in service to ERGs: (1) strategist, (2) evangelist, (3) innovator, (4) broker, and (5) mentor. Let's go into these a bit here:

The strategist partners with the group to articulate a mission, vision, and goals aligned with the organization's business, talent, or diversity and inclusion goals while also focusing the group's ambitions to strike an appropriate balance between the interests of local chapters and the goals of the national network. The strategist also helps to evaluate the group's structure and governance and recommend reengineering when necessary, with an eye toward enhancing effectiveness, visibility, and impact. Nicole Fuller, principal at Deloitte, has worked with the company's Black Employee Network to design a long-term strategy that will not be derailed by the next "flavor of the month" initiative. Sometimes, her role as executive sponsor is to pull back ERG leaders from taking on too much and emphasize a mission that will stand the test of time. She led the charge to change the way the Black Employee Network was perceived within the company, insisting the

Her role as executive sponsor is to pull back ERG leaders from taking on too much and emphasize a mission that will stand the test of time.

group identify and measure the previously unquantified bottom-line impact of its initiatives.

The evangelist persuades executives and middle managers of the value of the ERG, elevates discussions about growing membership and increasing engagement, and advocates for the ERG's position on signature issues. The evangelist also speaks up when he hears a colleague say something inappropriate and offers a way to reframe the conversation. In this way, the evangelist sets a precedent for inclusion. He might also ask about employees who are missing from the group and who should be included in the conversation. As we wrote in the white paper, Guillermo Diaz, Jr., CIO and senior vice president of information technology at Cisco, considers "telling the story, showing the ROI" for Cisco's Conexión his most important role as executive sponsor—both within the company and at technology industry events.

The innovator cuts through red tape, leverages her position's power to procure needed resources, and brings new resources and ideas to the table with the goal of encouraging the ERG leader and members to identify new ways to make a difference or look at an obstacle as a road to a new opportunity. As former Cisco Veterans' Network sponsor Michael Quinn explains, "Your job as an executive sponsor is to break down barriers for other people. This is a skill set that, as a leader, transitions well into your day-to-day role. I learn a lot every time I speak to these

> Your job as an executive sponsor is to break down barriers for other people . . . I learn a lot every time I speak to these individuals, and it enhances my knowledge of what's happening in the company.

individuals, and it enhances my knowledge of what's happening in the company."

The broker connects the ERG to funds and people in the company while connecting the company to the concerns of the ERG members, shares information about company priorities and initiatives, and makes introductions to important people and organizations outside the company. When Cisco's Disability ERG wants to pitch ideas to leaders in countries where diversity awareness is underdeveloped, Greg Akers, senior vice president and chief technology officer of Advanced Security Initiatives, gets out his Rolodex. Through one-on-one conversations with members of senior management, Akers can often win their support relatively quickly. "Because I'm a senior vice president and have been around a long time," he noted, "I can get to our CEO, COO, and president in a heartbeat."

The mentor role is probably the most familiar. In this capacity, the executive sponsor teaches professional and leadership skills, provides career advice, and models "bringing your whole self to work." AT&T's Kelly King, executive sponsor of the Asian Pacific Islanders (APCA) group, uses advisory board meetings as a practice ground for his ERG leaders and members to enhance their speaking skills. As sponsor of Walmart's Promoting, Respect, Inclusion, Diversity, and Equity (PRIDE) Network, Michael Cox tries to help LGBTQ employees overcome messages that they are not valued. He described the moment when he was inspired by an encounter on an airplane to "change the way I showed up in the workplace." Now he tries to

Michael Cox inspires LGBTQ employees to overcome messages that they are not valued and to "change the way they show up in the workplace."

be more consciously "out" at work and to model confidence in his identity as a gay man.

Ideally, all executive sponsors excel in more than one of these roles, with the goal of building beyond where they naturally gravitate to support their groups from all five roles, eventually. We hope sponsors are willing to acknowledge their own learning curves and take the risk of being vulnerable as they engage with ERG members. As consultants and coaches to executive sponsors, we work to help our clients see the possibilities and cultivate their own leadership skills while also serving the nascent or growing ERG. The value being exchanged is therefore mutual.

Executive sponsor participants in JBC's study agree that the composition of the "holy grail" of ERG business alignment includes the following components. We thought this was an exciting vision for the future potential of these groups:

- Company leadership (beyond the executive sponsor) would proactively seek out the ERG's input on marketing, product development, talent, and diversity issues.

- ERGs and leadership would develop formal processes for input and output. The company would inform ERGs about important strategic initiatives and priorities.

- The ERGs would deliver results-driven reports from the perspectives of their constituencies to help achieve business goals.

- Middle managers would come to fully appreciate the value of their employees' "volunteer" work with the ERG and grant members time from their daily responsibilities to work on ERG initiatives.

- The broad membership of the ERG would include diverse skill sets and representation from all levels, geographies, and units of the organization.

- Most of the members would be active contributors, and the energy and enthusiasm of ERG members would spread across the entire employee population.

With guidance from the executive sponsor, ERG members can gradually come to understand that working toward business goals ultimately aids their own professional development and enhances their personal brand. Executive sponsors are the link to the business for ERG leaders, and simultaneously, the sponsors become aware of emerging talent and cultural insight from the membership.

THE FUTURE OF ERGs

The current and potential future states of ERGs illustrate a workforce in transition that's actively seeking uncharted pathways to deliver its ideas and efforts. These groups straddle cultures and environments to innovate solutions for their respective companies. While resource groups often begin as a tribe seeking at least a moment of refuge, safety, and comfort, ERGs ultimately foster a sense of community that carries into the workplace at large. ERGs nurture leadership development skills and evoke customer insights. Members capitalize on their ambitions and, ultimately, drive the company as well as themselves forward.

ERGs nurture leadership development skills and evoke customer insights.

As the global economy continues to transform, we must excel at identifying value that is most meaningful to our companies, business partners, and communities of affinity. In constructing its 2016 list of "100 Best Companies to Work For," *Fortune* found that, while employees value perks of all kinds, the benefits that created the most excitement were those that engendered the greatest equality. One Googler said, "The company culture truly makes workers feel they're valued and respected as a human being, not as a cog in a machine."[8]

TEN ERG EVOLUTION PRACTICES

As ERG evolution accelerates, it's equally important to maintain them as it is to launch them in the first place. Failing to continue nourishing your ERGs sends the message to the groups that company leadership does not view their value in the same way ERG members do. The following practices are critical for managing ERG growth successfully:

1. Position ERGs as core to the cultural competency required for globalization and new market expansion. Use ERG leaders as subject matter experts, coaches, and mentors for international executive leadership, and as network builders in the new local economies and cultures.

2. Invest leadership development resources in ERG leaders and members. To help ensure that ERGs are prepared to partner effectively for achieving business goals, resources must be allocated to grow the skill sets, competencies, and networks of these groups.

3. Consider enhancing the importance of ERG leadership positions, including that of the executive sponsor. Treat the positions as opportunities, or high-potential development. Partner with talent management to help identify important diverse employees who might be relatively unknown to the

larger organization. Make sure that a percentage of ERG strong performers are regularly included in talent reviews, as well as intentionally mentored and sponsored.

4. Use ERGs and their multiple aspects of diversity (such as an employee's visibility or invisibility, experience, function, and geographic location) as models for how to use diversity of thought to serve innovation. Encourage idea generation and crowdsourcing efforts through ERGs to take advantage of their unique, cross-functional, highly loyal networks.

5. Explore including diversity and inclusion competencies in performance appraisal criteria, from the highest level of employees down. Make sure that middle management and rising diverse talent understand how to claim credit for participating in and leading ERGs.

6. Look for ways to count those with invisible diversity affinities (such as LGBT, disabilities, veterans, and more).

7. Even while cultivating and educating executive sponsors, begin to develop important stakeholder support. These stakeholders must be from a broad cross section of the business, perceive the unique value in collaborating with ERGs, and be willing to partner closely with ERGs to help enable their own business goals. This could also diversify the current funding sources for ERGs, spreading the accountability and the opportunity to a broader group. Develop nonprofit partnerships, from writing a check or attending a dinner to strategic alliances that provide a mutually beneficial business impact.

8. Establish a healthy balance of current and future metrics in every ERG's strategic plan. Next-generation metrics should include tracking business-development opportunities and sales revenue; encouraging product development, marketing, recruitment, and retention; and diversifying the supplier base of the company. Do not lose sight of basic metrics, such as number of events, attendance, size of membership, and more.

9. Work to rebrand ERGs as groups that can help increase business and profitability. Do not assume this is understood throughout the organization, even by ERG members and their executive sponsors. Push to position ERG stakeholders to succinctly describe the importance and significance of their contributions.

10. Look at your company's entire ecosystem for strategic partnerships, including customers, vendors, and industry competitors. For ERGs, same-industry associations can serve an important business function, channeling multiple insights and developing critical networks.

> Push to position ERG stakeholders to succinctly describe the importance and significance of their contributions.

Leading companies across nearly all industries are working to increase the autonomy and capacity of their ERGs. ERG leaders and business leaders have to work together to make significant progress and to create a more inclusive workplace. ERGs must speak up and make the case for how their efforts can affect—and effect—profitability. ERGs should be involved in everything from marketing to professional development to research and development (R&D). The ERG leadership can lobby for this, but the C-suite can also make it a key performance indicator for the heads of those departments to engage the ERGs. Not only must ERGs adequately prepare themselves for this level of engagement, but management must be enthusiastic and knowledgeable about using them as a strategic resource and value their input. When ERGs are healthy and winning in their missions, everybody will win.

■ ◤ ◣

CHAPTER TEN

TALKING DIVERSITY

Leading Your Diversity and Inclusion Revolution

"A leader takes people where they want to go. A great leader takes people where they don't necessarily want to go, but ought to be."

–ROSALYNN CARTER, FORMER FIRST LADY

In a recent session on covering, led by my respected colleague Kenji Yoshino, I was met with an unexpected question on the focus of inclusion. As Kenji was discussing the high percentage of covering behaviors exhibited by heterosexual white men in the workplace, a woman of color approached me. She had no patience for that statistic, or even for including men's experience as something worthy of consideration as we discussed the problem. She was frustrated that we are not making progress—and the statistics we've shared bear this out—on increasing representation of people of color specifically in the workplace, and she was fearful this new cohort would dilute attention to what she considered a more pressing problem.

With my deep belief that everyone has a diversity story, however, I couldn't agree with her contention that men, particularly white men, have no place in the diversity and inclusion discussion. As someone who is well-versed in today's organizational power structures and constantly mindful of who has the most positional power to create change, I usually respond with this: "We will need everyone. At whatever level, with whatever identity, or in whatever package they're born—everyone is needed to create true culture change."

> **We will need everyone. At whatever level, with whatever identity, or in whatever package they're born—everyone is needed to create true culture change.**

We all share commonalities in unexpected ways, which we should leverage to come together more effectively. As Kenji often points out to help simmer everyone down, "This is not the Pain Olympics." Everyone's story matters.

Inclusion, after all, isn't inclusion if we are excluding a majority of the team from the discussion. White men often perceive that diversity initiatives have nothing to do with them, and people in underrepresented groups sometimes judge that the last thing the diversity and inclusion movement needs is a bunch of white men trying to tell everyone what to do next. That might just replicate decades' worth of frustrations, they say. As a humorous side-note, the compulsion felt by some men to explain things to women on topics that affect women has been coined mansplaining, which has become popular as a hashtag on Twitter in the feminist blogosphere. A male writer on Everydayfeminism.com defines it as "a condition that affects many men who believe it is our natural born right to talk over, interrupt, and especially explain things to women on topics that affect women, are predominately about women, and that they're probably experts on in the first place, and that's condescending."[1]

In all seriousness, men discussing gender more often in the workplace, however inartfully, would count as progress, in my book. At least it would be talked about, and there would be lots of opinions circulating about what to do about it.

Every last one of us, though, knows what it feels like to be excluded. We have all experienced it, albeit some of us more often and, perhaps, more intensely than others. We have distinct differences, but our fundamental needs and wants as individuals are the same. We all want to be welcomed, valued, respected, and heard. And straight, white men, who happen to be the dominant demographic group in American business, are certainly no different. My colleague and good friend, Chuck Shelton, shares this insight on the topic: "No business strategy, including D&I, will deliver optimal results when many with position power (white men, in this discussion) disconnect from the strategy."[2]

> We all want to be welcomed, valued, respected, and heard. And straight, white men, who happen to be the dominant demographic group in American business, are certainly no different.

This will continue to be the case especially because of the high risk of self-advocacy that is still experienced by so many. In a study published in March 2016, David R. Hekman, Stefanie Johnson, Maw Der Foo, and Wei Yang found that women and members of minority communities who advocate for inclusion efforts are often punished in the workplace in ways that white men are not:

We found that women and nonwhite executives who were reported as frequently engaging in these behaviors were rated much worse by their bosses, in terms of competence and performance ratings, than their female and nonwhite counterparts who did not actively promote balance. For all the talk about how important diversity is within organizations, white and male executives aren't rewarded, career-wise, for engaging in diversity-valuing behavior, and nonwhite and female executives actually get punished for it.

Hekman and Johnson further clarify:

High status groups, mainly white men, are given freedom to deviate from the status quo because their competence is assumed based on their membership in the high status group. In contrast, when women and nonwhite leaders advocate for other women and nonwhites, it highlights their low-status demographics, activating the stereotype of incompetence, and leads to worse performance ratings.[3]

I think the message is clear: although the risks are high for all, (and for some more than others) if we are going to affect real change, we need the white men to participate. According to this research, they have the least to lose and the most freedom to engage with fewer consequences.

In talking about how white people can best serve as allies to communities of color, Brittney Cooper, cofounder of the Crunk Feminist Collective, regular contributor to *Salon*, and assistant professor of Women's and Gender Studies and Africana Studies at Rutgers, wrote:

White people should recognize that the best way to be good allies is to go work among their own people (white people) to create more allies. Too frequently, white allies think we are asking them to come into our communities to affirm our account of racist acts and structures. What we are really asking is for them to (1) affirm that account boldly among other white people; and (2) use their privilege to confront racial injustices when they see them happening, whether in the grocery store or the boardroom.

Diversity and inclusion in the workplace requires that white men help persuade other white men of its significance. Remember what Lesley Miley said back in chapter 1: "The moment you say 'diversity,' I think a lot of people think you're calling them racist or a bigot." Miley's describing his own experience, as a person of

> Diversity and inclusion in the workplace requires that white men help persuade other white men of its significance.

color; the person doing the speaking matters. We need white men as allies to help explain that we are calling out a system that has become encrusted with structures that cantilever opportunity away from large groups of people. Because of their positional power, white men have the opportunity and the honor of helping to change the conversation—and change the population—in almost any meeting room, any client meeting, and any recruiting and promotion activities.

LEAVING THEM BEHIND: WHITE MEN IN THE DIVERSITY AND INCLUSION REVOLUTION

A couple of years ago, Chuck Shelton led an in-depth leadership survey entitled, *The Study on White Men Leading through Diversity & Inclusion*.[4] He wanted to address four concerns about white men in the diversity and inclusion revolution, and because he was so succinct, I am going to quote him word for word here:

- White men possess more than 40 percent of the leadership jobs in most companies, and that percentage increases dramatically by leadership level. The position, power, and leadership skills that white men possess need to align with the value that diversity and inclusion delivers.

- White male leaders are less engaged with diversity and inclusion (D&I) than their diverse colleagues. As such, they represent a significantly underperforming asset in every company's global D&I investment portfolio.

- Progress is stifled by the perceived tension between the qualifications of diverse employees and the organizational commitment to diversity. Savvy leaders do not ignore or exaggerate dimensions of diversity; they lead with due regard for the way diversity operates in their relationships and sphere of influence. This is one way all leaders build trust.[5]

Chuck surveyed 670 leaders, 58 percent of whom were white men, and asked them ninety-four diversity and inclusion-related questions. Among his findings, Chuck observed,

White men bring their own safety concerns to diversity discussions, and their diverse colleagues may wonder if white male inclusion will open doors for everyone. Almost 80 percent of all respondents rated white male managers *highly on the ability to show respect for diverse co-workers.* In contrast, only 36 percent of white male respondents rated white male leaders positively for saying just *what needs to be said (candor) among diverse co-workers.*[6]

We're asking white men to change what is a relatively more comfortable workplace culture for them, as well as to become voracious students of other cultures, experiences, and insights. What they learn in becoming students of these cultures doesn't always cast a flattering light on white men as a leader population. But they don't share all of the burden; one survey respondent said, "I feel like we, as white men, are the forgotten group in the company, when it comes to diversity and inclusion." Exclusion is a powerful disincentive, and if white men imagine that they have been shut out of the inclusion conversation—and they do, even now—our current situation is instructive. Every member of an underrepresented community has felt excluded many, many times. Can white leaders harness the sense that they have been left behind long enough to begin to imagine what others have experienced routinely? White men can learn to accept and invite difference; the rest of us need to find a way to include the dominant group without sublimating ourselves. The leaders who will successfully adjust will have to embrace discomfort and address their own possible misperception that they are under threat. They will have to become "comfortable with being uncomfortable."

Can white leaders harness the sense that they have been left behind long enough to begin to imagine what others have experienced routinely?

CONFRONTING YOUR OWN DIVERSITY STORY

As a diversity and inclusion consultant, I was startled a while back to realize that I hadn't given white men a great deal of thought either. When you are surrounded as I am, given my work, by those who are passionate about distributing opportunity more equitably and the inclusion of traditionally underrepresented voices, you don't often find yourself talking with a group of white men. But this is changing, and there is no more important conversation to have in today's world. Is it always comfortable? Often, it is decidedly not. I meet some of my fiercest opposition in these rooms and often open my keynotes up with an anecdote about the physical response I have as the person presenting on diversity and inclusion to groups that are uncooperative, resentful, and frankly hostile to the concept. I might be equipped with a litany of facts and figures to back up my assertions about why diversity is great for business and why they should care, but the resistance can feel like a personal attack against everything that I am and that I stand for.

The resistance can feel like a personal attack against everything that I am and that I stand for.

While we continue to put ourselves into discomfort for purposes of change, my hope for all of us is to continue to notice how easy it is to stereotype, marginalize, or dismiss those who've been in a majority as not understanding or experiencing exclusion. Through seeking those conversations, we become aware of the assumption of advantage and privilege and challenge ourselves to be mindful that those who are advantaged have also experienced disadvantages. It is easier to view people in a one-dimensional way, but it's not accurate. The iceberg looms in all of us, with so much under the waterline that is not visible. I am ever mindful of my own story:

to a lot of people, my outward appearance suggests one thing, and, at my core, I am much more. Surely, that's true for others, as well.

But I am challenged about my identity too, even as I facilitate diversity conversations with other change agents, say, of different backgrounds than my own. Whether the questions are spoken or not, they are: "Who are you, and why are you, *as a white woman*, doing this work? Why do you care?" People often make assumptions about my privilege, and question my "real" intentions, as a result. I am an outsider to a group of insiders who've been doing this work for decades.

When I feel this dynamic, it reminds me of what many well-intentioned allies experience in attempting to enter conversations about difference. What they can't see is what's below my waterline. In my case, my sexual orientation often seems to be invisible unless I bring it up and talk about it. In my case, likely because of my *heteronormativity*, I don't match a stereotype in people's minds. When I am able to share a bit more about myself and my experiences as an outsider, given that I have been a member of the LGBTQ community for more than twenty years, and talk about the gender expression I feel most comfortable in, I am able to bridge a perceived gap, and the conversation opens up. This establishment of trust, through vulnerability and commonality, enables us to get the real work started. It acknowledges that we all have a voice in the conversation, and that the goal is not to

We all have a voice in the conversation, and the goal is not to compare relative oppression but, rather, to talk about our common commitment to inclusion for all.

compare relative oppression but, rather, to talk about our common commitment to inclusion for all.

That brings me to your diversity story. Yes, I am talking especially to my white, male colleagues. What is your diversity story? What aspects of yourself do you keep below the waterline?

> **Just as institutions have founding stories, so do people: lessons they learned along the way, the source of their values, their passion, what makes them unique, why they care about what they care about. You were forged by your experiences.**

Just as institutions have founding stories, so do people: lessons they learned along the way, the source of their values, their passion, what makes them unique, why they care about what they care about. You were forged by your experiences. I am always curious about these stories, as we often only see the final result: a passionate volunteer, a crusader for a cause, an enlightened executive who "gets it." But what is most important for us to see about each other is *how* we got to our clarity. There is power in the vulnerability within these stories to inspire others; leaders can use it to model the value they place on diversity, *adversity*, and inclusion. And yet few leaders, while striving to present an all-knowing, strong, and certain face to the organization and to the world, recognize the power of these stories.

It can feel counterintuitive to incorporate realness, and humanness, into our executive presence and the expectations we've all labored under to appear perfect, hard working, and all knowing—"in charge." It feels very risky for me to stand up and come out over and over, when there are clients and revenue on the line, and I have no idea whether an opportunity that can sustain and grow my business will be jeopardized by doing so—but I continue to do it.

It's no secret that we have a cultural bias against vulnerability, a fact that's especially true for men. I'm sure we've all had someone tell us or someone we know that "boys don't cry," to "man up," or that we shouldn't "let 'em see you sweat." Young boys are often steered away from nontraditional male occupations, such as a nurse or school-teacher, and instead are encouraged to be stern, withholding, and in charge—the providers and protectors of the pack. The patriarchal nature of our society's culture has taught us all. So revealing yourself to employees or even peers can be scary. And yet it is magical.

My good friend, Erin Weed, founder of Evoso and self-described "speaker midwife," asks us, as we write our talks, that we look at our lives and clarify things in a kind of arc that includes the following pieces: story, lesson, and truth. Each of us has a story—a narrative—whether we recognize it, or are comfortable looking at it and sharing it, or not. In decoding who we've become, we need to return to formative stories or events in our lives (story), assess the lesson or lessons we learned (lesson), and then translate it into a truth that we can share with others (truth). For others to learn from our story (that truth piece), we have to "show our work" just as we did in grade-school math: "Don't just show the answer, but show how you got there." Showing the work of yourself makes you a "living lesson." Your mistakes, epic failures, wrong turns, and successes—

Showing the work of yourself makes you a "living lesson." Your mistakes, epic failures, wrong turns, and successes—all can be unexpectedly instructive to others. As a leader, you start to step off the pedestal.

all can be unexpectedly instructive to others. As a leader, you start to step off the pedestal. You open yourself up to connection.

I realize that so much self-reflection can be disconcerting, or even frightening. I challenge myself to do it all the time, and not just about being LGBTQ but also other aspects I've kept hidden, that I assumed were irrelevant to others, or disempowering to my reputation. When I gave my first TEDx talk, in mining my story, lesson, and truth, I knew I had to share a big part of my most vulnerable story, which I detail on the following pages, but I wasn't sure it would interest anyone, nor transform anyone, certainly. In the years since, I have received countless comments about how the concept resonates for others, in ways I never could have foreseen. We don't always need to be certain how our stories will impact others. The focus should be on the telling of them.

> **We don't always need to be certain how our stories will impact others. The focus should be on the telling of them. Your courage may enable others to undertake their own journey, one step at a time.**

Your courage may enable others to undertake their own journey, one step at a time.

There is particular power in vulnerability and in sharing one's missteps and setbacks. Indeed, vulnerability is having a moment as a leadership competency, and it's exciting to see it resonating so broadly, in both the personal and business realms. As we've discussed extensively, millennials want to see in their leadership the kinds of leaders they aspire to be themselves, and this doesn't mean perfection. After all, 63 percent of the millennial respondents to a recent survey published by *Workplace Trends* said they want to be transformational leaders who challenge and inspire others with purpose and excitement. The second most desired leadership style was "democratic" (22 percent), defined as "sharing decision making with followers." Only 1 percent of those surveyed want to be autocratic leaders who impose strict control over policies and procedures.[7] Oops: this leadership style is the hallmark of traditionalist and baby boomer organizational architects, a legacy we've inherited and still labor under. That's a big and dangerous leadership disconnect that must be bridged in today's workplace, and quickly.

EMBRACING *DIFFERENT*: MY STORY

My diversity story began to crystallize for me in 2012. With the pressure of my first TEDx talk looming, I had to discover my "idea worth spreading" in order to create that precious eight minutes of content. At that point, JBC was seven years old, and we had grown successfully into specialists in building more inclusive organizations, with lots of impressive clients. But that's not enough—or even appropriate—for the TED stage, where it is truly verboten to brag or name-drop. This talk would need to be personal and deeply relevant to the times we live in. What would be compelling enough to others about my life? I found it intimidating but also energizing. I knew it was an honor to be invited to speak. If this were my opportunity to share my thoughts and to issue a call to action, what would I say? What was my message in a bottle?

What I felt compelled to share in being totally truthful was that, my whole life, I wanted to be a singer, dancer, and performer. The businesswoman part came much later. I grew up in a musical family, and from a very early age, I felt compelled to perform—to express myself, and to positively connect to and move others. I had hoped I could make my living in the world of opera and musical theater and practiced diligently to get there.

However, my dreams were cut short about ten years ago. As I started to build my career as a singer, I struggled continually with vocal problems. It turns out that my instrument is prone to injury and the only known remedy is a delicate but risky surgery directly on the vocal folds—which I endured, twice. I will never forget the recovery period, when I had to remain completely silent for two weeks. When I was finally allowed to make a sound, I could only make a tiny squeak at first. Starting with only five gentle minutes a day, I would hum to slowly work my way back into a normal register. After several rounds of this, even with a good surgical result, I discovered that my voice would be forever diminished.

In the opera world there is a lot of shame associated with getting this kind of surgery. Was I careless? Did I overtrain? Can a company count on me to deliver, night after night? Singers who undergo this surgery almost always keep it secret or cover it. I was hardest on myself, sure that I had been irresponsible or not disciplined enough.

I came to the edge of something more significant that would change my life: I was terrified that I had lost the means to express myself. It is deeply human—the craving to be seen and heard, to share your story, and to tell your truth. The experience of losing it and then seeking it clarified my understanding of what I am actually here to do.

I was meant to use my voice—just not as a singer.

As I sought a new career, I listened carefully to my mentors and colleagues who saw my love of being in front of audiences and helping others and who encouraged me toward what would be my new field and my professional home to this day: consulting to organizations about how leadership leveraging diversity drives innovation. I spent some time in corporate jobs and then saw that I could have greater impact from the outside. I founded my company, where my team and I dedicate our energy to building more inclusive workplaces for the future, which, enabled by *all* kinds of talent, will ultimately produce better business results.

That energy pulled me toward giving my first TEDx, in a way. The seed was planted: I was co-facilitating one of JBC's flagship training programs for high-potential LGBTQ leaders of a large banking client, and we were teaching our storytelling module. It made sense for me to lead by example and tell my story.

Let me back up; this program is unique. One of its biggest gifts is the safe space that participants and faculty create together. Teaching it for the last five years, we've seen over and over again that the intentional creation of a homogenous group of LGBTQ individuals means we all can remove our protective armor and learn together that we have rich stories to tell and yet very few places to share them. Every single cohort has the same energy: participants can barely contain their enthusiasm to be in this room, guards down, reflecting together and supporting one another. It is such a rare experience for them; some of them have *never* been in a room like this before in their professional lives. This training is an unusual opportunity for all of us—faculty and participants alike—to connect our experiences to our development as leaders, unifying the disparate pieces of our identities as people and as professionals. We are literally reuniting parts of ourselves we've kept separate for, in some cases, much of our profes-

We are literally reuniting parts of ourselves we've kept separate for, in some cases, much of our professional lives.

sional lives. It is some of the most rewarding and transformational work we have the privilege to do at JBC.

All of that support notwithstanding, even I was as frightened as anyone else in that room to share my story. I knew I couldn't give the glossy version of my life—not when we were teaching the power of vulnerability. I gave it a shot though, speaking to one of the rawest, most painful periods in my life: losing my voice and having to give up my pursuit of a professional singing career. As I told it and related it to my current situation, I realized suddenly that there was a beautiful, colorful thread sewing my "selves" together. Here is a bit of the talk that grew out of the story I told in the corporate classroom that day:

> Every day, my team and I work with our clients to build strategies to retain and develop their upcoming leaders, and I have the privilege of knowing certain allies and CEOs who, as we say, "get diversity," such as EY's former Global Chairman and CEO, Jim Turley.

> I am frustrated, though, when I hear how many people still don't feel comfortable "bringing their whole selves to work," how many people still feel compelled to cover, to conceal, to deflect, to evade.

> Marianne Williamson once said, "As we are liberated from our own fear, our presence automatically liberates others." At some point in the early days of running my company, I had to liberate myself from my deepest fear, which meant coming out professionally as a member of the Lesbian, Gay, Bisexual, and Transgender community. I had come out to family and friends years earlier. However, declaring this publicly felt much riskier to me, as my name was now

"on the door." I imagined that clients and contracts that can make or break a small company, especially during a recession, were at stake in these very early days of my fledging consultancy. I had been warned once before that I could never come out as who I was, as a performer, that I would be judged as "inauthentic" if I tried to play traditional roles, that I wouldn't get certain offers. Due to my vocal type and my petite stature, casting directors saw and heard me as the definition of feminine heteronormativity: I was destined to play the ingénue. I could play those roles competently, but inside, I'd felt like I was maintaining a lie offstage. As a singer, I had needed to keep telling that lie in order to succeed. I didn't know any successful "out" role models in the opera world. As a business owner later on, I wanted to model bringing my full self to work for our clients and their stakeholders once my name was on the door. Today, I finally have the freedom to lead from and with my truest self.

SO, I ASK AGAIN, WHAT'S YOUR STORY?

I know this might be uncomfortable. Get comfortable with it. Here are a few prompts to help you find your diversity story:

- **It's your story, and you have the right to tell it.** Let the guide star of vulnerability lead you, with the spirit of building connection, plus knowing your audience—these are the ingredients to start with. But most importantly, don't judge your story as irrelevant or not powerful enough before you share it.

- **It's not always the story you think it is.** When I was invited to give my TEDx talk, I knew it was important to the organizers that I come out in the talk. My personal identity and my history with the LGBTQ community have been formative for me, but I also challenged myself to reach another plateau of fear and vulnerability by revealing my experience as a singer. I had told just a few people about my heartbreak over my performance career, and here I was, preparing to tell one thousand strangers. It conflicted with my instincts to protect myself and my image, which was how I knew I needed to do it.

> It conflicted with my instincts to protect myself and my image, which was how I knew I needed to do it.

- **Shock value can work in your favor.** The mere fact that I show up to talk about diversity surprises many who don't know me and don't know what I do. They don't know how deeply it resonates for me and that I can't imagine dedicating every day of my working life to anything else. But I am reminded constantly that we create shortcuts about people, almost immediately, and are often embarrassingly wrong. I see that shocked look when I tell someone what I do; bewildered, they might ask, "However did you get into that?" The question lurking behind the first one is, "Why do you do that?" They have made many assumptions about who I am, what my story is, and who they imagine labors in the corridors of diversity and inclusion. They can't connect the puzzle pieces, but their effort to reconcile all the parts of who we are—remember we discussed this as our intersectionality—creates new pathways in our audiences' hearts and minds about what makes up their clients, their colleagues, their family members. You yourself can be the lesson and plant the seed. The more we can show all of our diversity dimensions, even if apparently contradictory (or especially if so), the more impact we'll have.

> **You yourself can be the lesson and plant the seed.**

THOUGHT STARTERS FOR YOUR STORY

Tapping into your own vulnerability isn't easy. You have to do a lot of reflecting and thinking about who you are and why, which is harder than it may sound on the surface. We're not, after all, asking you to tell people your name, age, job title, and hobbies. This is not a corporate bio. You must dig deeper than that, and to do so, it helps to give yourself some focal points before you begin shoveling. We like to call these thought starters, and they're designed for leaders and executives to ponder as they explore their diversity story:

- When have you felt the sting of exclusion? How did adversity in any form shape you as a leader? As a human being?

- Where are your diverse employee voices? How conscious were you of inclusiveness when hiring those individuals? Whom have you reached out of your comfort zone to nurture and guide?

- Can you share a story that reveals a bias you've overcome?

- Which rising star can you speak about who has authentically leveraged a non-majority identity to engage and impress?

- Have you had an encounter with someone from a different culture, background, or orientation that has influenced you? This person may be a mentor, friend, manager, high-potential performer, customer, or partner. Has that experience altered your leadership style in any way?

- Have you mentored a woman, a Hispanic/Latino employee, a transgender worker? What was the outcome?

- Are you proud of your company's diversity commitment? What does it mean to you?

- How will you engage your peers in the conversation?

- How did your intentional inclusion of someone not "of the majority"—say, a disabled woman or a service veteran—improve that employee's experience, better their team, and better the organization?

- How has heightened awareness of diversity of style and approach changed the assumptions you make about the ways work gets done?

Notice one thing about these questions; I am recommending that you are intentionally inclusive in choosing *the people you tell stories about*. It's easy to fall into the habit of telling the stories of people that look like us; indeed, as we've documented so thoroughly in this book, many upper-level leaders are surrounded by others who share their background, and reaching outside of this inner circle, across difference, may not be a part of a leader's everyday life (yet another reason to get involved in your company's employee resource groups—see chapter 9). Building trusting relationships with those different from us and sharing stories of those experiences takes intentional time and effort.

Whom we choose to tell stories about not only says something about us but also bolsters those who don't see their stories shared. As a leader, you can provide that platform and elevate those voices to greater visibility.

My last piece of advice here is to remember the old adage, "What gets measured, gets done." I recommend to CEOs and executive teams to consider committing to the following:

> **Whom we choose to tell stories about not only says something about us but also bolsters those who don't see their stories shared. As a leader, you can provide that platform and elevate those voices to greater visibility.**

- Involve your team and hold them accountable.

- Add inclusive behaviors and results to performance goals.

We often think our differences set us apart from everyone else—usually in a negative way. But it may be very much the opposite. Our diversity story can connect us with many other aspects people are keeping beneath their waterlines. So take the risk to lead through being vulnerable. See how peculiar you are, or even how peculiar you're not.

EXECUTIVE STORYTELLING ABOUT DIVERSITY IN ACTION

What does this look like in practice? I had the opportunity to witness the CEO of a large utility company provide the opening remarks at a diversity summit where I was the keynote. He shared the following observations about his own diversity and inclusion journey as a white, heterosexual man, and I wrote them down verbatim because I was so inspired to hear such competency, spoken with conviction and authenticity. Here are some of his quotes:

- "On cultural competency, I began my learning by showing up and listening, first and foremost."

- "Some of our leadership still come up and ask me, 'Why does this matter?' I take a deep breath and say, 'Okay, let's go through it again.' Some have asked me this multiple times, but good news: some of those are finally getting it. I find it helps to describe it in terms of imagining we hire someone and asking why we'd want that person to just give us 70 percent and not capture the other 30 percent? It's illogical. They usually get that."

- "When I think about what's changed, it's the relationship between businesses and the social environments they exist in. McKinsey's gender research shows that $12 trillion in GDP would be unlocked if we had female equality in the global workplace."

- "I recently had the chance to talk to Lord Browne in the UK, ex-CEO of BP, who was hiding all his life and is now a champion and an out gay man. Imagine how he would have been an even better leader if he could have been transparent? I attended the Stonewall parade in London that same trip."

- "When I joined the company fifteen years ago, all I saw were other white middle-aged men, no diversity, and now I see a fantastic mix. But we still have work to do; our employee surveys tell us that we have many people who can't bring their full selves to work."

- "Actually, I'm happy to bias our recruiting. If we go back to how we did it historically, we won't end up in a different place, and that isn't acceptable. It might feel harder, initially, but through adhering to this principle we have uncovered assets and people we already had in this organization."

He covered a lot of terrain in his remarks. What I most noticed was humility, a listening stance, peer accountability, and knowledge of the business case. I especially appreciated the window into his unwavering commitment in speaking to his executive peers, as well as his knowledge of the facts and cultur-

"I'm happy to bias our recruiting. If we go back to how we did it historically, we won't end up in a different place, and that isn't acceptable."

ally significant community examples that landed on me as authentic, heartfelt, and well researched.

In Chuck Shelton's research, 55 percent of "White Men" and 79 percent of "All Other" respondents, including white men themselves, negatively rated white men who lead without relying on diversity and inclusion:

White male leaders self-marginalize when they fail to find their self-interest in diversity and inclusion, missing the career advantage and business results. They risk their influence when they habitually ignore an inescapable human reality: diverse colleagues generally perceive white men as white men, whether or not the white guys see that being white and male could be important.[8]

Leaders, this is the perfect moment to think about what comprises your diversity story and how you may want to let it inform your leadership style and choices. Chuck also documented what I have certainly found to be true: candid conversations around diversity are essential, but we often dodge or deflect the opportunity to have substantive discussions because of the perceived risk of something going sideways.

WHAT'S IN IT FOR EXECUTIVES TO GET INVOLVED

It's a valuable experience to sponsor an employee resource group or serve as an executive champion for firm-wide efforts, and it is a great way to build one's competencies as a diversity and inclusion-driven leader. As pointed out by the executives we featured in our 2015 white paper, *Executive Sponsors Fuel High-Performing ERGs*, sponsoring a group changed them in profound ways. Balaji Ramarao, a Cisco executive at the time, said about working with the company's millennial ERG: "Just to get to coach others, to see the passion and energy is great. I learn about how the younger folks think, [their] work ethic, and [their] sense of politics, people, success, and achievement."

Nitin Kiwale, also at Cisco at the time, further expanded on the value proposition of serving as an executive sponsor:

I have definitely learned what's important in an employer for this generation. I blog now, [including] video blogging; the way I communicate and interact with employees… has changed. My own work processes have changed. I've gotten what I want out of it, and now I want to make a difference with it…change the way we recruit.

As we mentioned previously in our "Thought Starters for Your Story" section, many CEOs have begun to require the involvement of their direct reports in taking this journey with them. I predict involvement will become much more systemically measured and tied to compensation in the future. Measuring progress is critical to reinforcing an organization's commitment to inclusion and to establishing the pivotal path of accountability at the highest echelons of the company. Sometimes, some folks need a little nudge.

Leaders of tomorrow will need to take charge of the evolving corporate culture. They need to cultivate the capacity for network management, relationship building, influencing without authority, cultural competence, allyship, and seeking what's different to fuel innovation and growth. A diverse workforce and a multicultural marketplace are already looking for leaders who have the ability to be vulnerable and carry a sort of humility in their work. The ability to listen and heighten one's sensitivity to multiple realities and derive the best way forward from an overwhelming amount of input are the key competencies of the future. The executive on the ground level, comfortable among the broadest and

The ability to listen and heighten one's sensitivity to multiple realities and derive the best way forward from an overwhelming amount of input are the key competencies of the future.

furthest sections of the company pyramid, with an exceptional emotional intuition, is already garnering greater respect, commitment, and loyalty than the traditional hardened, distant, commander-in-chief is. The female, non-white, LGBTQ, differently abled executive might be the exception today, but the demand for transparency and leadership that reflects the larger world is growing louder by the day. If we can rebrand what it means to lead, placing inclusion as a core value, then we may find the leaders we need right now among us. Those of us incumbents in the leadership ranks must transform. Even if it is long overdue, it may be just in time.

IN CLOSING

I have tried to articulate the overpowering workforce, workplace, and marketplace imperatives that should influence every leader's strategy in thinking differently about who and how we hire, lead, and conduct our businesses. I want to see women and people of color thrive in engineering. I want to see men teach school and become nurses and *boys* aspire to be them someday. I want to see all parents take full advantage of parental leave and feel less stressed, and more fulfilled, in how they are balancing all of their priorities and their health. I want less covering of stigmatized identities. I want workplaces that seek and invest in people with disabilities. I want us to work within our own organizations and across our society as a whole to dismantle the false binaries and unconscious biases that separate us so that we might celebrate together all the differences that enrich us—while still being aware of the importance of safety in community. But above all, I want each of us to feel welcomed, valued, respected, and heard at work—and in life.

I know it can be frightening to think about making these multiple and systemic changes, but we must, lest change happens without us—or to us. We have a window of time where we can get involved, deepening our leadership and broadening our horizons to include the rich, transformative power of difference. Choosing to sit on the sidelines of this shift means that all the richness of *your voice and your story* will be missed in the evolution. The evolution will not be complete.

This begins with you.

GLOSSARY

I have selected the following list of terms as some of the many concepts that must be learned to truly understand the impact diversity and inclusion can have within a company—and family life. While this list is certainly not all-encompassing of the important words related to diversity and inclusion, I do hope it helps you on your journey to learning others' stories—and telling your own.

affinity: a group of people who share interests, issues, and a common bond or background and offer support for each other. These groups can be formed between friends or people from the same community, workplace, or organization. Affinity groups can represent a narrow or broad definition of a dimension of diversity: African ancestry or black employees, Asian Indian, Chinese, gay and lesbian, Hispanic or Latino, people with disabilities, Mideast and Southeast Asian, veterans, and women, to name just a few.[1]

ally: someone who uses their power to advocate on behalf of someone who otherwise would not have an equal voice; someone who uses his or her platform to help move the discussion of diversity and inclusion forward.

allyship: one's position to stand for and drive outcomes that many lack the positional power or social capital to lead.

B Corp: for-profit companies certified by the nonprofit B Lab to meet rigorous standards of social and environmental performance, accountability, and transparency.[2]

business resource group (BRG): a concept that is gaining in popularity as companies begin to more fully recognize the potential business impacts of Employee Resource Groups (ERGs) and want those employees to be associated with driving real business results. There is still at this time a wide variety of names utilized for these networks, besides BRG and ERG.

change agent: related to diversity and inclusion, an individual who helps an organization convert itself into a more inclusive workplace, from whatever level in the organization.

C-Suite: term used to collectively refer to a corporation's most important senior executives; the name is derived from the "C" that often begins senior executives' titles (chief executive officer, chief financial officer, chief operating officer).

cisgender: denoting, or relating to, a person whose self-identity conforms with the gender that corresponds to that individual's biological sex.[3]

co-mentoring: the act of pairing talent and senior leaders of different backgrounds. See also ***reverse mentoring*** on page 273.

conscious capitalism: a business strategy focused on the interests of its customers, employees, investors, communities, suppliers, and the environment.[4]

corporate philanthropy: any act in which a corporation promotes the welfare of others.

corporate social responsibility: a business strategy prioritizing the sustainable expansion or reinforcement of economic, social, and environmental benefits for all its stakeholders.

covering: downplaying a known stigmatized identity.

cultural competency: the ability to interact effectively across difference.[5]

diversity of thought: a function of an individual's physical and experiential identities and the impact they have on work and life experience in terms of problem solving and bringing new insights to the workplace.

employee resource group (ERG): any employee-led group with the purpose of supporting its members and organizations by cultivating a diverse, inclusive workplace aligned with organizational mission, values, goals, business practices, and objectives. See also *business resource group (BRG)* on page 270.

executive sponsor: a member of the executive level who serves as a mentor for an individual or group, particularly an ERG, especially when advocating for them in the C-suite and other organizational management levels.

flat organization: a management structure with no or very few levels of middle management separating staff and executives.

gender expression: the personal manifestation of masculinity or femininity, especially when evincing one's gender identity, our innermost sense of being male or female. One's gender identity can be expressed or suppressed, both consciously and unconsciously, through gender expression, such as physical mannerisms, hair and clothing styles, language, and other outward displays.[6]

gender identity: how individuals experience or perceive their personal gender.

heteronormative: relating to the view that heterosexuality is the normal, or at least preferred, sexual orientation.[7]

holacracy: an organizational management strategy in which a company's governance and decision making are distributed evenly among self-organized teams. Individual employees are viewed as both a whole group and part of a larger group.

human capital: the skills, knowledge, and experience possessed by an individual or population, viewed in terms of their value or cost to an organization or country.

intersectionality: the idea that someone can be privileged in some ways but not in others, or have multiple identities that intersect, including gender, race, and sexual orientation.

intrapreneurial: those who take hands-on responsibility for creating innovation of any kind, within a business.

LGBTQ: lesbian, gay, bisexual, transgender, queer; although the Q can stand for queer or questioning, it is most often seen as queer. The word queer is about intersectionality, as not everyone identifies as L, G, B, or T; therefore, the inclusion of queer better reflects more individuals outside gender and sexuality norms.

majority: those who hold the majority of positions, particularly positions of power, in a company or society; often an identity group that comprises the majority of workforce or social demographics.

minority: any group or member of a group whose social identity is underrepresented in the workplace, especially relative to its general population.

microaggression: brief, everyday exchanges that send denigrating messages to certain individuals because of their group membership.

microinequity: the casual degradation of any socially marginalized group.

mutualism: the doctrine that the interdependence of social elements is the primary determinant of individual and social relations, especially the theory that common ownership and property, or collective effort and control governed by sentiments of brotherhood and mutual aid, will be beneficial to both the individual and society.[8]

personal brand: the experience of someone having a relationship with who you are and what you represent as an individual and as a leader.

queer: queer is an umbrella term encompassing a variety of sexual orientations and gender identities excluding heterosexuality. The word queer is in the process of being reclaimed (since the mid 80s); it has evolved from decades ago when queer was used as an anti-gay epithet. The term has been reclaimed by younger generations to also refer to political ideologies not adhering to heteronormativity or a gender binary.[9]

reverse mentoring: the generation-based pairing of older executives with younger employees to be mentored on topics such as technology, social media, and current trends.

sexual orientation: a person's sexual identity in relation to the gender to which they are attracted; the fact of being heterosexual, bisexual, or homosexual.[10]

slate: individuals the organization intends to interview for an open position. Diverse slates include women and minorities; inclusion of diverse candidates often has to be done intentionally.[11]

sponsorship: the act of using executive influence to advocate for an individual or group, usually by initiating introductions, funneling opportunities, and offering invitations to decision-making discussions and meetings.

stereotype threat: the sense that one might be judged in terms of negative stereotypes about one's group instead of on personal merit.

transgender: denoting or relating to a person whose self-identity does not conform unambiguously to conventional notions of male or female gender.

triple bottom line: centers on three main components: people, planet, and profits.

unconscious bias: our set of attitudes toward and stereotypes of other social groups that affect our understanding, actions, and decisions in an unconscious way, especially negatively.

virtual worker: an employee or team of employees who work(s) outside the physical workplace, sometimes across time zones and countries, but connect through various forms of technology to perform work-related tasks.

RESOURCES

We have compiled a handful of helpful resources for you in this section. For easier access to an online version of these resources please visit: www.jenniferbrownspeaks.com/inclusion-book-resources

CHAPTER 2

Project Implicit: Assess Your Unconscious Biases

https://implicit.harvard.edu/implicit/takeatest.html

Project Implicit is a nonprofit organization and international collaboration between researchers who are interested in implicit social cognition: thoughts and feelings beyond one's awareness and control. The goal of the organization is to educate the public about hidden biases and to provide a virtual laboratory for collecting data on the Internet.

The Change Adoption Curve (a.k.a. The Five Stages of Grief)

https://www.cleverism.com/understanding-kubler-ross-change-curve/

See "The Kubler-Ross Change Curve" on page 279.

CHAPTER 3

JBC's Engagement Best Practice: Welcomed, Valued, Respected and Heard

See the "Best Practices: Engagement" chart on page 280.

Employee Resource Groups That Drive Business: ERG Benchmarking Study

http://jenniferbrownconsulting.com/cisco-jbc-driving-business-next-practices-for-ergs/

CHAPTER 4

Uncovering Talent: A new model of inclusion[1]

http://gender.stanford.edu/sites/default/files/06%20UncoveringTalentPaper.pdf

JBC Allies Initiative: Allies "Come Out"

http://jenniferbrownconsulting.com/jbc-allies-initiative-allies-come-out/

Just as LGBTQ employees have made great strides in creating more inclusive policies and practices at the corporate level, allies have quietly—and not so quietly—been laboring, bringing their influence as well as sweat equity to create organizational change.

CHAPTER 5

Lean In

www.leanin.org/

Great resources can be found here for women and their allies on moving gender parity forward.

"The Power of We: Building Ally-Focused Inclusion Initiatives that Engage the Broader Workforce"

https://www.stthomas.edu/workplaceforum/wp-content/uploads/2015/03/S5H_final-handout.pptx
Presentation by Shavondalyn Givens and Jennifer Brown

CHAPTER 6

JBC's Diversity Starter Kit for CEOs: A Step-by-Step Guide for Facilitating the D&I Conversation with Your CEO.

http://jenniferbrownconsulting.com/diversity-starter-kit-for-ceos/

The starter kit will help you encourage your CEO to ask and answer questions and affirm action steps—all in under thirty minutes.

The Iceberg That Sinks Organizational Change[2]

http://www.torbenrick.eu/t/r/jxm

The Purpose Economy: How Your Desire for Impact, Personal Growth and Community Is Changing the World[3] by Aaron Hurst

https://www.imperative.com/index2015

CHAPTER 8

How to Engage LGBTQ ERGs in Supplier Diversity

http://jenniferbrownconsulting.com/diversity-executive-how-to-engage-lgbt-ergs-in-supplier-diversity/

Insight to Impact: Connecting Diversity and Inclusion to Organizational Impact

http://jenniferbrownconsulting.com/insight-to-impact-connecting-di-to-organizational-impact/

Generations in the Workplace: The Next Wave of Diversity

http://jenniferbrownconsulting.com/generations-in-the-workplace-the-next-wave-of-diversity/

Diversity & Inclusion: The Big Six Formula for Success[4] by D.A. Abrams

> https://www.amazon.com/Diversity-Inclusion-Big-Formula-Success-ebook/dp/B00E42UGAO#nav-subnav

CHAPTER 9

Progressing towards Success: Maximize Your ERG for Business Impact

> http://jenniferbrownconsulting.com/progressing-towards-success-maximize-your-erg-for-business-impact/

Executive Sponsors Fuel High-Performing ERGs: Executive Summary

> http://jenniferbrownconsulting.com/executive-sponsors-fuel-high-performing-ergs-executive-summary/

"100 Best Companies to Work For"[5]

> http://fortune.com/best-companies/

CHAPTER 10

The Study on White Men Leading Through Inclusion[6]

> http://www.whitemensleadershipstudy.com/
> https://www.youtube.com/watch?v=aAxeDkoeaxo

THE KÜBLER-ROSS CHANGE CURVE

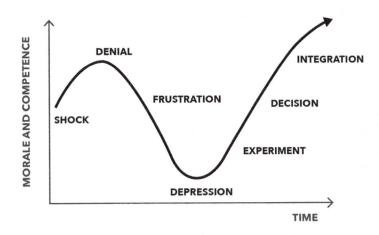

SHOCK	Surprise or shock at the event
DENIAL	Disbelief; looking for evidence that it isn't true
FRUSTRATION	Recognition that things are different; sometimes angry
DEPRESSION	Low mood; lacking in energy
EXPERIMENT	Initial engagement with new situation
DECISION	Learning how to work in the new situation; feeling more positive
INTEGRATION	Changes integrated; a renewed individual

BEST PRACTICES: ENGAGEMENT

	WELCOMED →	VALUED →	RESPECTED →	HEARD
MEANINGFUL WORK	Customize onboarding, and continue to check in periodically on engagement.	Offer visible assignments; intentionally leverage skills.	Give credit where it is due, and promote successes as visibly as possible.	Share employee success stories.
GREAT MANAGERS	Solicit and consider new ideas; reward process improvements.	Provide clear, concise, specific, timely feedback; rally membership or teams toward aligned goals.	Offer to coach ERG leaders; invest in skills and advancement.	Implement new ideas; give credit; ask for feedback.
INCLUSIVE CULTURE	Encourage colleagues to bring more of their full selves to work.	Utilize ERGs as an employee referral resource, thus enabling more diverse candidate slates.	Understand work and family balance; encourage utilization of flex policies.	Collect and share feedback regularly about a job well done to supervisors and executives.
INSPIRE TRUST IN LEADERSHIP	Learn and use people's names and know the job they do.	Lead by walking around; speak with and get to know ERG members and other champions.	Demonstrate openly that you care about who people are and what they do.	Participate regularly in diversity initiatives; mention in communications what you learn from what you hear.

REFERENCES

We have compiled all references from each chapter of the book for your convenience. For easier access to an online version of these references please visit: www.jenniferbrownspeaks.com/inclusion-book-references

CHAPTER ONE

1   Philip Bump, "Here Is When Each Generation Begins and Ends, According to the Facts," *The Atlantic*, March 25, 2014, http://www.theatlantic.com/national/archive/2014/03/here-is-when-each-generation-begins-and-ends-according-to-facts/359589/.

2   African American is used to indicate ethnicity, while black indicates race. Either one is acceptable, but when discussing ethnicity it is advisable to use African American. If you are referring to a group of people of African descent that are not necessarily African American (i.e., Haitian, African, Afro-Caribbean), it is preferable to use black.

3   Megan Rose Dickey, "Twitter Engineering Manager Leslie Miley Leaves Company Because Of Diversity Issues," Tech Crunch, November 3, 2015, https://techcrunch.com/2015/11/03/twitter-engineering-manager-leslie-miley-leaves-company-because-of-diversity-issues/.

4   Janet Van Huysse, "We're Committing to a More Diverse Twitter," Twitter, August 28, 2015, https://blog.twitter.com/2015/we-re-committing-to-a-more-diverse-twitter.

5   Dickey, "Twitter Engineering Manager Leslie Miley Leaves."

6   Karen Grigsby Bates, "Q&A with the Black Twitter Engineer Who Left over Diversity Problems," Code Switch (online section), National Public Broadcasting, November 6, 2015, http://www.npr.org/sections/codeswitch/2015/11/06/454949422/a-q-a-with-lesley-miley-the-black-twitter-engineer-who-left-over-diversity-probl.

7   Natalie Thorenson, quoting Derald Sue, "Unearthing and Combatting Microaggressions in Work with Youth," Instructor Bio page, City College of San Francisco website, https://www.ccsf.edu/en/educational-programs/contract-education/title4e/title4e_instructor_bios/title4e_bios_thoreson.html.

8   Aimée Lutkin, "Facebook Releases Their Yearly Diversity Numbers, Blames Stagnation on the Educational Pipeline," Jezebel, July 14, 2016, http://jezebel.com/facebook-releases-their-yearly-diversity-numbers-blame-1783683109.

9   US Census Bureau, *Disparities in STEM Employment by Sex, Race, and Hispanic Origin*, report (2000 to present), http://www.census.gov/prod/2013pubs/acs-24.pdf.

10   Jessica Guynn, "Airbnb Diversity Chief: Tech Should Reflect 'Diverse Tapestry of America,'" *USA Today*, March 4, 2016, http://www.usatoday.com/story/tech/news/2016/03/04/airbnb-hires-first-chief-diversity-officer-from-peace-corps/81242224/.

11   Barney Ely, "Breaking the Rules," Hays, https://social.hays.com/2016/04/12/breaking-the-rules/.

12   Caroline Fairchild, "What Davos Is Like for a Female CEO," *Fortune*, January 20, 2015, http://fortune.com/2015/01/20/davos-female-ceo/.

13   Adrienne Selko, "Confidence Is Top Leadership Difference between Women and Men," *Industry Week*, March 8, 2016, http://www.industryweek.com/leadership/confidence-top-leadership-difference-between-women-and-men.

14   Betsey Guzio, "Xerox: What We Lose When Ursula Burns Steps Down," Bizwomen, American City Business Journals, March 23, 2016, http://www.bizjournals.com/bizwomen/news/latest-news/2016/05/xerox-what-we-lose-when-ursula-burns-steps-down.html.

15a US Census Bureau, "FFF: Hispanic Heritage Month 2015," September 14, 2015, http://www.census.gov/newsroom/facts-for-features/2015/cb15-ff18.html;

15b Ahiza Garcia, "Only 9 Hispanic CEOs at Top 500 Companies," CNN Money, September 9, 2015, http://money.cnn.com/2015/09/09/news/hispanic-ceo-fortune-500-companies/;

15c McDonald's CEO to Retire; "Black Fortune 500 CEOs Decline by 33% in Past Year," DiversityInc, January 29, 2015, http://www.diversityinc.com/leadership/mcdonalds-ceo-retire-black-fortune-500-ceos-decline-33-past-year/;

15d Emily Cohn, "Here Are All the Openly Gay CEOs In The Fortune 500," *The Huffington Post*, October 30, 2014, http://www.huffingtonpost.com/2014/10/30/gay-ceos-fortune-500_n_6074768.html;

15e Benjamin Snyder, "Apple's CEO becomes the Fortune 500's only openly gay CEO. Here are 11 other workplace stats," *Fortune*, October 30, 2014, http://fortune.com/2014/10/30/apples-ceo-becomes-the-fortune-500s-only-openly-gay-ceo-here-are-11-more-workplace-stats/.

16   Richard Feloni, "Here's Everything Facebook Is Doing This Year to Address Its 'Pathetic' Diversity Numbers," *Business Insider*, January 20, 2016, http://www.businessinsider.com/facebooks-2016-strategy-for-improving-diversity-2016-1.

17   Vivian Hunt, Dennis Layton, and Sara Prince, "Why Diversity Matters," McKinsey & Company, January 2015, http://www.mckinsey.com/business-functions/organization/our-insights/why-diversity-matters.

18   Crustian Dezso and David Gaddis Ross, "Does Female Representation in Top Management Improve Firm Performance? A Panel Data Investigation," *Strategic Management Journal* 33, no. 9 (September 2012), https://www0.gsb.columbia.edu/mygsb/faculty/research/pubfiles/3063/female_representation.pdf.

19   Gregory Wallace, "Only 5 Black CEOs at 500 Biggest Companies," CNN Money, January 20, 2015, http://money.cnn.com/2015/01/29/news/economy/mcdonalds-ceo-diversity/?iid=EL.

20   Nick Wingfield, "Intel Allocates $300 Million for Workplace Diversity," *New York Times*, January 6, 2015, http://www.nytimes.com/2015/01/07/technology/intel-budgets-300-million-for-diversity.html?_r=0.

21   "Diversity Makes Us Stronger Every Day," Apple Inc., http://www.apple.com/diversity/.

22   Feloni, "Here's Everything Facebook is Doing."

23   Megan Rose Dickey, "Facebook Launches TechPrep to Grow the Pipeline by Empowering Black and Latino Parents," TechCrunch, October 20, 2015, http://techcrunch.com/2015/10/20/facebook-launches-tech-prep/.

24   Li Zhou, "Pinterest's Data-Driven Approach to Improving Diversity," *The Atlantic*, January 15, 2015, http://www.theatlantic.com/technology/archive/2016/01/pinterest-diversity/424203/.

25   Steve Crabtree, "Worldwide, 13% of Employees Are Engaged at Work," Gallup, October 8, 2013, http://www.gallup.com/poll/165269/worldwide-employees-engaged-work.aspx.

26   Cameron Keng, "Employees Who Stay in Companies Longer Than Two Years Get Paid 50% Less," *Forbes*, June 22, 2014, http://www.forbes.com/sites/cameronkeng/2014/06/22/employees-that-stay-in-companies-longer-than-2-years-get-paid-50-less/#5a5169a6210e.

27   Tessa L. Dover, Brenda Major, and Cheryl R. Kaiser, "Diversity Policies Rarely Make Companies Fairer, and They Feel Threatening to White Men," *Harvard Business Review*, January 4, 2016, https://hbr.org/2016/01/diversity-policies-dont-help-women-or-minorities-and-they-make-white-men-feel-threatened.

28   Ibid.

CHAPTER TWO

1   Delece Smith-Barrow, "Problems with Retention Block STEM Workforce from being More Diverse," US *News & World Report*, June 30, 2015, http://www.usnews.com/news/stem-solutions/articles/2015/06/30/problems-with-retention-not-just-recruitment-inhibit-stem-workforce-diversity.

2   Austin Carr, "The Inside Story of Starbucks's Race Together Campaign, No Foam," Fast Company, June 15, 2015, http://www.fastcompany.com/3046890/the-inside-story-of-starbuckss-race-together-campaign-no-foam.

3   Jon Kamp and Cameron McWhirter, "Business Leaders Speak Out against North Carolina's Transgender Law," *The Wall Street Journal*, March 30, 2016, http://www.wsj.com/articles/business-leaders-speak-out-against-north-carolinas-transgender-law-1459377292.

4   Alexander Kaufman, "Here Are The 379 Companies Urging The Supreme Court To Support Same-Sex Marriage," *The Huffington Post,* March 5, 2015, http://www.huffingtonpost.com/2015/03/05/marriage-equality-amicus_n_6808260.html.

5   Sara Ashley O'Brien, "Sam's Club CEO Takes Heat for Diversity Comments," CNN Money, December 16, 2015, http://money.cnn.com/2015/12/16/news/companies/rosalind-brewer-sams-club-diversity/.

6   Doktor Zoom, "All Of America Boycotting Sam's Club For Hating White Men, Says Stupid White Man," Wonkette, December 22, 2015, http://wonkette.com/597246/all-of-america-boycotting-sams-club-for-hating-white-men-says-stupid-white-man#ZR6o1kETc0Du4bvU.99.

7   Louise Jury, "Nike to Trash Trainers That Offended Islam," *Independent,* June 24, 1997, http://www.independent.co.uk/news/nike-to-trash-trainers-that-offended-islam-1257776.html.

8   "Slogan Translations," http://www.subgenius.com/bigfist/answers/articles2/X0010_Slogan_Translations.html.

9   Joyce Park, "Diversity Is Not Some PC BS," Be yourself (Medium), January 2015, https://byrslf.co/diversity-is-not-some-pc-bs-abb03271f8d3#.qalvamb11.

10   "HR KPIs: The good, the bad and the ugly," mortenkamp, March 30, 2012, https://mortenkamp.com/2012/03/30/hr-kpis-the-good-the-bad-and-the-ugly/.

11   "Allyship," The Anti-Oppression Network, https://theantioppressionnetwork.wordpress.com/allyship/.

12   "What is the ROI of Diversity and Inclusion Strategies?: Voices from thought leaders," December 10, 2015, http://www.aperianglobal.com/what-is-the-roi-of-diversity-inclusion-strategies/.

13   "Johari Window," *Pegasus Vertex, Inc.,* February 18, 2014, http://www.pvisoftware.com/blog/wp-content/uploads/2014/02/Johari_Window-01.png.

CHAPTER THREE

1   Jennifer Brown, "Finding Your Voice in the Workplace: Jennifer Brown at TEDx Presidio," TEDx Talks, September 11, 2012, https://www.youtube.com/watch?v=b03DrOYWC_w.

2   Bim Adewunmi, "Kimberlé Crenshaw on intersectionality: 'I wanted to come up with an everyday metaphor that anyone could use,'" NewStatesman, April 2, 2014, http://www.newstatesman.com/lifestyle/2014/04/kimberl-crenshaw-intersectionality-i-wanted-come-everyday-metaphor-anyone-could.

3   Google, "You Don't Know What You Don't Know: How Our Unconscious Minds Undermine the Workplace," Google Official Blog, September 25, 2014, https://googleblog.blogspot.com/2014/09/you-dont-know-what-you-dont-know-how.html.

4   Ibid.

5   Matt O'Brien, "Q&A: Google's Nancy Lee, on Diversifying the Tech Workforce," The Mercury News, Business section, February 13, 2015, http://www.mercurynews.com/business/ci_27521277/q-googles-nancy-lee-diversifying-tech-workforce.

6   Google, "You Don't Know What You Don't Know."

7   Ian Sample, Rebecca Ratcliffe, and Claire Shaw, "The Trouble with Tim Hunt's 'Trouble with Girls in Science' Comment," Guardian, June 12, 2015, https://www.theguardian.com/science/2015/jun/12/tim-hunt-trouble-with-girls-in-science-comment.

8   Merrill Miller, "#ILookLikeAn Engineer: A Campaign to End Gender Stereotyping in STEM," The Humanist, August 19, 2015, http://thehumanist.com/commentary/ilooklikeanengineer-a-campaign-to-end-gender-stereotyping-in-stem.

9   Isis Anchalee Wenger, "You May Have Seen My Face on BART," The Coffeelicious (Medium), August 1, 2015, https://medium.com/the-coffeelicious/you-may-have-seen-my-face-on-bart-8b9561003e0f#.kg0pbzvrb.

10   Ibid.

11   Steven Stroessner, Catherine Good, and Lauren Webster, "What is stereotype threat?", http://www.reducingstereotypethreat.org/definition.html.

12   Sunnivie Brydum, "The True Meaning of the Word 'Cisgender,'" Advocate, July 31, 2015, http://www.advocate.com/transgender/2015/07/31/true-meaning-word-cisgender.

13   Peggy McIntosh, "White Privilege and Male Privilege: A Personal Account of Coming to See Correspondences through Work in Women's Studies," Working Paper 189, Wellesley College Center for Research on Women, Wellesley, Massachusetts, 1988; excerpt quoted in "White Privilege: Unpacking the Invisible Knapsack," De Anza College, 1988, https://www.deanza.edu/faculty/lewisjulie/White%20Priviledge%20Unpacking%20the%20Invisible%20Knapsack.pdf.

14 Desmond Tutu, *No Future without Forgiveness* (London: Doubleday, 1999).

15 These programs identify and pair talent with more senior leaders of different backgrounds.

16 Lisa Quast, "Reverse Mentoring: What it is and Why it is beneficial," *Forbes,* January 3, 2011, http://www.forbes.com/sites/work-in-progress/2011/01/03/reverse-mentoring-what-is-it-and-why-is-it-beneficial/#22bc60d653aa.

17 Jennifer Brown, "JBC's Interview with Jim Turley," https://vimeo.com/64647492.

18 Katherine W. Phillips, "How Diversity Makes Us Smarter," *Scientific American,* October 1, 2014, http://www.scientificamerican.com/article/how-diversity-makes-us-smarter/.

CHAPTER FOUR

1 Christie Smith and Stephanie Turner, *The Radical Transformation of Diversity and Inclusion*, report, Deloitte University, 2015, http://www2.deloitte.com/us/en/pages/about-deloitte/articles/radical-transformation-of-diversity-and-inclusion.html#.

2 Ibid.

3 US Equal Employment Opportunity Commission website, https://www.eeoc.gov/employers/recordkeeping.cfm.

4 Smith and Turner, *The Radical Transformation of Diversity and Inclusion.*

5 Punit Renjen, "Millennials and Purpose: The Message Is Clear for Business Leaders," Politico, September 24, 2015, http://www.politico.com/sponsor-content/2015/09/millennials-and-purpose-the-message-is-clear-for-business-leaders#ixzz462xEV8mB.

6 Jeffrey S. Passel and D'vera Cohn, "U.S. Population Projections: 2005–2050," Pew Research Center, Febrauary 11, 2008, http://www.pewhispanic.org/2008/02/11/us-population-projections-2005-2050/.

7 Sandra L. Colby and Jennifer M. Ortman, *Projections of the Size and Composition of the U.S. Population: 2014 to 2060*, report, US Census Bureau, https://www.census.gov/content/dam/Census/library/publications/2015/demo/p25-1143.pdf.

8 Ashley Broughton, "Minorities expected to be majority in 2050," CNN, August 13, 2008, http://www.cnn.com/2008/US/08/13/census.minorities/.

9 "Colin Powell Biography," Biography, August 3, 2016, http://www.biography.com/people/colin-powell-9445708.

10 Brooks Barnes and John Koblin, "Channing Dungey to Succeed Paul Lee as Chief of ABC Entertainment," *The New York Times,* February 17, 2016, http://www.nytimes.com/2016/02/18/business/media/paul-lee-resign-abc-entertainment.html?_r=0.

11   Mona Chalabi, "Three Leagues, 92 Teams And One Black Principal Owner," FiveThirtyEight, April 28, 2014, http://fivethirtyeight.com/datalab/diversity-in-the-nba-the-nfl-and-mlb/.

12   Alicia Montgomery, "America Is Obsessed with Identity. Thanks, Obama?" Code Switch (online section), National Public Radio, February 17, 2016, http://www.npr.org/sections/codeswitch/2016/02/17/466950838/america-is-obsessed-with-identity-thanks-obama.

13   Sheryl Sandberg and Adam Grant, "Why Women Stay Quiet at Work," The New York Times, January 12, 2015, http://www.nytimes.com/2015/01/11/opinion/sunday/speaking-while-female.html.

14   Claude Steele, "How Stereotypes Affect Us and What We Can Do: An Introduction to Stereotype Threat," Facing Today, http://facingtoday.facinghistory.org/how-stereotypes-affect-us-and-what-we-can-do-an-introduction-to-stereotype-threat.

15   Ibid.

16   Glenn Llopis, "Personal Branding Is A Leadership Requirement, Not A Self-Promotion Campaign," Forbes, April 8, 2013, http://www.forbes.com/sites/glennllopis/2013/04/08/personal-branding-is-a-leadership-requirement-not-a-self-promotion-campaign/#6856b2b415c0.

17   Kenji Yoshino and Christie Smith, "Uncovering Talent: A new model of inclusion," report, Deloitte University, December 6, 2013, http://www2.deloitte.com/content/dam/Deloitte/us/Documents/about-deloitte/us-inclusion-uncovering-talent-paper.pdf.

18   Ibid.

19   Deena Fidas and Liz Cooper, The Cost of the Closet and the Rewards of Inclusion: Why the Workplace Environment for LGBT People Matters to Employers, report, Human Rights Campaign Foundation, May 2014, http://hrc-assets.s3-website-us-east-1.amazonaws.com//files/assets/resources/Cost_of_the_Closet_May2014.pdf.

20   Karlyn Borysenko, "The Cost of Employee Turnover," LinkedIn, July 1, 2014, https://www.linkedin.com/pulse/20140701121556-17497251-the-cost-of-employee-turnover; Cameron Keng, "Employees Who Stay in Companies Longer Than Two Years Get Paid 50 percent Less," Forbes, June 22, 2014, http://www.forbes.com/sites/cameronkeng/2014/06/22/employees-that-stay-in-companies-longer-than-2-years-get-paid-50-less/#5a5169a6210e.

21   Julie Battilana and Tiziana Casciaro, "The Network Secrets of Great Change Agents," Harvard Business Review, July-August 2013, https://hbr.org/2013/07/the-network-secrets-of-great-change-agents.

22   Ken Mandel, "Bill Clinton Inaugural Address Highlights: 7 Quotes From Speeches," newsmax, March 20, 2015, http://www.newsmax.com/FastFeatures/Bill-Clinton-Inaugural-Speech-Highlights-U-SPresident/2015/03/22/id/631609/.

23   "Woodrow Wilson," Wikiquote, https://en.wikiquote.org/wiki/Woodrow_Wilson.

24   Julie Battailana and Tiziana Casciaro, "The Network Secrets of Great Change Agents," *Harvard Business Review*, July-August 2013.

25   Ibid.

26   "Intrapreneurship," Wikipedia, https://en.wikipedia.org/wiki/Intrapreneurship.

27   Seth Godin, *Tribes: We Need You to Lead Us*, quoted in Good Reads, https://www.goodreads.com/work/quotes/3873014-tribes-we-need-you-to-lead-us.

28   "Remarks by the First Lady at Tuskegee University Commencement Address," the White House, May 9, 2015, Tuskegee University, press release, https://www.whitehouse.gov/the-press-office/2015/05/09/remarks-first-lady-tuskegee-university-commencement-address.

29   "Remarks by the President at Morehouse College Commencement Ceremony," the White House, May 19, 2013, Morehouse College, https://www.whitehouse.gov/the-press-office/2013/05/19/remarks-president-morehouse-college-commencement-ceremony.

30   Ernest Owens, "Lucky or Proud to Be a Minority in College," *The Huffington Post*, February 16, 2013, http://www.huffingtonpost.com/ernest-owens/campus-diversity_b_2282629.html.

CHAPTER FIVE

1   Ellen Pao, "Ellen Pao Speaks: 'I Am Now Moving On,'" Recode, September 10, 2015, http://www.recode.net/2015/9/10/11618452/ellen-pao-speaks-i-am-now-moving-on.

2   David Streitfeld, "Ellen Pao Loses Silicon Valley Bias Case Against Kleiner Perkins," *The New York Times*, March 27, 2015, http://www.nytimes.com/2015/03/28/technology/ellen-pao-kleiner-perkins-case-decision.html.

3   Ibid.

4   Pao, "Ellen Pao Speaks: 'I Am Now Moving On.'"

5   David Streitfeld, "Ellen Pao Loses Silicon Valley Bias Case against Kleiner Perkins."

6   "Women and Leadership," Pew Research Center, January 14, 2015, http://www.pewsocialtrends.org/2015/01/14/women-and-leadership/.

7   Ibid.

8   Stefanie K. Johnson and David R. Hekman, "Women and Minorities Are Penalized for Promoting Diversity," *Harvard Business Review*, March 23, 2016, https://hbr.org/2016/03/women-and-minorities-are-penalized-for-promoting-diversity.

9   "The AAUW Foostepss Project: Elect HER!", Saint Lawrence County Branch, http://stlawrence.aauw-nys.org/electher.htm.

10 Kimberly Weisul, "Globally, women gain corporate board seats – but not in the US," *Fortune,* January 13, 2015, http://fortune.com/2015/01/13/catalyst-women-boards-countries-us/.

11 "Women CEOs of the S&P 500," Catalyst, July 1, 2016, http://www.catalyst.org/knowledge/women-ceos-sp-500.

12 "How Women Leading the Business World Are Changing the Face of Technology," Women in Business & Industry, October 23, 2015, http://www.wib-i.com/index.php/articles-online-magazine/articles/work/425-how-women-leading-the-business-world-are-changing-the-face-of-technology.

13 Sandrine Devillard and Sandra Sancier-Sultan, "Moving mind-sets on gender diversity : McKinsey Global Survey results," McKinsey, January 2014, http://www.mckinsey.com/business-functions/organization/our-insights/moving-mind-sets-on-gender-diversity-mckinsey-global-survey-results.

14 "Gender Pay Gap: Recent Trends and Explanations," *Council of Economic Advisers Issue Brief,* April 2015, https://www.whitehouse.gov/sites/default/files/docs/equal_pay_issue_brief_final.pdf.

15 Rich Henson, "Eleven Surprising Statistics about Women in the Workplace," Resourceful Manager, April 19, 2015, https://www.resourcefulmanager.com/women-workplace-statistics/.

16 Jessica Roy, "Microsoft CEO to Women: Don't Ask for a Raise," *New York* magazine, October 9, 2014, http://nymag.com/daily/intelligencer/2014/10/microsoft-ceo-to-women-dont-ask-for-a-raise.html.

17 McKinsey & Company, "Women Matter: Gender Diversity, a Corporate Performance Driver," report, 2007, http://www.mckinsey.com/global-themes/women-matter.

18 "Why Diversity Matters," Catalyst, July 2013, http://www.catalyst.org/system/files/why_diversity_matters_catalyst_0.pdf.

19 Renée B. Adams and Daniel Ferreira, "Women in the Boardroom and Their Impact on Governance and Performance," Journal of Financial Economics 94 (2009): 291–309.

20 "Why Diversity Matters," Catalyst.

21 Anita Williams Woolley, Christopher F. Chabris, Alexander Pentland, Nada Hashmi, and Thomas W. Malone, "Evidence for a Collective Intelligence Factor in the Performance of Human Groups," *Science* 330, no. 6004 (October 29, 2010), DOI: 10.1126/science.1193147; "Collective Intelligence: Number of Women in Group Linked to Effectiveness in Solving Difficult Problems," *Science Daily* (October 2, 2010), https://www.sciencedaily.com/releases/2010/09/100930143339.htm.

22 McKinsey & Company, "Moving Mind-Sets on Gender Diversity: McKinsey Global Survey Results," report, January 2014, http://www.mckinsey.com/business-functions/organization/our-insights/moving-mind-sets-on-gender-diversity-mckinsey-global-survey-results.

23 Matt Egan, "Still missing: Female business leaders," CNN Money, March 24, 2015, http://money.cnn.com/2015/03/24/investing/female-ceo-pipeline-leadership/.

24 McKinsey & Company, "Women Matter: Gender Diversity, a Corporate Performance Driver."

25 Egan, "Still missing: Female business leaders."

26 Kim Park, Juliana Menasce Horowitz, Wendy Wang, Anna Brown, Claudia Dean, Rich Morin, Eileen Patten, *Women and Leadership: Public Says Women Are Equally Qualified, but Barriers Persist*, report, Pew Research Center, January 14, 2015, http://www.pewsocialtrends.org/2015/01/14/chapter-3-obstacles-to-female-leadership/.

27 McKinsey & Company, *Moving mind-sets on gender diversity: McKinsey Global Survey results*, January 2014, http://www.mckinsey.com/business-functions/organization/our-insights/moving-mind-sets-on-gender-diversity-mckinsey-global-survey-results.

28 "Companies with More Women Board Directors Experience Higher Financial Performance, According to Latest Catalyst Bottom Line Report," Catalyst, http://www.catalyst.org/media/companies-more-women-board-directors-experience-higher-financial-performance-according-latest.

29 Joanna Barsh and Lareina Yee, *Unlocking the Full Potential of Women in the U.S. Economy*, McKinsey & Company, 2011, www.mckinsey.com/womenineconomy.

30 Sylvia Ann Hewlett, "Black Women: Ready, Willing, and More Than Able to Lead," *Inc.*, June 8, 2015, http://www.inc.com/center-for-talent-innovation/black-women-ready-willing-and-more-than-able-to-lead.html.

31 Barsh and Yee, *Unlocking the Full Potential of Women in the U.S. Economy*.

32 Hewlett, "Black Women: Ready, Willing, and More Than Able to Lead."

33 Ibid.

34 Ibid.

35 Ibid.

36 Sheryl Sandberg, "Why we have too few women leaders," TED, December 2010, https://www.ted.com/talks/sheryl_sandberg_why_we_have_too_few_women_leaders/transcript?language=en.

37 Sheryl Sandberg, *Lean In: Work, Women, and the Will to Lead* (New York: Alfred A. Knopf, 2013).

38 Adam Grant, "Why So Many Men Don't Stand Up for Their Female Colleagues," *The Atlantic*, April 29, 2014, http://www.theatlantic.com/business/archive/2014/04/why-men-dont-stand-up-for-women-to-lead/361231/.

CHAPTER SIX

1   Karl Moore, "Millennials Work for Purpose, Not Paycheck," Forbes, October 2, 2014, http://www.forbes.com/sites/karlmoore/2014/10/02/millennials-work-for-purpose-not-paycheck/#58ba5c9e5a22.

2   "Seven Must-Watch Trends at the Intersection of Sustainability and Purpose," http://events.sustainablebrands.com/sb16sd/updates/7-must-watch-trends-at-the-intersection-of-sustainability-and-purpose.

3   Aaron Hurst and Anna Tavis, 2015 Workforce Purpose Index, Imperative, 2015, https://www.imperative.com/index2015.

4   Ibid.

5   Ibid.

6   Rajendra S. Sisodia, David B. Wolfe, and Jagdish N. Sheth, Firms of Endearment: How World-Class Companies Profit from Passion and Purpose (Indianapolis: FT Press, 2007).

7   "Patagonia's Mission Statement," Patagonia, http://www.patagonia.com/company-info.html.

8   "Our Business and Climate Change," Patagonia, https://www.patagonia.com/climate-change.html.

9   "Patagonia's Mission Statement."

10   "Becoming a Responsible Company," Patagonia, https://www.patagonia.com/responsible-company.html.

11   "About the IKEA Group: Welcome inside our company," IKEA, 2016, http://www.ikea.com/ms/en_US/this-is-ikea/company-information/.

12   "IKEA Reviews," glassdoor, August 3, 2016, https://www.glassdoor.com/Reviews/IKEA-Reviews-E3957.htm.

13   Reid Hoffman, "The Power of Purpose at Work," LinkedIn, November 5, 2015, https://www.linkedin.com/pulse/power-purpose-work-reid-hoffman.

14   Sandy Hoffman, "LinkedIn's 2015 Workforce Diversity," LinkedIn blog, June 8, 2015, https://blog.linkedin.com/2015/06/08/linkedins-2015-workforce-diversity.

15   Stacy Jones, "See how the big tech companies compare on employee diversity," Fortune, July 30, 2015, http://fortune.com/2015/07/30/tech-companies-diveristy/.

CHAPTER SEVEN

1   Kathy Caprino, "Six Essential Ways to Build a Positive Organization," Forbes, December 13, 2013, http://www.forbes.com/sites/kathycaprino/2013/12/13/6-essential-ways-to-build-a-positive-organization/#76a0e8a45df6.

2   Salvador Rodriguez, "Why Silicon Valley Is Failing Miserably at Diversity, and What Should Be Done about It," *International Business Times*, July 7, 2015, http://www.ibtimes.com/why-silicon-valley-failing-miserably-diversity-what-should-be-done-about-it-1998144.

3   Ibid.

4   "How Aetna CEO Brings health and healing to the workplace," CBS News, March 26, 2015, http://www.cbsnews.com/news/aetna-ceo-mark-bertolini-healthy-workplace-healing-meditation-yoga/.

5   Jacob Morgan, *The Future of Work: Attract New Talent, Build Better Leaders, and Create a Competitive Organization*, Hoboken, New Jersey: John Wiley & Sons Inc., 2014, http://www.wiley.com/WileyCDA/WileyTitle/productCd-1118877241.html.

6   Ibid.

7   Ibid.

8   Gary Hamel, "Innovation Democracy: W. L. Gore's Original Management Model," MIX, Sep. 23, 2010, http://www.managementexchange.com/story/innovation-democracy-wl-gores-original-management-model.

9   "Responsibility," Gore-Tex, http://www.gore-tex.com/en-us/experience/responsibility.

10   "How It Works," HolacracyOne, 2016, http://www.holacracy.org/how-it-works/.

11   Richard Feloni, "Zappos' CEO Says This Is the Biggest Misconception People Have about His Company's Self-Management System," Business Insider, February 2, 2016, http://www.businessinsider.com/zappos-ceo-tony-hsieh-on-misconception-about-holacracy-2016-2.

12   Ibid.

13   Lisa Wirthman, "Is Flat Better? Zappos Ditches Hierarchy To Improve Company Performance," *Forbes,* January 7, 2014, http://www.forbes.com/sites/sungardas/2014/01/07/is-flat-better-zappos-ditches-hierarchy-to-improve-company-performance/#475f0d2c24d9.

14   Alison Coleman, "Banishing the Bosses Brings Out Zappos' Hidden Entrepreneurs," *Forbes,* April 7, 2016, http://www.forbes.com/sites/alisoncoleman/2016/04/07/banishing-the-bosses-brings-out-zappos-hidden-entrepreneurs/2/#14d2797d6ed6.

15   Robert Goffee and Gareth Jones, *Why Should Anyone Be Led by You?: What It Takes to Be an Authentic Leader,* Boston: Harvard Business Review Press, 2006.

16   Jason Fried, "Why I Run a Flat Company," *Inc.,* April 2011, http://www.inc.com/magazine/20110401/jason-fried-why-i-run-a-flat-company.html.

17   Ibid.

18   Maria Konnikova, "The Limits of Friendship," *The New Yorker*, October 7, 2014, http://www.newyorker.com/science/maria-konnikova/social-media-affect-math-dunbar-number-friendships.

19   David Ward, "Beyond the Open Office," SHRM, April 1, 2015, https://www.shrm.org/publications/hrmagazine/editorialcontent/2015/0415/pages/0415-open-office.aspx#sthash.DLAfOhNa.dpuf.

20   Jungsoo Kim and Richard de Dear, "Workspace Satisfaction: The Privacy-Communication Trade-Off in Open-Plan Offices," Journal of Environmental Psychology 36 (December 2013): 18–26.

21   William Kremer, "The pleasures and perils of the open-plan office," BBC News, March 28, 2013, http://www.bbc.com/news/magazine-21878739.

22   "Speech Privacy in Office Environments," CBE, July 18, 2007, http://www.cbe.berkeley.edu/research/acoustics.htm.

23   Sherri Anne, "Debunking the Myth of the Open-Plan Office," OBlog, February 28, 2014, https://blog.nus.edu.sg/audreyc/2014/02/28/debunking-the-myth-of-the-open-plan-office/.

24   Tom Lowry, "Bloomberg: The CEO Mayor," Bloomberg, June 14, 2007, http://www.bloomberg.com/news/articles/2007-06-14/bloomberg-the-ceo-mayorbusinessweek-business-news-stock-market-and-financial-advice; Michael Howard Saul, "Murky Future For 'Bullpen,'" *The Wall Street Journal*, March 22, 2013, http://www.wsj.com/articles/SB10001424127887324557804578376793784458224.

25   Dan Buettner, "Are Extroverts Happier Than Introverts?", Psychology Today, May 14, 2012, https://www.psychologytoday.com/blog/thrive/201205/are-extroverts-happier-introverts.

26   James B. Stewart, "Looking for a Lesson in Google's Perks," *The New York Times*, March 15, 2013, http://www.nytimes.com/2013/03/16/business/at-google-a-place-to-work-and-play.html.

27   Curt Rice, "How Blind Auditions Help Orchestras to Eliminate Gender Bias," *The Guardian*, October 14, 2013, http://www.theguardian.com/women-in-leadership/2013/oct/14/blind-auditions-orchestras-gender-bias.

28   Vivienne Ming, "The Tax on Being Different," http://moment.vivienneming.com/2015/05/the-tax-on-being-different/.

29   Ibid.

30   Ibid.

31   Ibid.

32   Katherine L. Milkman, Modupe Akinola, and Dolly Chugh, *Temporal Distance and Discrimination: An Audit Study in Academia, research report*; abstract reprinted in Psychological Science (May 21, 2012), http://pss.sagepub.com/content/early/2012/05/18/0956797611434539.abstract.

33   David R. Francis, "Employers' Replies to Racial Names," NBER, http://www.nber.org/digest/sep03/w9873.html.

34   Ming, "The Tax on Being Different."

35   Dean Schabner, "Americans Work More Than Anyone," ABC News, May 1, 2016, http://abcnews.go.com/US/story?id=93364&page=1.

36   David G. Javitch, "The Benefits of Flextime," *Entrepreneur*, June 5, 2006, https://www.entrepreneur.com/article/159440.

37   Scott Behson, "Flex Time Doesn't Need to Be an HR Policy," *Harvard Business Review*, December 4, 2014, https://hbr.org/2014/12/flex-time-doesnt-need-to-be-an-hr-policy.

38   Katherine Reynolds Lewis, "How Men Flex," *Working Mother*, July 23, 2015, http://www.workingmother.com/content/how-men-flex.

39   Brad Harrington, Fred Van Deusen, Beth Humberd, *The New Dad: Caring, Committed and Conflicted*, report, Boston College, 2011, http://www.bc.edu/content/dam/files/centers/cwf/pdf/FH-Study-Web-2.pdf.

40   Mike Ramsey, "Men Need Work/Life Balance, Too," SHRM, November 1, 2014, https://www.shrm.org/hr-today/news/hr-magazine/pages/1114-paternity-leave.aspx.

41   Jason Hall, "Why Men Don't Take Paternity Leave," *Forbes*, June 14, 2013, http://www.forbes.com/sites/learnvest/2013/06/14/why-men-dont-take-paternity-leave/#5b65453d3270.

42   Claire Cain Miller, "Paternity Leave: The Rewards and the Remaining Stigma," *The New York Times*, November 7, 2014, http://www.nytimes.com/2014/11/09/upshot/paternity-leave-the-rewards-and-the-remaining-stigma.html?_r=0.

43   Reed Hastings, "Freedom & Responsibility Culture," LinkedIn SlideShare, June 30, 2011, http://www.slideshare.net/reed2001/culture-2009.

CHAPTER EIGHT

1   Tyler Atkinson, David Luttrell, and Harvey Rosenblum, "How Bad Was It? The Costs and Consequences of the 2007–09 Financial Crisis," *Staff Papers* no. 20 (July 2013), Dallas Fed, https://dallasfed.org/assets/documents/research/staff/staff1301.pdf.

2a   *Vanguard's economic and investment outlook*, The Vanguard Group, December 2015, https://personal.vanguard.com/pdf/ISGVEMO_122015.pdf;

2b   Walter Updegrave, "Why you shouldn't abandon bonds," CNN Money, June 29, 2016, http://money.cnn.com/2016/06/29/retirement/retirement-bonds/;

2c   Pooja Gupta, "Strategic default and unemployment: What factors affect the likelihood that homeowners will default on their home mortgages?", Journalist's

Resource, April 11, 2016, http://journalistsresource.org/studies/economics/personal-finance/strategic-default-unemployment-home-mortgage.

3   Phillip Cohen, "Fewer births and divorces, more violence: how the recession affected the American family," The Conversation, December 12, 2014, http://theconversation.com/fewer-births-and-divorces-more-violence-how-the-recession-affected-the-american-family-34272.

4   Paul Flatters and Michael Willmott, "Understanding the Postrecession Consumer," *Harvard Business Review*, July-August 2009, https://hbr.org/2009/07/understanding-the-postrecession-consumer.

5   Phil LeBeau, "Americans Holding onto Their Cars Longer Than Ever," CNBC, July 29, 2015, http://www.cnbc.com/2015/07/28/americans-holding-onto-their-cars-longer-than-ever.html.

6   Glassdoor Team, "Glassdoor Outpaces CareerBuilder.com in U.S. Traffic," Glassdoor, April 30, 2015, https://www.glassdoor.com/blog/glassdoor-outpaces-careerbuilder/.

7   Inc. Staff, "How a Business Can Change the World," *Inc.*, http://www.inc.com/magazine/20110501/how-a-business-can-change-the-world.html.

8   Tina Rosenberg, "Ethical Businesses with a Better Bottom Line," *Opionator* (blog), *New York Times,* April 14, 2011, http://opinionator.blogs.nytimes.com/2011/04/14/ethical-businesses-with-a-better-bottom-line/.

9   "What are B Corps?", B Corporation, https://www.bcorporation.net/what-are-b-corps.

10   Ryan Honeyman, "Has the B Corp Movement Made a Difference?" *Stanford Social Innovation Review*, October 13, 2014, http://ssir.org/articles/entry/has_the_b_corp_movement_made_a_difference.

11   "Triple bottom line," *The Economist*, November 17, 2009, http://www.economist.com/node/14301663.

12   Timothy Erblich, "The Next Decade of Corporate Ethics," *The Huffington Post,* April 20, 2016, http://www.huffingtonpost.com/timothy-erblich/the-next-decade-of-corpor_b_9739882.html.

13   "CSR RepTrak®," Reputation Institute, https://www.reputationinstitute.com/thought-leadership/csr-reptrak-100.

14   Beyond the Boundary Wheelchairs, "Corporate Social Responsibility (CSR)," http://www.beyondtheboundarywheelchairs.com/corporate-social-responsibility-csr/.

15   "A Focus on Early Learning," PNC, https://www.pnc.com/en/about-pnc/corporate-responsibility/grow-up-great/our-great-story.html.

16   Sylvia Ann Hewlett, Melinda Marshall, and Laura Sherbin, "How Women Drive Innovation and Growth," Thinkers 50, http://thinkers50.com/blog/how-women-drive-innovation-and-growth/; "Case Study: Supporting women in our markets,"

Standard Chartered, http://reports.standardchartered.com/sustainability-review-2012/beingaresponsiblecompany/peopleandvalues/diversityandinclusion/casestudysupportingwomeninourmarkets.html.

17 John Mackey, *Conscious Capitalism* (Boston: Harvard Business School Publishing Corporation, 2014).

18 Aaron Hurst, *The Purpose Economy: How Your Desire for Impact, Personal Growth and Community Is Changing the World* (Boise: Elevate Publishing, 2014).

19 Corporation for National & Community Service, "One in Four Americans Volunteer; Three in Five Help Neighbors," press release, December 8, 2015, http://www.nationalservice.gov/newsroom/press-releases/2015/new-report-1-4-americans-volunteer-3-5-help-neighbors.

20 Deloitte, "The Deloitte Millennial Survey 2016," http://www2.deloitte.com/global/en/pages/about-deloitte/articles/millennialsurvey.html.

21 Honeyman, "Has the B Corp Movement Made a Difference?"

22 "The Making of a Multicultural Super Consumer," Nielsen Insights, March 18, 2015, http://www.nielsen.com/us/en/insights/news/2015/the-making-of-a-multicultural-super-consumer-.html.

23 Phebe Dowels, "Nielson report: multicultural spending power at an all-time high," Urban Geekz, April 1, 2015, http://urbangeekz.com/2015/04/nielsen-report-multicultural-spending-power-at-all-time-high/#sthash.ZRI1v9nX.dpu.

24 "Out in the World: Securing LGBT Rights in the Global Marketplace," Center for Talent Innovation, http://www.talentinnovation.org/_private/assets/OutInTheWorld_Infographic-CTI.pdf.

25 Denis Markman, "Values-based diversity: The challenges and strengths of many," LinkedIn SlideShare, February 6, 2014, http://www.slideshare.net/DenisMarkman/values-based-diversity.

26 Cathy Gallagher-Louisy, "Measuring the Dividends of Diversity," *PeopleTalk* 20, no. 3 (Fall 2013), http://www.hrvoice.org/wp-content/uploads/2013/10/PeopleTalk-Fall-2013.pdf.

27 Josh Bersin, "Becoming Irresistible: A New Model for Employee Engagement," *Deloitte Review* 16 (January 26, 2015), http://dupress.com/articles/employee-engagement-strategies/.

28 D. A. Abrams, *Diversity & Inclusion: The Big Six Formula for Success* (Charleston: CreateSpace, 2013).

29 Braden Goyette, "Cheerios Commercial Featuring Mixed Race Family Gets Racist Backlash (VIDEO)," *The Huffington Post*, May 31, 2013, http://www.huffingtonpost.com/2013/05/31/cheerios-commercial-racist-backlash_n_3363507.html.

CHAPTER NINE

1   Priscilla H. Douglas, "Affinity Groups: Catalyst for Inclusive Organizations," *Employment Relations Today* 34, no. 4 (January 24, 2008): 11–18, DOI:10.1002/ert.20171

2   "Diversity and Inclusion: Employee Affinity Networks," Goldman Sachs, http://www.goldmansachs.com/who-we-are/diversity-and-inclusion/employee-affinity-networks.html.

3   Jennifer Brown, "Employee Resource Groups that Drive Business," Jennifer Brown Consulting, http://jenniferbrownconsulting.com/cisco-jbc-driving-business-next-practices-for-ergs/.

4   Susan L. Colantuono, "News and Insights about Closing the Leadership Gender Gap," Leading Women, http://www.leadingwomen.biz/blog/bid/72612/Require-Diverse-Slates-of-Candidates-to-Minimize-Gender-Bias.

5   Rajat Taneja, "How Visa Attracts the Top Minds in Tech," Visa, https://usa.visa.com/visa-everywhere/innovation/visa-attracts-top-tech-minds.html.

6   "Global Diversity and Inclusion: Fostering Innovation Through a Diverse Workforce," Forbes Insights, http://images.forbes.com/forbesinsights/StudyPDFs/Innovation_Through_Diversity.pdf.

7   Jennifer Brown, "Executive Sponsors Fuel High-Performing ERGs," Jennifer Brown Consulting, http://jenniferbrownconsulting.com/executive-sponsors-fuel-high-performance-ergs/.

8   "100 Best Companies to Work For 2016," *Fortune*, http://fortune.com/best-companies/.

CHAPTER TEN

1   Adam Levine-Peres, "What's Mansplaining? Here's How (And Why) You Need to Stop Privileged Explaining," Everyday Feminism, October 4, 2015, http://everydayfeminism.com/2015/10/what-is-mansplaining/.

2   Aimee Hansen, "What's keeping white male leaders from leading Diversity & Inclusion efforts?", The Glass Hammer, http://theglasshammer.com/2015/07/07/whats-keeping-white-male-leaders-from-leading-diversity-inclusion-efforts/.

3   Stefanie K. Johnson and David R. Hekman, "Women and Minorities Are Penalized for Promoting Diversity," *Harvard Business Review*, March 23, 2016, https://hbr.org/2016/03/women-and-minorities-are-penalized-for-promoting-diversity.

4   Chuck Shelton, *The Study on White Men Leading Through Diversity & Inclusion,* Greatheart Labs, February 2013, http://www.whitemensleadershipstudy.com/pdf/WMLS%20Results%20Report.pdf.

5   Ibid.

6   Ibid.

7   Workplace Trends, "The Millennial Leadership Survey," press release, July 20, 2015, https://workplacetrends.com/the-millennial-leadership-survey/.

8   Shelton, *The Study on White Men Leading Through Diversity & Inclusion.*

GLOSSARY

1   "Glossary of 'A,'" Work and Family Researchers Network, 2016, https://workfamily.sas.upenn.edu/glossary/a/affinity-groups-definitions.

2   "What Are B Corps?" B Corporation.

3   Sunnivie Brydum, "The True Meaning of the Word 'Cisgender,'" *Advocate*, July 31, 2015, http://www.advocate.com/transgender/2015/07/31/true-meaning-word-cisgender.

4   Jeff King and Jeff Fromm, On Marketing, "Only Conscious Capitalists Will Survive," December 4, 2013, http://www.forbes.com/sites/onmarketing/2013/12/04/only-conscious-capitalists-will-survive/#69fc823443bf.

5   Jalena Keane-Lee, "Diversity can be helped through 'cultural competency': Experts," CNBC, August 23, 2015, http://www.cnbc.com/2015/08/21/diversity-can-be-helped-through-cultural-competency-experts.html.

6   "Sexual Orientation and Gender Identity Definitions," Human Rights Campaign, http://www.hrc.org/resources/sexual-orientation-and-gender-identity-terminology-and-definitions.

7   "heteronormative," Merriam Webster, http://www.merriam-webster.com/dictionary/heteronormative.

8   "mutualism," dictionary.com, http://www.dictionary.com/browse/mutualism.

9   Lori Grisham, "What Does the Q in LGBTQ stand for?", *USA Today*, July 22, 2016, http://www.usatoday.com/story/news/nation-now/2015/06/01/lgbtq-questioning-queer-meaning/26925563/.

10   "Sexual Orientation and Gender Identity Definitions," Human Rights Campaign.

11   Susan Colantuono, "News & Insights about Closing the Leadership Gender Gap," Leading Women, http://www.leadingwomen.biz/blog/bid/72612/Require-Diverse-Slates-of-Candidates-to-Minimize-Gender-Bias.

RESOURCES

1   Kenji Yoshino and Christine Smith, "Uncovering Talent: A New Model of Inclusion," report, Deloitte University, 2013, http://gender.stanford.edu/sites/default/files/06%20UncoveringTalentPaper.pdf.

2   Torben Rick, "The Iceberg that Sinks Organizational Change," January 16, 2015, http://www.torbenrick.eu/blog/change-management/iceberg-that-sinks-organizational-change/.

3   Aaron Hurst, *The Purpose Economy: How Your Desire for Impact, Personal Growth and Community Is Changing the World* (Boise, Idaho: Elevate Publishing, 2014).

4   D. A. Abrams, *Diversity & Inclusion: The Big Six Formula for Success* (CreateSpace Independent Publishing Platform, 2013).

5   "100 Best Companies to Work For," *Fortune*, 2016, http://fortune.com/best-companies/.

6   Chuck Shelton, *The Study on White Men Leading Through Diversity & Inclusion, Greatheart Labs*, February 2013, http://www.whitemensleadershipstudy.com/pdf/WMLS%20Results%20Report.pdf.

29842085R00183

Made in the USA
Columbia, SC
24 October 2018